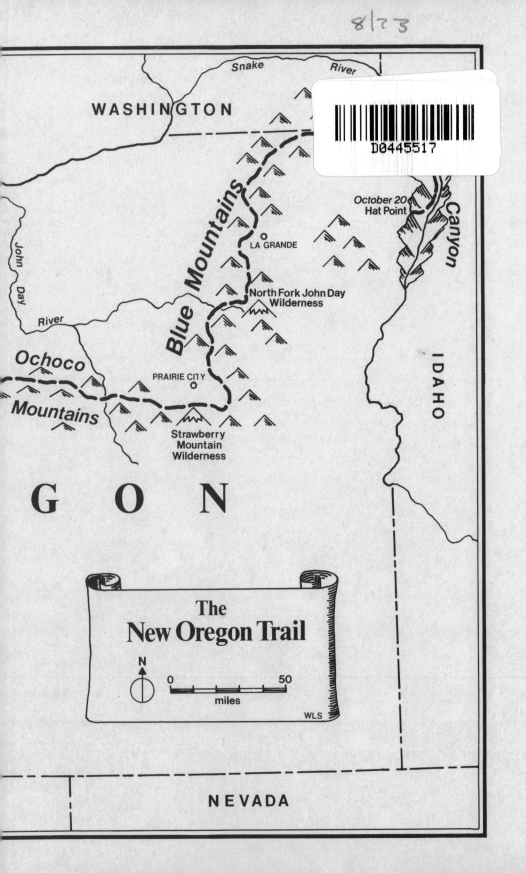

Snake River

WASHINGTON

October 20
Hat Point

Canyon

Blue Mountains

LA GRANDE

North Fork John Day
Wilderness

John Day River

IDAHO

Ochoco

PRAIRIE CITY

Mountains

Strawberry
Mountain
Wilderness

G O N

The
New Oregon Trail

N

0   50
miles

WLS

NEVADA

LISTENING

FOR COYOTE

ALSO BY WILLIAM L. SULLIVAN

The Cart Book: with Plans & Projects
Exploring Oregon's Wild Areas

LISTENING

A Walk Across

William Morrow and Company, Inc.

FOR COYOTE

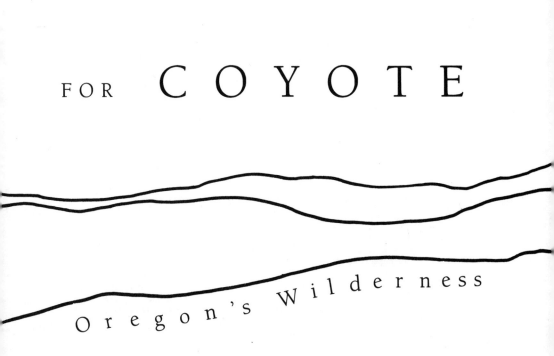

Oregon's Wilderness

William L. Sullivan

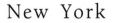

New York

Library of Congress Cataloging-in-Publication Data

Sullivan, William L.
  Listening for coyote : a walk across Oregon's wilderness / William
L. Sullivan.
     p.   cm.
  ISBN 0-688-07880-X
  1. Hiking—Oregon. 2. Backpacking—Oregon. 3. Wilderness areas—
Oregon. 4. Oregon—Description and travel—1981– I. Title.
GV199.42.07S74   1988
917.95—dc19   88-8599
                                                                           CIP

Printed in the United States of America

First Edition

1 2 3 4 5 6 7 8 9 10

BOOK DESIGN BY MARIA EPES

To
J. Wesley Sullivan,
who took this hike in spirit

Contents

PROLOGUE

There are times when daydreams of wilderness loom so enticingly they might be Atlantis at a rare low tide.

It was a rainy Oregon winter and I was thirty-two, rewriting an unpublished novel in the unheated basement of my Eugene apartment, when my thoughts suddenly wandered off by themselves toward the mountains.

That night, sleepless, I paced our rooms. I was as happy married to Janell as any man had a right to be. Four-year-old Karen and two-year-old Ian, tangled in the covers from their bedtime struggle against sleep, looked as fragile as two pale eggs in a nest. But my daydream lingered before me, raising questions that could not be answered at home.

I knew the United States has set a world record for wilderness preservation—over eighty-five million acres in forty-three states—but I wondered, could the *spirit* of wilderness within us have flickered out in the meanwhile?

Poring over maps that night, I realized the Old Oregon Trail is now overlain by an interstate freeway. The adventure of that mighty western route is gone. But scattered across the map were islands of recently designated Wilderness I didn't recognize. Grassy Knob? Black Canyon? What's more, I saw a string of them forming a scraggly W-shaped line from the Pacific Ocean to the Snake River's Hells Canyon.

Surely, I thought, that meandering line would be the wildest route across Oregon. It would traverse four mountain ranges and eighteen designated Wilderness Areas. It would lead through fog-bound rain forests, windswept glacial cirques, and sunbaked desert canyons. It would extend for more than 1,300 miles, from Oregon's western shore at Cape Blanco to the state's easternmost point in the depths of Hells Canyon.

To me, it was irresistible. If the spirit of American wilderness still lived, I would find it hiking that route.

In the morning Janell, to her everlasting credit, did not find my plan altogether insane. She even wished she could come. After all, we had once bicycled five thousand kilometers through Europe together. And we had built a log cabin together on Oregon's Siletz River using only hand tools. But that was before we had children. Now, she agreed to stay home—if I promised to give her a chance to "escape" someday, too.

I assembled a stack of topographic maps an inch thick to esti-mate what lay ahead. There would be some bushwhacking, but a surprising 57 percent of the route was already in trail. Federal land ownership along the way was so complete I could lay out a path entirely on public land and existing public rights-of-way.

Why had no one thought of a west–east hiking route here be-fore? The Oregon State Parks' Recreational Trail Advisory Council wondered, too, and invited me to report on the trail's feasibility. To-day, the "New Oregon Trail" I scouted is part of Oregon's recreational trail plan.

I began to prepare for a 1,300-mile backpack in earnest. Six months before the start of my trip I started my training with what seemed like a very long five-mile walk across town. After three months I could knock off the five miles in sixty-five minutes. I moved up to eleven-mile hikes with a light pack. I added weight to the pack until I could make the eleven-mile trip in two hours and twenty-five minutes, packing fifty pounds of firewood. I hoped that would be good enough. Crossing the state in the two and a half months I had set aside would mean averaging seventeen miles a day. But time for training was running short.

The pile of gear I accumulated looked frighteningly heavy. I grumbled at the three pounds of camera gear and lenses. I left out the extra jeans, the flashlight, the mittens, and the hat. I threw out all the cooking pots but one for boiling water; food would have to be simple.

I left the suntan lotion and mosquito repellent. I left all of the first-aid kit except a single elastic bandage, three Band-Aids, and a bottle of water-purification tablets. My biggest health danger, I imagined, would be hypothermia, so I took a three and a half-pound backpacking tent, a tiny butane stove, and a down coat. Janell sewed me an entire outfit of waterproof outerwear. I have no doubt it saved my life.

Obviously I could not carry all the food at once. So I divided it into nine piles, and mailed eight of them ahead to relatives and friends who would meet me at checkpoints. My maps and research notes weighed an agonizing ten pounds. I divided the 120 maps and four journal notebooks among the food packages. Then I put stamped manila envelopes in the food packages, too, so I could mail back maps, journals, and camera film when I was finished with them.

At two o'clock in the morning of August 17, I squeezed the alarm clock silent. The night bus—the only bus to Port Orford on the Oregon coast—would be leaving soon. My wife rolled over in bed as I put on my jeans and hiking boots. "Come back soon," she said.

I kissed little Ian and Karen in their sleep. They had nodded innocently when I had told them I would be leaving on a long trip. Time meant nothing to them. But when I was really gone, what would they think?

Ian would start his first preschool class while I was gone. Karen would start kindergarten and have her fifth birthday. Their mother would have to watch them both, run the house alone, and keep her part-time job. And what would I find?

I fought back the lump in my throat, balanced the huge, sixty-pound pack on my back, and walked out into the night streets toward the bus station. The red patch on the back of the pack—the patch Janell had sewn on for me—read: HELLS CANYON OR BUST!

I.

THE KLAMATHS

And the Coyote singing
   is shut away
   for they fear
   the call
   of the wild.

—GARY SNYDER

4:12 P.M. Cape Blanco State Park. 68°F. Day's mileage: 12.7.

I hike along the beach toward Oregon's westernmost point, en-joying the crisp sea air, the curling surf, and the solitude. Dark green mountains loom to the east; forests sweep right down to the sand. Ahead, Cape Blanco is as flat-topped and huge as a beached aircraft carrier. Its conning tower—a white lighthouse—blinks my way every thirty seconds.

I smile to think that this dark ocher headland was named Cabo Blanco ("White Cape") by an Spanish sea explorer in 1603. Perhaps it was wrapped in fog when he saw it. Certainly the Spaniards did not find this rugged coast as impressive as tourists do today. Oregon, the early explorers complained, was a wilderness. There was no farmland visible behind the harborless seashore. The unfriendly Indians had no gold. After 1603 no white man returned to Oregon for 172 years.

I stop to study my topographic map. It identifies a small slough on my right as a backwater of the Elk River. The map assures me the slough will end soon, and it seems that it surely must, since the cliffs behind it are rising taller and my beach is growing narrower with every step.

However, at the end of the slough, I discover with astonishment that it does not end at all. Instead, the slough right-angles across my path and runs straight into the ocean. And then I realize this is not a backwater at all, but rather the entire Elk River, which has changed course since the 1957 map was published. I haven't yet reached the starting point of my hike, and already my maps are failing me.

I frown at the water. The ocean waves are rolling in over a choppy bar with the rising tide, and have begun to fill the river mouth with what looks like hip-deep water. I should turn back to look for a bridge.

But there is a force within every hiker that makes the thought of backtracking odious. Solemnly, I take off my boots and tie them to my pack. I survey the river bar, and take off my pants as well. Finally I grab a stout walking stick and slosh into the river in my underwear.

The river is salt here, of course, and has the North Pacific's characteristic goose-bump chill. Halfway across, the river is only thigh-deep—I jump the little waves rolling in over the bar. But suddenly the water darkens and I slip to my waist. Immediately I fear for the pack. If it gets wet, along with my maps, camera, clothes, and food, I would be delayed for days. If the current catches it, I could swim free, but my trek across Oregon would be over before it begins. Still, I *can't* turn back now. The far shore is hardly a dozen feet away. On tiptoe I feel my way forward with the water lapping against my chest. I hitch up the pack, but hear the cover of my sleeping bag slap into the salt water—and then, just as suddenly, I reach the upslope.

I sprawl out on the dry sand. With relief I determine that the waterproof cover of my sleeping bag has kept it dry. I celebrate by breaking out my daily allotment of lunch—a few handfuls of granola and nuts. Then I put on my pants and boots and march victoriously toward Cape Blanco, now only two miles away.

The white sand on this side of the river is dotted with extravagant tufts of pioneer grass and huge gray driftwood logs. The shiny wet edge of the beach arcs into the cape ahead. A black cormorant flies across the wavetops. A sandpiper banks out around me. I can't resist a game of my boyhood: stomping on the washed-up seaweed bulbs of kelp to hear them pop. It is my twenty-one-gun salute to the world's largest ocean.

And then I see a head in the waves. *Foop!* it's gone. Pause. *Foop!* it's back. Shiny, black, earless, but with the big watchful eyes of a puppy. *Foop!* it's gone. Then a big breaker lifts the entire animal up for an instant, holding its body lengthwise to the light—and I can see the whole speckled, blubbery cigar shape, complete with two built-in swim fins at the end. It is too fat for a sea otter, and has no tail. It is a harbor seal, the one marine mammal on this coast that does not seem frightened by these strange men-things—only curious. The seal eyeballs me for a few more foops, keeping pace with me, and then barrel-rolls off and away.

Anytime you can win the confidence—or even just the curiosity—of a fellow mammal, it gives a certain smiling glow. But I had hoped to spot a sea otter here.

Sea otters were what finally brought white men back to Oregon's wilderness coast. Between 1775 and 1823, over 100,000 sea otters were killed for their pelts, which sold in Paris for as much as one thousand dollars apiece. In 1900 the harvest had dropped to just 127 animals. By 1911 the sea otter was classified as extinct south of the Aleutians. At that point, federal laws were passed giving sea otters complete protection. Today it is a crime even to own a strip of sea otter fur.

So how could I hope to find an otter here? In 1970 the Atomic Energy Commission announced plans to test a nuclear bomb on an Aleutian island. After studying the test's environmental impact, the AEC trapped ninety-five sea otters from the bomb site and released them in Oregon, near Cape Blanco. Then they detonated the Aleutian island, instantly killing all the sea otters that remained there.

I had been told Oregon's new sea otters loll in the surf, never more than two hundred yards from shore, nor in water more than 150 feet deep. Their favorite position is floating on their backs, feet up and paws folded behind their heads, like lazy men on swimming-pool air mattresses. They even eat in that lazy pose, placing mussels on their upturned tummies, and whacking the shells open with a rock held in one paw.

When the beach ends at the great dark base of Cape Blanco, I hike up a state park road. The stunted plants along the road are dramatic evidence of the force of the Pacific's winter storms. Sitka spruce trees, which grow two hundred feet tall inland, here have been so blasted by the ocean wind that they only form a contorted, waist-high mat. Where even this tree-carpet cannot grow, salal brush struggles on, hugging the ground but still producing its thick-skinned, edible, dark blue berries. Finally, at the cape's flat crest, there is a meadow, eternally mown smooth by the wind. Heroic yarrow and aster spangle the field with summery blooms.

Determined to begin my hike at the absolute tip of the cape, I walk up the little road to the tall, neatly whitewashed lighthouse. Just short of my goal, however, I am stopped by a fence and a gate with the sign U.S. COAST GUARD PROPERTY. TRESPASSERS WILL BE PROSECUTED. I dump my pack in frustration and peer through the gate. A woman with binoculars is wandering through the brush on the far side of the lighthouse.

"Hello!" I call. "How did you get through without getting arrested?"

She comes nearer. I see she is wearing a down vest and an

orange-and-blue knit cap. "We're from the local Audubon Society," she tells me. "We wrote to the Coast Guard office in Coos Bay and got permission to watch for vagrant warblers."

I ponder this a moment. "Do you suppose I could come look for vagrant warblers, too?"

"I don't see why not."

In a minute I'm past the fence and walking with her toward the end of Cape Blanco. The farther out we walk, the more I am aware of being surrounded by water. The little field at the end of this narrow headland is two miles out to sea, and two hundred feet above the waves. We make our way through some very weather-beaten thimbleberry bushes, and then she says, "Let's see. There's really no good way out here to Jim."

We crash through the brush to a ravine on the north face of the cape, and there, in a patch of grass, is her Jim. The man's head is wreathed with long, wavy salt-and-pepper hair. An enormous square beard gives him a dauntless aspect. All in all, if he only had a robe, he could pass for Moses. This image is so forceful, it is jarring to see him lean over a 22-power wide-angle telescope on a tripod and squint at some chattering yellow and gray birds.

"There's that little gray one again," he announces, and for a moment I nearly accept this as some strange eleventh commandment. "I still can't tell if it has an eye ring or not. Oh-oh, here comes Yellow-cheek."

When I am introduced, the two birders explain why their warblers tend to stray out to this unlikely spot. In mid-August these songbirds are supposed to be migrating south overland, but on overcast days they seem to get confused and fly west, soon ending up out at sea. Then the warblers see the light from the lighthouse, and it attracts them here. "All up and down the Oregon coast," the woman says, "you'll find lost warblers on overcast days at headlands with lighthouses."

I remark that I always thought birds migrated by magnetic bearings or by the stars or something.

They exchange a nod with lifted eyebrows. "These are all guesses," she says. "We still know very little about—" Suddenly she breaks off her sentence with a frantic duck of her head. "My God, Jim, it's a *gos*!"

We all cringe together as the goshawk swoops past us at the little warblers. They scatter like shrapnel from a bomb. Then all is quiet.

I speak first. "Have you seen any sea otters today?"

Jim stares at me, as if trying to register what I have said. "Sea otters?" His hands leave the telescope and hide in his beard as he thinks. "Well, there used to be some. But the fishermen in town shot most of them. They thought the otters were eating salmon. Yeah, a few years back there were still some otters north of here, but I haven't seen any lately."

When I leave the two birders and wander toward the end of the cape, I am thinking otter thoughts. Perhaps the otters are really still here. Perhaps they swam back to their detonated Aleutian home. Or perhaps wildness, once lost, is simply gone.

Ahead, at the westernmost tip of Cape Blanco, the meadow I am crossing suddenly disappears into thin air. The only way I can be sure the edge is not a crumbling overhang is to go look. I creep to the brink, one step at a time, and peer over.

Huge waves erupt on the rocks a very long way directly below. A half dozen jagged rock islands start up out of the foam. Twenty-foot breakers off the North Pacific roll in against them and explode in slow motion. Cormorants stand in the thick of the spray in stoic poses. Seagulls wheel around the rocks' white-stained summits. Kelp bobs in slithery fields between the islands. It looks like the perfect home for sea otters to me.

Several dozen larger islands—Orford Reef—cluster two miles out to sea. One of them is cut into an arch. Another looks like a whale with a two-hundred-foot-tall back. The islands, made of the same rock as Cape Blanco itself, must have been an extension of the cape long ago. The sea has crumbled away the softer land, much as a wave on a beach reduces a sand castle to the pebbles that decorated its towers.

These islands are in fact Oregon's westernmost wilderness—one that man will never visit. In all, Oregon has 1,477 such rocky offshore islands. And all the ones I can see from Cape Blanco have been officially designated as Wilderness by Congress. But in this case the ban on motorized travel seems superfluous, for no boat could land on such steep, waveswept cliffs. The islands are the retreat of sea lions

and sea birds: petrels, auklets, grebes, murrelets, pelicans, and
scoters. It has been estimated that Oregon was home to more than
two million sea birds as recently as 1940, but the development of the
coast has trimmed that number by a factor of ten. On these islands,
their refuge is secure.

Perhaps it is appropriate that I should begin my journey through
Oregon's wilds with a wilderness forever out of reach. Wilderness is
not intended for man. It is a reminder that the world is not our toy,
or even a safe shell to hide under. We need a place where we do *not*
belong, just as children delight in sneaking into forbidden rooms and
attics, for a glimpse of the unknown.

It is late afternoon. I carry my pack back to the state park, set up
my little tent in the hiker-biker campsite, and fall to work on my
journal. As I write, a harried robin swoops down on the lawn before
me, pursued by two fat, pestering sparrows. Hop hop hop, goes the
proper robin, and cocks its head to listen for worms. But up come the
two followers, cheeping so loudly and insistently the poor robin is
obviously having trouble hearing the subtle noise of worms digging.
Then I look closer. Ah, yes—the followers are not sparrows at all, but
rather, immature robins themselves. *Cheep! cheep!* they beg. To my
surprise, Mother Robin actually pulls up a worm and sticks pieces of
it into their noisy beaks. The sight makes me think of home, and the
two small children who only now are realizing I am gone. But then a
black bicycle clicks into the campsite and the robins fly away.

The rider of the black bicycle does not join me at once at the
one picnic table reserved for nonmotorized campers. Instead, after he
dismounts, he leaves the bike and its heavy load of traveling gear
against a fence and walks around the campsite writhing and making
peculiar moaning sounds. He stretches his legs; he rolls his shoulders;
he lies briefly on the ground and groans. While continuing his gyra-
tions, he takes off his white plastic helmet, strips off his skintight
shirt, and peels down his thigh-length black cycling pants. With these
hung on a salal bush to dry, he calisthenics his way over to me in his
underwear.

"Ooh," he says.

"Long ride?"

"Unh."

When he becomes more communicative, I discover that he is a

pre-med anatomy instructor from Simon Fraser University in Van-
couver, Canada, on a holiday between terms. He is bicycling the
Oregon coast from north to south in five 100-mile days; I have met
him at the bottom of the fourth. With great enthusiasm and dismay,
he explains to me there's been fog along the coast every day—he's
even seen a baffling satellite photo that showed clouds nowhere else
but on the route of his trip. I explain the phenomenon to him gently:
The warm summer sea breeze condenses to fog along the cool coast
each night, and does not burn off on most summer days.

Then I ask what he has been able to see through the fog today.
He looks thoughtful. "There's been some lovely farm meadows. The
bridges over the rivers aren't as pretty by bike as they probably are by
car, where you don't have to worry about wood chip trucks from the
sawmills whooshing you over the railing." Then he brightens. "But I
did pass a car wash in Bandon run entirely by girls in hot pink hot
pants and tiger-striped tank tops." We share a smile at the thought of
those nymphs sudsing down his bicycle in wild a-Bandon.

He produces a bottle of Chenin Blanc from his bag, and we tell
of bicycle tours we have undertaken abroad—he in New Zealand, I in
Europe. I drink from my plastic orange mug, but he pours his wine
into a two-pint plastic measuring bowl, which he claims is his standard camping cup. There is a small hole melted through it at the one-
cup mark. The hole, he says, is the work of comrades from a group
bike trip who feared the cup would hold more than his fair share of
wine.

We finish the bottle. He brings up Simon Fraser, the Scottish
explorer who crossed Canada in the vanguard of the British fur company expansion. Only five feet four, Fraser was compulsively active,
writing in his journal each night until three A.M., then rousing the
camp at six A.M. for another hard day of canoeing or trekking. I muse
that my two favorite western explorers, David Douglas and John
Muir, were also diehard Scots. The bicyclist and I shake our heads,
and conclude soggily that such men could only have been so driven
because they were misfits in their homeland—or vice versa. And the
days of the great explorers are over anyway, aren't they?

In the dark the roar of the ocean is overwhelming, crashing ever
louder. I walk out from the camp's shelter of gnarled Sitka spruce and
stand on the park road's center line. The great beacon of the light-

house swings its beam through the fog that boils up over the cape—
and the light bursts upon me for an instant, as if it had to cast its
great curious eye upon me, too.

There are lights at sea. Ships in the dark, untouchable islands,
misfits adrift. And I wonder: Am I the only one born out of time, out
of place? Or is the mystery deeper—is each of us secretly adrift? And
if so, are we not all explorers?

AUGUST 18

*7:27 A.M. Inland from Cape Blanco. 58°F. Mileage so far today: 2.0.
Total: 14.7.*

I awake at first light. The drizzly fog has left everything damp.
While my little butane burner boils a teapot of water for oatmeal, I
stuff my wet tent. By 6:30, all is ready. It takes two tries to swing the
huge backpack into place—I must rest it on my knee halfway up to
do it at all. Then I walk out through the sleeping campground and
follow the road east.

On the silent road, doubts loom up through the fog. Suddenly it
seems like someone else—someone very naïve—drew the 1,300-mile
route in red ink across my maps. That red line blithely wanders cross-
country through canyons and mountains I've never seen—perhaps
over cliffs or into impossible brush. Hundreds of unanticipated prob-
lems could keep me from ever reaching the nine checkpoints laid out
for me across Oregon. What if I break my leg, or get shot by a
drunken hunter? And I'd told everyone weather would not change my
schedule—but, but, but! Maybe I started too late in the year. I had
wanted to spend most of the summer with my family, and now as a
result, my schedule crowds perilously close to winter. On October 29
my route climbs six thousand feet out of Hells Canyon—past the
ominous label Freezeout Saddle—to its finish atop Hat Point.

Last week my father insisted on buying a $100,000 life insur-
ance policy for me, with my wife as beneficiary. At seventeen dollars a
month, he said it was a deal he couldn't pass up.

A white picket fence appears out of the fog, with a sign: CAPE
BLANCO PIONEER CEMETERY. My shoulders are already so sore, I set

down my pack to rest. Only five or six thin white tombstones stand crooked in the grass. The first one reads: WILLIAM O'SULLIVAN, BORN IRELAND, DIED 1900, AGE 86."

For a moment I just stare at my name chiseled in the marble. I have found my own tombstone.

Then I smile: At least I lived to old age.

Then I laugh out loud. Suddenly all my doubts and fears seem ridiculous. My only real obstacle has been myself!

I breathe deep the cool, fresh air of the Pacific. Ahead lies some of the most glorious wild country in the world. And by God, I'm going to charge into it whistling "The Happy Wanderer."

7:15 P.M. Atop Grassy Knob, elev. 2,342'. Day's mileage: 17.8. Total: 30.5.

The climate and plant life change drastically as I hike inland from Cape Blanco.

At the cape, Sitka spruce and salal fight to survive in a harsh environment alongside twisted lodgepole pine, salmonberry, and bracken fern: It could be the Alaska Panhandle. Just two miles inland is a foggy rain forest, with western red cedar and alder spreading a canopy over sword fern, huckleberry, and red elderberry: It feels like western Washington. Four miles inland, where I suddenly hike out from under the curtain of coastal fog, sunshine pours down into a Douglas fir forest, with rhododendron, blackberry, goldenrod, blue mint, and spirea still in bloom: It is undeniably Oregon.

I cross Highway 101 amid the rumblings of trucks, and follow a narrow road uphill, toward one of Oregon's least-visited Wilderness Areas, Grassy Knob. There are no houses along this quiet forest road. So I am surprised when a long-haired woman in cutoffs appears momentarily from the roadside foliage, and then disappears.

"Hello?" I call.

There is a pause. Then a branch is pushed aside and the woman is watching me again.

"What are you doing?" I ask.

"What are *you* doing?" she asks, rather guiltily, I think.

"I'm hiking."

A muffled voice from farther back asks, "*What's* he doing?" The long-haired woman calls over her shoulder, "He's hiking." Then she speaks to me. Suddenly her tone is secure, even superior. "We're foraging."

"Foraging? For berries?"

"No, for ferns."

I notice she really does have a bundle of fern fronds in her hand. I give her a baffled look, and she adds, "Lady ferns and cedar sprays. A florist wholesaler buys them for flower arrangements."

"Does it pay?"

"Yes."

"Is it—is it legal?"

She tosses her head and disappears into the brush. So I never find out.

I hike on, looking back from time to time. Behind me, the fog has lifted from Cape Blanco. I can see down to the four-mile-wide coastal plain I crossed in the morning. The plain looks like a huge, dry beach, and it is. It was cut smooth by ocean waves when the land was lower. In fact, the little plateaus I am climbing past—some of them more than a thousand feet above the current sea level—are all wave-cut terraces.

The entire Pacific coastline of North America is slowly rising, stranding beaches such as this one from California to Alaska. At the same time, the Atlantic coastline is sinking, drowning valleys as at Chesapeake Bay. Our continent is listing like a ship run aground.

Up here, close to the wilderness boundary, the Douglas fir forest is mixed with bushy, leathery-leaved trees that belong in the hot, dry northern California chaparral: madrone, with its red peeling bark; chinkapin, with spiny, yellow golfball-sized fruits known locally as "porcupine eggs"; and canyon live oak, with small holly-shaped leaves that stay a dusty green all year. The foggy rain forest of Cape Blanco seems a thousand miles away.

A year-old buck steps out into the road, looks at me, but does not even raise its white tail in alarm as it walks back into the forest.

The ridge narrows; the canyons on either side steepen; and then a small metal sign, posted in the middle of the road, announces: U.S. FOREST SERVICE WILDERNESS—MOTORIZED VEHICLES AND EQUIPMENT PROHIBITED. The sign is bolted to a steel highway barricade. Beyond the barricade, the freshly built gravel road continues just the same, with galvanized culverts and one hundred-foot road cuts, into the forest. Wilderness? My map shows this as a footpath leading to the summit of Grassy Knob.

I sigh. I had been warned about this. In the waning months of the wilderness designation battle of 1984, when Grassy Knob was being considered for inclusion in the Wilderness Bill, a Forest Service supervisor suddenly ordered the area's only trail replaced with a thirty-foot-wide logging road. No matter that the Forest Service admitted that road construction in this steep area would cost more than logging revenues would return. No matter that a court injunction was in the works to stop construction. The road went in.

For a time it seemed that a single bureaucrat's antiwilderness bias had forever disqualified Grassy Knob. The Wilderness Act is very clear: An official wilderness must be "an area where the earth and its community of life are untrammeled by man, . . . retaining its primeval character and influence, without permanent improvements." But conservationists objected that this particular road amounted to "legislation by bulldozer." The U.S. Congress, which had previously considered excluding Grassy Knob, put the area back in.

I crawl over the barricade. It is nearly evening, and the clouds have settled over the hills in a mysterious fog. I walk on into the designated Wilderness, another two miles according to the pedometer hanging on my belt. The strange logging road nearly levels the misty summit of Grassy Knob, then dips to a saddle, where it ends with a flourish, in a two-acre turnaround of crushed rock. Slash has been bulldozed into the forest on all sides. If there ever was a level spot for a tent here, it has been buried by this wilderness parking lot. However, tiny clumps of blue lupine and white chickweed are coming up defiantly in the little desert. With a smile I join them, and pitch my tent smack in the middle, using rocks as anchors.

Food is a celebration after the day's seventeen-mile hike. I cook up my only packet of freeze-dried lasagne. Although the package claims to be a two-man dinner, it leaves me hungry. I think of the reconstituted mashed potatoes I threw away in disgust the night before. I wish I had them now.

In the twilight, to shake down my sore leg muscles, I walk back to Grassy Knob, a little bare-topped hummock above the steep, forested ridges. The fire lookout tower that was once here is gone, and it is too foggy to see far. Still, I can well imagine the terror of the lookout rangers who, in September 1942, were attacked by the Japanese.

Grassy Knob was one of only two places in the lower forty-eight United States that were targeted and bombed during World War II. An odd place to attack? Well, yes and no. The whole story was only recently told by the man who planned the raid: Nobuo Fujita.

In 1942 Fujita was a Japanese Navy pilot when the Americans pulled off a daring bombing raid on Tokyo. Fujita thought he could retaliate in kind by bombing the American mainland. He routinely flew reconnaissance missions from a submarine, scouting targets for his shipmates to torpedo. His plane had to be catapulted off the submarine's deck for each mission. Upon his return, the plane's pontoons and wings were detached, and its waterproof fuselage was bolted back onto the deck. It was a strange little aircraft, but it had a three hundred-mile range, and it could carry one bomb.

So Fujita loaded an incendiary bomb and flew toward the closest, westernmost shore he could find. It would be too risky to bomb a city. He planned to start a forest fire, hoping to detract manpower from the U.S. war effort.

The lookouts atop Grassy Knob must have gaped at the little Japanese plane buzzing their tower. It might be the vanguard of a great attack. Some of the rangers rushed outside. Others raced to the lookout telephone. Meanwhile, the plane dropped its bomb into the forest.

The U.S. Army Air Corps scrambled into full alert. Within minutes, fighters armed with antisubmarine depth charges were in the air. However, because of some confusion about the names of the towns nearest to Grassy Knob—Bandon and North Bend—the Army Air Corps dispatched the fighters not to the coast, but rather to the town of Bend, some two hundred miles inland, in Oregon's high desert plateaus. One fighter got things sorted out in time to attack the Japanese submarine as it dived. Fujita's plane had already been mounted to the deck, and he escaped in the damaged sub alive.

Nobuo Fujita recently returned to Oregon as a tourist. He talked over old times with the old Grassy Knob lookout personnel and invited a local high school class to visit him in Japan. All animosity was forgotten.

But—what of Fujita's incendiary bomb? It never went off. Despite many searches, it has never been found.

As I walk back down to my tent on the rock road, I think of the bomb dropped here—the bomb that would have destroyed these forests. Perhaps it is merely biding its time, like the log trucks waiting for their wilderness road to open.

AUGUST 20

6:15 A.M. Near Iron Mt. Mileage yesterday: 23.5. Total: 54.0.

Yesterday was beautiful, but so arduous I could not write. If the seven miles I had to bushwhack yesterday morning are typical of the trailless stretches ahead, I will not reach Hells Canyon.

It was drizzling at dawn, so I put on my rain pants, raincoat, and the red waterproof pack cover. Hunched over, I studied the topographic map. There are no trails at all in the Grassy Knob Wilderness, and the fog was so thick I could not see across the gravel turnaround. The red line on my map roller-coastered east along a ridgeline for four miles, then dived off to the south, down a creek canyon to the Elk River and a forest road. I would have to walk with a compass in hand, checking direction every few hundred yards, and verifying my position by the slope of the ground under my feet. I clambered through the slash at the end of the road, and launched myself ahead into the brush.

I was immediately thrown back by a tangle of branches. From a distance, the huge, old-growth trees gave the impression that the forests on these ridge crests were open. But underneath was a ten-foot-thick layer of intertwined madrone, rhododendron, and live oak. The only feasible way through this wet chaparral, I decided, was to act like a bear, wallowing forward by sheer weight. So off I wallowed.

The method worked for downhill travel; uphill was harder. Occasionally I was able to climb on open slopes, under gnarled live oaks that dripped with moss. There the ground glowed a brilliant green from its mossy carpet. But on most uphill slopes, I had to pull my way through with my hands, as if I were climbing up a jungle gym.

I invented two rules of bushwhacking. First, when in doubt, stay on high ground, since the lower slopes dive down to who knows where. Second, keep cool-headed enough to believe the map and not take hunches based on shapes seen through the fog. Of course, every hill and pass is a little farther away, and a little bigger than it seems from the map, especially when it can take a quarter hour just to cross a hundred feet of snarled blowdown.

After five hours the map showed me just four miles from my start, though I'd jiggled the pedometer so much in my struggles it said I'd hiked six and a half miles. I simply had to rest. With a defeated sigh, I went limp in the brush, my arms draped about the branches. I hung there like a fly in a web, the drizzle dripping from my coat, hair, and nose. Inside my "breathable" rain gear I was soaked with sweat. Then I saw an old, blackened frying pan lying on the ground ahead.

Incredibly, I was not the first to reach this remote spot. I looked again at my map, and suddenly realized this was the pass I had been searching for. Here I would leave the ridge crest and go down Sunshine Creek.

The creek canyon was a completely different rain forest world of deep greens, with delicate maidenhair ferns and sweeping cedars. Lovely little creeks disappeared under gravel beds only to reappear later in chutes or falls down curved, smooth bedrock.

The canyon was not easier to travel. Deadfall choked the narrow gorge—often bridging it from side to side—and there was waterfall after waterfall. Each cascade was beautifully fresh and white, but after a while it was hard not to see them also as mountaineering challenges, for the cascades were often thirty feet tall, in a sheer-sided canyon. At times I could climb downward past the falls, feeling my way on ledges and slick moss; at other times I had to make long uphill detours around them.

I was climbing over the snaky limbs of a huge and very grand cedar when I noticed the tree was not of the ordinary variety. There were little white Xs on the underside of its leaf scales. It was a Port Orford cedar—a rare find in the wild.

This fragrant tree is one of the most popular landscaping cedars in the world. In the city it is easily tamed to form neat, elliptical bushes. Here in the wild, however, it can grow to be five hundred years old and 190 feet tall. Its native range is restricted to the remote parts of five coastal counties near the Oregon-California line, and that range is rapidly shrinking.

Part of the Port Orford cedar's problem is its cash value. The Japanese are willing to pay as much as $10,000 for a single tree. The

Port Orford cedar is a close substitute for Japan's native hinoki cypress, whose wood the Japanese admire so greatly they have nearly driven this cypress to extinction.

A bigger threat to the wild Port Orford cedar, however, is *Phytophthora lateralis,* a root-rot fungus carried on the wheels of civilization. Every Port Orford cedar this fungus touches dies. Because the fungus spreads easily through groundwater, every tree in an infected drainage will die.

The fungus, first noticed in tree nurseries in Portland, was accidentally introduced in this area in 1944. For a time, foresters were puzzled because the blight did not stay confined to one drainage but spread along logging roads, and jumped from campground to campground. Then they realized that every log truck, bulldozer, and four-wheel-drive vehicle in an infected area was carrying tiny bits of infected soil on its tire treads and fenders. The roadless side of Grassy Knob may be the wild Port Orford cedar's last stand.

Finally Sunshine Creek became continuous, and full of four-inch, darting trout. Then the canyon opened onto the Elk River. The river was unrecognizable from my earlier fording on the beach, for here it was a rushing mountain stream with mossy cliff banks and clear, startlingly green pools.

I waded, calf-deep, barefoot, then sat on the round river rocks to collect my thoughts. I had spent eight and a half hours and all of my energy crashing through seven miles of forest. But my schedule required me to go on. The following day I was supposed to reach the tiny settlement of Agness on the Rogue River by noon, to meet a newspaper reporter and check in with my wife by telephone. Wearily, I rolled up my rain gear—the clouds had lifted again—and set off up the logging road.

Now I could understand the troubles of the government's 1851 expedition into these hills. The U.S. Navy had dropped off a force of twenty men near Cape Blanco with orders to blaze a supply trail inland to the newly discovered gold mines in the Klamath Mountains. The mines lay near the headwaters of the Rogue River, so the men started up the Rogue. But the central canyon of that river is one of the most rugged on earth. After bushwhacking as far as Agness, the men gave up and turned north instead (toward the Grassy Knob forests!). They abandoned their packhorses. They became completely lost in the dense underbrush. When they finally staggered back to the sea, the Indians killed all but five of them.

The U.S. Navy reported the expedition's failure with embarrassment. The following year, in 1852, the U.S. Army was sent out instead.

Last night, after coming down from Grassy Knob, I dragged myself another sixteen and a half miles on a logging road, climbing three thousand feet out of the Elk River Canyon to Iron Mountain. The stars were out at 9:30 P.M. when I stopped, utterly exhausted, and collapsed into my sleeping bag. The stars were still out this morning when I awoke and began writing.

12:16 P.M. Agness General Store. 88°F, sunny. Mileage so far today: 12.7. Total: 66.7.

Iron Mountain, like most of the taller hills in the Klamath Mountains, is unforested on the southwest side of its summit. None of these hills are above timberline, and they all have forest on their other sides, so it makes one wonder why they are grassy on only the southwest face. Is it lack of moisture on the sunny south side? Exposure to lightning storms on the windy west side? I don't know. But I do know the phenomenon once caused hundreds of treasure seekers a great deal of trouble.

The treasure story began with a report filed by Dr. John Evans, a geologist doing surveys for the U.S. Department of the Interior in 1856. He had just completed an expedition from Port Orford inland to Eugene, and sent some of his rock samples to the Smithsonian Institution. They wrote back that one of the rocks was extraterrestrial in origin: a Pallasite meteorite. In great excitement, Evans announced the fragment had come from an eleven-ton rock projecting four or five feet above the grassy, boulderless west slope of a very prominent "Bald Mountain," some forty miles from Port Orford. The Smithsonian commissioned Evans to return to the site, but he died before the expedition could get under way. Two Smithsonian geologists who followed his instructions failed to find the rock.

The whole affair was forgotten until a reporter for the *Oregonian* discovered the tale in 1937, and printed it, along with the observation that Pallasite material had since increased in value to one hundred

was reported incorrectly that first time, and the post office is slow to change. Mail delivery has always been by boat, up the river from Gold Beach. Now, however, the mail boats have jet engines, and carry mainly loads of tourists, bouncing up the white water to look at the canyon for a few hours. There is much talk here that the Rogue River and its biggest tributary, the Illinois River, may be declared part of a new National Park. From Agness south to the California line, these rivers cut through the Kalmiopsis and Wild Rogue wildernesses in the largest roadless forest in Oregon.

I hose off my head and chest. Then I go to the phone booth, standing out among the dry weeds, and call my wife.

She has been waiting by the phone. She says our four-year-old daughter begs for Papa's bedtime stories every night, and then cries herself to sleep. Our two-year-old son, however, seems to enjoy having Papa gone so he can be man of the house. I don't know which behavior troubles me most.

"Oh, and there's a message from the insurance company," she adds. "They say your policy's void if you do any hang gliding or mountain climbing."

"Did you tell them I'm walking, not hang gliding?"

"Yes, but they can't find any restrictions on *walking*."

The operator breaks into the line. "Three minutes," she says. I just have time to say good-bye.

I eat my lunch under a tree, thinking of the miles I will have to walk before I reach another telephone. Then I look at the digital watch in my pocket. The newspaper reporter I'm supposed to meet should be here by now. Our rendezvous is at the Agness ranger station; I wonder if the station's not right here in town?

AUGUST 21

6:38 A.M. Illinois River. 48°F. Mileage yesterday: 27.0. Total: 81.0.

This morning I am recovered enough to write again.

When I stopped writing yesterday, I went into the general store to ask directions. The woman told me the ranger station was moved across the river last year. It was six and a half miles, she said, by way of the new bridge. Time was short. Without my pack, I might have been able to swim the river and save an hour. As it was, I set off on the road at a fast walk. Three times, pickup trucks pulled up to a dusty halt beside me to offer a lift. Each time I said no, thanks—for I still hope to walk every step of the way across Oregon. The drivers only shook their heads.

When I reached the station, my pedometer read twenty miles for the day. The reporter came out of the shade with a grin and a handshake. "I wondered if you were coming. Do we still have time to take our little hike?"

I had agreed to backpack with him seven miles up the Illinois River Trail this afternoon. How could I have misjudged the significance of these distances so badly? The soles of my feet were burning. True, I already had calluses on my heels from my warm-up hikes earlier in the summer, but I was getting sneaky blisters in unlikely spots: between my toes or at the edge of a callus. Since Agness, I had been limping on both feet at once, like a man trying to walk barefoot over a field of hot gravel.

Still, I wasn't about to limp and groan in front of this reporter. I could imagine his article calling me a tenderfoot. "Sure, Bob," I said, and led off toward the trailhead with a very firm smile.

Bob, a clean-shaven man about my age, followed with his light pack. As we walked he asked questions about the New Oregon Trail I am scouting, but often he just smiled at the sky, as if smirking that he had bamboozled his editor into paying him to go camping.

Snow apples overhung the road—I was hungry and ate three. They were so soft and ripe and plentiful, a mash of the fallen fruit littered the road, attracting yellowjackets.

A curious Monarch butterfly fluttered our way, and pursued us for a quarter of a mile. It flitted ahead, lagged a bit as it got distracted, then sailed past us again. It didn't really flap its wings often, but soared like a delicate, orange-and-black paper airplane. Monarchs are uncommon here, since their caterpillars only eat milkweed, and I haven't seen any milkweed on my hike.

Just before the trailhead, Bob pointed out a historical marker by the road: OAK FLAT, SITE OF PEACE TREATY, 1856. He asked if I knew which peace treaty it meant, and I nodded. However, I had never heard the Battle of Oak Flat called a peace treaty before.

The battle was the U.S. Army's first real difficulty after building a fort near Cape Blanco in 1852. The army never tried to blaze a supply line to the mines. Instead, it concentrated on taming the wilderness and Indians along the coast. After four years, the army celebrated its success by holding a Washington's Birthday dance. While the soldiers were dancing, however, the Indians burnt sixty cabins along the southern Oregon coast and killed all the new white settlers they could find.

It took the soldiers a month to chase the Indians up the Rogue River to Oak Flat. Here they held a parley. The army's Captain Smith informed the assembled chiefs that they would have to go to the Siletz reservation on the northern Oregon coast. They would have a good life there, he said. They would receive free blankets, plows, and seeds, and white agents would teach them to farm. The bad news was that any Indian found off the reservation would be hanged.

Some of the chiefs thought they might go to the reservation; one, Tyee John, thought they should not. Both sides agreed to meet again in the morning.

In the morning one of the soldiers' sentinels fell. There was a puff of powder and a rifle crack. Without orders, the white soldiers began frantically digging rifle pits with bayonets and tin plates. The Indians charged, were repelled, and charged again all that day.

After a sleepless night the soldiers counted eleven of their number dead and sixteen wounded. The wounded men moaned for water, but the supply of water was gone.

Between charges, the Indians taunted the soldiers in a mixture of English and Chinook jargon, the trade language of the Oregon frontier: "Mika hias ticka chuck (you sure would like some water). One more sun no water, no muckamuck (food), no soldier. All dead."

Captain Smith bellowed back that they would all hang.

Tyee John made a cedar-bark noose and waved it, yelling, "Oh, Captain Smith! If you promise to go on the reservation and not travel around the country, I will not hang you! See this rope? It is for you, because you do not want to stay on a reservation where you can have plenty of plows and wagons and plenty to eat, and white men to teach you." Finally the Indians drew up ranks for a final charge to wipe out the whites.

At that moment seventy-five additional white soldiers came into sight, marching up the Rogue River Canyon. Captain Smith's men jumped from their shallow pits and charged down the hill. The surprised Indians, caught in a crossfire, were taken captive.

The army herded the Indians together, tied their hands, and assigned guards to march them three hundred miles to the reservation. The prisoners had only marched a few days when a group of white settlers overpowered the guards, and all the Indians were shot.

The Illinois River Trail we were hiking climbed through deep forest to Buzzard's Roost, a crag high above the thin green river. Bob was silent now, for he had already run through two rolls of film and exhausted his supply of questions.

My legs were wobbling when we reached a meadow campsite beside Indigo Creek. I dropped my pack, took off my boots and socks, and cautiously felt the soles of my feet. To my surprise, they were neither bloody nor covered with blisters. They were mostly just red, complaining that they did not wish to hike twenty-seven miles a day.

That evening we lay in the meadow, watching a sickle moon go down and the stars come out. We talked into the darkening sky, the way boys do on summer evenings in the backyard, relating their innermost feelings to the compassionate night air, unaware that the neighbors are listening out their windows and chuckling. Finally the huge silence of the wilderness became more important than words.

It was the first clear night of the trip—and what a spectacle it was! Blue-white Vega beamed precisely overhead, yellow Arcturus shimmered to one side, and across the whole blazed the Milky Way, glowing so brightly that the dark, mottled dust clouds of the galaxy's arm stood out in sharp relief.

In the stillness of the night, the unseen gravity pressing our backs against the dark meadow seemed like an untrustworthy force—as if it might suddenly fail, and we would go hurtling off into the galaxy on edge before us.

11:23 A.M. On the Illinois River Trail. Mileage so far today: 6.8. Total: 87.8.

Bears today.

I get off to a late start this morning, writing, waiting for the

reporter to wake up. Suddenly I notice a woman on horseback, leading a packhorse quietly across the far end of the meadow. She is
perhaps in her thirties, with strong, handsome features and her hair
tied back. She wears jeans and a simple jacket. She looks ahead only,
with a serious expression. Remarkably, I recognize her.

Seven years ago I hiked the Illinois River Trail with my wife, and
camped at this same spot. Since we had made camp in the early
afternoon, we had time to wander up Indigo Creek. A mile upriver we
came to a fallen fence, a tepee, and three very inquisitive goats. The
goats lifted papers and gloves right out of our pockets and butted us
gently, as if begging to be petted. "Anyone home?" we called. At that,
two naked little boys jumped out of the tepee and danced about us in
the dust. Then a young woman came out, with a confused, friendly
smile. She wore a great bunch of beads around her neck and a volu-
minous peasant dress that reached to her bare feet. She talked about
birds and wildflowers as the friendly goats pushed her one way and
then the other. In answer to our questions, she said she was camping
on the land as a squatter; the area was an island of private land in the
National Forest, and was owned by someone back east who had never
been there.

Seven years later, she is still here. I smile, expecting a greeting.
She simply rides past, her eyes set sternly forward. Probably she is
still raising goats and boys. Certainly she is still a squatter. But the
starry-eyed flower child of the 1970s is gone.

When Bob crawls out of bed, I shake his hand in farewell. I
follow the forest trail in silence for two miles.

Then I am startled by a huge black squirrel. The squirrel climbs
ten feet up a trailside tree before I realize it is actually a black bear
cub, no bigger than a fuzzy pillow. It hitches up the tree a few more
feet and peers at me fearfully with its tiny black eyes and light brown
snout.

The cute cub presents me with a problem. Its mother is surely
nearby, and would likely interpret my hiking past this tree as an act
of aggression. Mother black bears are said to be extremely dangerous
when protecting their cubs. And I'd have little defense, for black bears
can run thirty miles per hour, and climb trees much better than people. So I retreat backward, around a corner. I whistle an appeasing
tune loudly while I wait. I think about *bears*.

The most famous of all Oregon bears was Old Reelfoot, a grizzly that limped from the effects of a steel trap. According to legend, he was first sighted in 1846 by the great western explore Frémont. Old Reelfoot terrorized southern Oregon stockmen between Crater Lake and the Klamath River for decades. Finally, in 1891, he was killed by two hunters in a hair-raising battle at the base of Pilot Rock on the California line. Old Reelfoot's eight-foot carcass was carefully stuffed and exhibited at the Columbian Exposition in Chicago in 1893. Not long afterward, the grizzly bear became extinct in all of Oregon.

Black bears fuel a lesser terror. They are never much more than five hundred pounds, and are never taller than three and a half feet at the shoulder. They are quite capable of killing a man, but I've never heard of it happening.

My first plan after retreating from this black bear cub is that I will rush past it, holding my burning butane stove before me like a torch against demons. Now that I've calmed down a bit, the plan seems silly. I've given the little bear half an hour to itself. I put my pack back on, and walk past the tree. The cub and its unseen mother have understood my courtesy, and are gone.

The trail crosses a creek amid huge outcroppings of rock, hot in the sun. All along the rock there are little scurryings, tiny creatures escaping from the trail like minuscule, uphill rockslides. I pause, and one of the creatures pauses, too. It is a Western fence lizard—*Sceloperus occidentalis*—mottled exactly the color of the brown rock. The camouflage would make him invisible, if he didn't insist on doing little push-ups with his front legs the whole time he's watching me. I take his picture. He bows again, and becomes another uphill rock-slide.

After that I watch the rocks more carefully. I'm just starting to think I've got these lizards pretty well figured out when I come across one that's bright blue. Well, only its tail, perhaps, but the tail is absolutely iridescent. I flip through the research notes in the front of my journal.

It is a juvenile skink. And why is its tail so stunning? Like the fence lizards, it's thinking about the hawks that swoop down and grab little reptiles by their tails. Both skinks and lizards are able to detach their tails in that moment of need, and so to scurry to safety, where they can grow a new tail. Young skinks have taken the added precaution of making sure the hawk sees the tail first. Presumably an older skink would know enough not to get caught at all.

The trail climbs into the dry forest again, past several worrisome piles of bear scat. I've had my encounter with a bear today, and want no more. But when I reach the crest of a steep ridge, two black bear cubs tumble over each other in their haste to scramble up a tree. Again, they are hanging right over my trail. Again, the slope is so steep that the tree cannot be easily circumvented. I take a slow step backward. But I am too late. The mother bear, as big as a gorilla, is charging down the trail at me.

The adrenaline of terror rushes in. But for that one instant I cannot run. As if in slow motion, the great bear reaches the tree where its cubs are clinging, lifts her snout to me, and lunges.

She lunges onto the tree. With a huff and a grunt, she climbs up past her two trembling cubs. Then she hides on the far side of the big trunk, and peers out.

I back down the trail, my heart pounding, my mouth dry. When I am out of sight, I hear the scratch of claws on bark. There are more huffs and heavy crunchings in the dry leaves as the bears take off down the far side of the ridge at what sounds like a terrific pace.

I have been outclimbed and outrun.

3:54 P.M. Atop Bald Mountain. Mileage so far today: 10.5. Total: 91.5.

The Illinois River Canyon is so steep and rugged here that the "river trail" finally gives up trying to get through at all, and instead detours over the top of Bald Mountain. The sun is blazing as I switchback up this 3,600-foot climb; my T-shirt and socks are soon soaked with sweat. However, I know there is a cool spring near Bald Mountain's wilderness summit and push on.

I am practically at the spring when a black-bearded man in baggy clothes steps out of a green dome tent beside the trail.

"Well, hello," he says. "I knew there was a reason I made extra spaghetti sauce. You prefer coffee or Red Zinger?"

"Um—" I stall. "Water?"

He waves to the spring beyond his tent. "Help yourself. And by the way—the name's Lou. Lou Gold."

I limp to the spring and fill my cupped hands over and over. It gives me some time to survey this sudden host.

Lou seems to be in his forties, wears sandals, and has a vaguely East Coast accent. His curly black hair is tied back with a blue-white-red bandanna. Lou's camp is dominated by a fire pit with a big iron grate and blackened pots. Logs and planks form shelves for neat stacks of firewood and canned goods. Lined up against a huge Douglas fir nearby are twenty long sticks, decorated with strange carvings and colored ribbons. Like Lou himself, the sticks are puzzling but not threatening.

"Are you serious about the spaghetti?" I ask.

"Absolutely."

He has won me over. I sit on one of the logs, put my sore feet into a pair of tennis shoes, and we talk.

Lou tells me he is camped here as a sentinel for Earth First!, an environmental group that fears Bald Mountain will be logged. Even though Bald Mountain appears to stand deep in the wilderness, the official Wilderness designation cuts the mountain in half. A five-mile-long logging road already has been built precisely on the wilderness boundary, to within three miles of Bald Mountain's summit. Lou shows me photocopies of Forest Service plans that would convert much of the trail I hiked this morning into yet more road and would clear-cut the old-growth forest where I met the bears.

"Some of those slopes are almost vertical," I recall, looking at his map skeptically. "They couldn't really log it."

He points to a label on the map: HELICOPTER LOGGING AREA. "Cost is no object," he says.

I frown. "So what do you plan to do about it?"

He smiles and leans back. "Earth First! has its ways."

"Like what?"

"Nonviolent civil disobedience."

"Meaning—?"

"We stopped the road in '83 by chaining ourselves to the bulldozers. The federal judge put a condition on my probation that I not reenter the area." He shrugs. "I've been living up here every summer since then. You know, to sound the alarm if the bulldozers come back."

I shift uneasily on my log. Lou is breaking the law just by being here. On the other hand, I can't help thinking about the Grassy Knob Trail, which was bulldozed into a useless logging road while conservationists wrung their hands, and about the Agness Trail, which is being turned into a logging road at this very moment. Now here is a Bald Mountain road, drawn on the map in such a way that it would clear-cut the absolute center out of the proposed Siskiyou National Park. The remarkable thing about the controversy, it seems to me, is that this road has been stopped, half built, for three years, by a black-bearded hermit who serves spaghetti to strangers.*

"What do you do while you wait?" I ask.

"Oh, a lot. The first summer I backpacked out a quarter ton of glass and metal left after they burned the old fire lookout tower. Last year I fixed up the trails, and rolled up five miles of wire from the old lookout telephone. This summer I found a rusted motorcycle up here. I'm tearing it apart with WD-40 and box wrenches, packing it out piece by piece."

Mention of the motorcycle jolts loose another memory for me. Seven years ago I had met a motorcyclist on the Illinois River Trail. I had asked the man if motor vehicles weren't prohibited there, and he had nodded but said he was hired to patrol Bald Mountain for lightning fires. Then he had grinned and confided he was growing a little patch of marijuana on the mountain, too.

Lou nods when I tell him. "Could be the same bike. This one was by a spring with a clever little marijuana irrigation system."

Then Lou strokes his bushy black beard thoughtfully and looks straight through me. "I have a deeper calling here. Most of my time is spent learning the Earth."

I hesitate. "How do you 'learn the Earth'?"

"Every evening I have an appointment with the sunset. I sit in the medicine circle I've built on the summit and meditate in the four directions until dark. In May, when the snow has melted enough for me to set up camp here, the dark comes early. In those days it rains and stays below thirty-five degrees. Then I hike the Pilgrim's Trail I've been roughing out. The route is a vast square, connecting four peaks

---

*Since my hike, an Oregon conservation leader (who opposes Lou's illegal methods) confided that Lou's presence not only has stopped the Bald Mountain road, but that the initial Earth First! road blockade sparked a lawsuit over the Forest Service's handling of roadless lands throughout the West—a lawsuit that led to the Oregon Wilderness Bill of 1984.

in the four directions." As he speaks, he points across the canyon to mountains that I know can only be reached by swimming the Illinois and scrambling up three thousand-foot canyon walls.

"I study my fellow animals. I watch the plants. I pray. That is how I learn the spirits of the Earth."

He looks at me again. Now it is clear to me why Lou has risked his liberty to camp here: He does not merely love the wilderness, as I do, he reveres it. It is everywhere alive. I have unwittingly hiked into the temple of a strange guru.

Suddenly he releases me from his gaze. "So what have you seen on the trail today?"

"Well, I met four bears on my way up."

He lifts an eyebrow. "What were they eating?"

I think back. "There were reddish-brown berries in their droppings. And they left torn-up ponderosa pinecones all over the trail."

"Yes, it is time they began eating pine nuts and manzanita berries. Manzanita berries will only grow after they have been passed by a bear. In May the bears were up on the summit prairies, eating grain from the grasses. In June they got a taste for protein and began digging up yellowjacket nests. In July they went downhill after rodents and fish. Now they are returning to the mountain."

Lou stands up and takes a towel off a line. "Dinner is after my solar shower. I'm afraid there's only water for one."

He crosses the meadow to a black water bag hanging from a limb in the sun. He shucks his clothes with a shrug and turns on the water from a spigot below the bag.

I am writing in my journal when he returns to fetch clean clothes off the line. "Didn't you hear anything?" he asks.

"Hear what?"

He points out a pair of shredded socks in the middle of the clothesline. "The mice walked the line and ate the toes out of my socks while you were sitting there."

"I'm sorry."

He shrugs. "It comes, it goes."

It takes him only ten minutes to light the fire and cook the spaghetti. The sauce is meatless and full of odd leaves and spicy berries, yet it is amazingly good. I tell him of my trip, and in return he tells me about himself.

Lou grew up in Chicago, then took a degree in political science from Columbia University in New York City. He taught fiery political-science courses for eight years at Oberlin and Illinois, back in the late sixties when colleges were scrambling for political relevance in the face of anti-Vietnam protests. Then came the issue of tenure.

Lou searches for words. "The university and I finally conspired to liberate me from it. I've never been sorry. There were parts of me and parts of the universe that were best explored by getting out. I did carpentry for six years, and then wandered for a while. I visited friends in southern Oregon. I wasn't here three days before I realized everything I was looking for in the universe could be found right in the Illinois Valley."

"Then you spend the winters here, too?"

"Not on Bald Mountain. In a community on the upper Illinois, toward the High Siskiyous. I live in a yurt on a friend's land."

"Do you still support yourself with carpentry?"

"My needs are few. Two nights a week I fire up a little sweat lodge, and people come. Not for money, of course, but they sometimes bring gifts. It's like here at Bald Mountain. When I need food, it comes. When I have enough, I share."

As soon as I clean my spaghetti bowl, I thank him for the dinner, but tell him I have to hike a few miles yet today. I share a few pieces of hard butterscotch with him—it is all I have to share—and assemble my pack.

"Wait," he says, and walks to the row of decorated sticks leaning against the tree. "Everyone who visits Bald Mountain takes a peace stick. Each stick has seven colored ribbons, representing the four directions, as well as the Earth, the Sky, and the Sunset Breeze—the spirit at the center. Choose the one that touches your spirit."

I look over the sticks with some misgivings. They are between four and six feet long—straight and freshly barked. It occurs to me they might serve as walking sticks, but I have always shunned walking sticks as just one more thing to carry. But it also occurs to me that he has an awful lot of sticks, and probably very few visitors. I take the lightest one and thank him for his generosity.

The trail passes the summit of Bald Mountain. White rocks are arranged there on the ground in the shape of a fifty-foot wheel with four spokes. Lou's prayer site, I realize, straddles the wilderness boundary. Sticks like the one I am carrying mark the cardinal directions on the rim of the circle, their ribbons fluttering in what will soon be the Sunset Breeze.

AUGUST 22

8:15 A.M. Briggs Creek trailhead. Mileage yesterday: 18.5. Mileage so far today: 3.5. Total: 103.0.

I continue my hike down from Bald Mountain this morning. Dry leaves crunch on the trail. The sound sends little red-brown Douglas squirrels scampering; they make their worried, whirring squirrel noises all through the trees. Orange sunlight slices through the low canopy of gnarled, moss-shagged canyon live oak. Poison oak adds splashes of bright red in an autumn forest now too dry for most wildflowers.

Poison oak is really one of the prettiest shrubs in the western Oregon forests, with its flaming autumn-leaf triplets and minute, starry white spring flowers. I don't know if *Rhus diversiloba*'s poison would give me a rash, since I've never touched it to find out. It did not seem to bother the local Indians. They wove baskets from its vines and stained basketry with its black juice. One Indian name for it was *Ma-tu-ya-ho,* or Southern Fire Doctor, because its juice, dripped on warts and ringworm, burned them out. I stop to photograph a fiery clump of poison oak, but through the viewfinder it just looks like a scraggly weed.

It's frustrating how few things in this huge canyon country seem to fit into my camera's rectangular box. A picture of a rocky slope with a forested ridge in the background would capture none of the awe I feel. The awe is in being *entirely surrounded* by rocky slopes and forested ridges. There is no snowcapped peak here at which to aim a camera. Instead, I am dropped among endless hills that seem to be focusing down on *me.*

I leave my peace stick at the Briggs Creek bridge, at the end of the Illinois River Trail. I have arranged to meet Len Ramp here, the state geologist for southern Oregon. I have been told he knows more about the Kalmiopsis Wilderness than anyone. I suspect he will know very different things than Lou.

9:52 A.M.—A little four-by-four pickup bumps down the dirt road and slows to look me over. The door reads: STATE OF OREGON, GEOLOGY.

> 7:07 P.M. Kalmiopsis Wilderness. 78°F. Day's mileage: 19.9. Total: 119.4.

Len Ramp is a lean bantam of a man with dark eyes and a trim black moustache. His weathered face is older than I had expected. A dozen pockets in his red canvas vest bulge mysteriously. A geologist's pick, the tool of his trade, hangs from a loop on his belt.

He smiles, but waits for me to speak.

"Len Ramp? I'm Bill."

He shakes my hand with a firm grip, and gives a signal to the driver of the pickup. The pickup growls back up the dusty road. Finally Len speaks. "He'll meet us ten miles up the road, at the edge of the Kalmiopsis. You didn't want to toss your pack in the truck, did you?"

I look at the dust cloud left by the truck. How could I have failed to think of it myself? The pack's straps have worn searing red grooves into my shoulders. But now I just shake my head.

"I didn't think you would. Anybody backpacking all the way across Oregon's not likely to cut corners. Well?" Len flashes another smile. "Ready?"

He leads the way up the road at an amazingly brisk pace. I don't want to criticize—after all, he's taken a day off from his office work in Grants Pass to hike and talk with me—so I jolt my pack along, trying to keep up.

While I try to pretend this semijogging is my normal gait, Len does most of the talking. He says he usually runs five miles before breakfast, but he didn't today, knowing he'd get in some hiking with me. He is fifty-nine, and each summer he competes in marathons. In the winters he climbs the peaks of the Cascade Range wearing crampons, and skis down. "Had a close call climbing a glacier on Shasta not long back," he says. "Fell through the snow into a deep crevasse.

Only survived because I'd strapped my skis crosswise on my back-pack. Bridged the crevasse right near the top."

"You hike a lot in the Kalmiopsis?" I ask.

He smiles again. "I mapped it for the state. Walked every stream, trail, road, and ridge for two hundred square miles. Learned the land like the palm of my hand."

For a moment I am reminded of Lou Gold, who had "learned the Earth" on his hikes from Bald Mountain. Maybe these two out-doorsmen have more in common than I thought.

"What did you learn about the land?" I ask.

"Well," he says, assuming a serious look, "the Klamath Moun-tains are complex. The geological formations date to the Paleozoic, the strata are heavily folded, and the mineral outcroppings include numerous economically valuable elements."

I stare at him, puffing from the pace. I can't absorb this sudden technical jargon while I'm trotting under a sixty-pound pack. "Len, could we slow down a bit?"

"Was I walking too fast?"

The sun is high now, and heat rises from the road in waves. I wipe my brow with the back of my hand. "A little, I guess." I take a deep breath at the new pace. "Now you can go ahead about the Klamath Mountains—but start at the beginning, all right?"

The earth's crust, he explains, is broken into about a dozen huge plates that float around on the currents and eddies in the molten rock underneath. Two hundred million years ago the Atlantic Ocean began to widen, sending the North American plate—and the ancient Klamath Mountains—westward right over the Pacific plate. At the rate of an inch a year, the West Coast has been rammed over 1,500 miles of Pacific seafloor, buckling up new mountain ranges clear to the Rockies.

No wonder our continent lists to starboard. And no wonder the Klamaths, in the forefront of all this action, have plowed up great masses of old seafloor rock. The whole range was kneaded like bread dough.

What makes the Klamaths even stranger, Len says, diagraming the whole process with his hands while we walk, is that they were an island for fifty million years. The collision between the North Amer-ican and Pacific plates is not quite head on, but rather shears to the

north. The resulting slip zone, which includes the famous San An-
dreas Fault, has ripped Baja California away from Mexico, and Van-
couver Island from Washington. Similarly, the Klamaths must have
once been torn away from the coast, for there are sixty miles of sea
fossils between them and the rest of the continent. Strata from the
southern Klamaths match perfectly with strata in the northern Sierras—but they are separated by the sixty-mile gap, cut as neatly as if
by a huge knife. Time, and the eruption of Mount Shasta, have filled
in the "Klamath Strait." But the Klamaths still have the strange plant
life, and the mystery, of an island.

"Len Ramp!" a harsh voice shouts.

I turn and see an overweight man hustling up from a barbed-
wire gate. He wears a very clean and very taut white T-shirt over his
great, jolting stomach.

"Well howdy, Sam," Len says, smiling.

The man puffs a moment, then says, "I just been out checkin'
cabins for the Bar Sixty-six—you got any more of them eight-dollar
maps?"

"You mean the geologic quadrangles?" Len asks. "Sure, I've got a
few." He unzips a hidden pocket inside the back of his red vest and
pulls out a large manila envelope.

The overweight man opens the multicolored map on top of his
stomach. "Goddam! Looks like a baby spit up on it, all the colors.
Fella's got to have it, though. It tells where there's gold." He shakes
his head. "What are you up to today?"

Len waves his hand toward me. "I'm hiking with Bill. He's just
come down the trail from Bald Mountain."

I smile and nod.

"Goddam!" the man says. "Had a coupla Mexicans wanted to go
up that trail not long back, let 'em borrow Willy for the trip. Now,
Willy, he's OK, you understand, but he's a donkey—that's all there is
to it, he's a donkey. So the fellas load up Willy with all their stuff and
start out fine, 'cause they brought along some apples as donkey incentive, you know? Well, when they run out of apples they have a dis-
agreement. Willy takes a bite out of one of 'em and hightails it home,
scattering their gear all down the trail."

The man wheezes—is it a laugh?—and asks, "Where you
headed next, kid?"

"The Kalmiopsis."

"Up *there*? Goddam!" He jerks his head back to stare at me. His crewcut seems to bristle. "Had a coupla young prospectors head up there last year. They had it all figgered out how they was going to get rich. Took along backpacks like you're doing, too. They wandered around lost for ten days before I went in and dragged 'em back out. They'd been down to eatin' *toothpaste*."

The man gives me a meaningful look. Then he nods to the geologist beside me. "Well, see ya, Len." And he leaves.

As I continue down the road with Len, I comment, "You seem to be well known around here."

Len shrugs. "Almost everybody in these parts is a prospector, at least part time. And I'm the only state geologist south of Salem. So everybody talks to me sooner or later. They all want to know where to find gold."

I think about that, and then ask, "Where *do* you find gold?"

"No secret to it. There are traces of gold in almost every rock on earth. The problem is finding where it's concentrated enough to mine. A good place to look is in ranges like the Klamaths and the Sierras and the Blue Mountains, where chunks of the old continent have gotten sucked deep down into the earth at the edge of a moving plate. When that light, continental rock gets deep enough, it starts to melt, releasing volatiles that collect some of the gold. Then the hot rock floats back up like a bubble. If the bubble is still molten when it reaches the surface, it's a volcano, and you'll probably never find the gold. But if it cools just below the surface, it's a granite intrusion, and there'll be gold in the quartz veins that crystallize all around the edges. Parts of the Klamaths are striped with quartz."

It sounds clear enough to me. "Then you just look for quartz?"

He shakes his head. "Most quartz veins haven't concentrated enough gold to make hard rock mining pay. It's easier to let erosion do all the sorting for you. Spring floods quarry out the rock and send it down the creeks. The gold's so heavy it catches in the chinks and crevices in the bedrock. Most prospectors just stake a claim in a creek and clean the gold out of the cracks. That's placer mining."

"But once all the cracks have been cleaned out, that's it, isn't it?" I ask. "No more placer mining for another million years?"

"Not at all. Some people clean out the bedrock cracks every

year, and get new gold after each spring flood. I was shown a pill bottle of gold dust this morning by a guy who does just that."

I raise my eyebrows. "Do people like that make much at it?"

"Couple hundred dollars a month, with luck and hard work. Of course, the government won't allow new claims in the wilderness anymore."

Len pulls a quart bottle from a pocket inside his red vest, and takes a drink. Then he takes a bandanna from another pocket and mops his brow.

I am beginning to marvel at this vest of his, which easily conceals a supply of large maps and bottles. Then he spots a screwdriver and two empty beer cans in the ditch and stashes them somewhere in the vest, too.

"How many pockets do you have in that vest?" I ask.

"My vest?" He looks down at it, as though he were just discovering it. "Well, I don't know. This pocket's got rock specimen bags. Here's a first-aid kit. This little zippered thing's got an altimeter and a barometer. This pouch has my transit compass and mirror. Here I've got my hand lenses. My lunch is in this back compartment. And there's—let's see—seven pens and pencils in these loops, including a magnetic one to check ferrous samples."

My marvel has turned to awe. The vest's an entire geologic field station. It must contain twenty pounds of gear.

"Oh, and there's this hidden pocket," Len adds, "with my Sasquatch weapon."

"Your *what?*" I had not known defense was necessary—or possible—against the mythic apeman of the Klamath wilderness.

"Well, it's a sling, actually." He pulls out a long thong attached to a small patch of leather. Then he loads a peach-pit–sized piece of gravel in the leather patch, whirls it fiercely over his head, and lets go of one end of the thong. The rock crashes into the forest one hundred yards across the river.

"It'd stop Bigfoot, if I met him. I've put rocks through a three-quarter-inch board. I worry a whole lot more about meeting marijuana growers, though."

We hike around a corner above the Illinois River, and suddenly the vegetation looks crippled. The big Douglas firs have disappeared, and the other trees are no more than struggling shrubs.

"Well, now we're into ultramafic rock," Len says.

"What's that?"

"A slab of sub-seafloor. Makes very poor soil. But it does have some heavy minerals you don't often find on dry land. Magnesium, nickel, chromite, and sometimes platinum. Here, I'll show you."

Len leads me down a short side road. Sunk into the hillside is a ruin of timbers and rock tailings.

"Big mine," I say.

"Robertson's Oregon Chrome Mine," Len says.

The name rings a bell. "Funny. I remember my grandpa in Grants Pass talking about a miner named Robertson."

Len's eyes twinkle. "I knew your grandfather. This mine was one of his better investments. It and others nearby turned out two hundred thousand long tons of high-grade chromite back in the fifties, when the government was stockpiling ore at an incentive price. You can't make stainless steel without chrome, and the only other places you find very much chrome are South Africa, Turkey, and Russia. The government didn't want our supply cut off by a war, so they offered one hundred fifteen dollars a ton."

I am not surprised that Len knew my grandfather, for the towns in southern Oregon are small, and Len is the only local geologist. But what he has told me is unsettling. I look at the desolate tailings and pits with new, mixed feelings. This is not merely an ugly blot at the edge of the wilderness. It is what paid for my college education.

Len tosses me a shiny black rock from the tailings as we leave; it is surprisingly heavy. We hike down the quiet dirt road another five miles, and Len turns up dozens more of the shiny black rocks from the dust. "A lot of ore bounced out of Robertson's trucks." Len smiles. "The road to the wilderness is paved with chrome."

We cross a high, swaying footbridge over the turbulent green-pooled Illinois River, and make our way across a hot, boulder-strewn bar.

"We better stop in to see Betty before heading up to the wilderness."

"Who?"

"Betty McCaleb. She and her husband bought a hardscrabble ranch out here in the twenties, wound up prospecting for a living. The husband died years ago, but Betty stayed on."

An ancient, unpainted-plank mining cabin sags against the hill-side ahead. When we climb up the hill, I can see the house is surrounded by a well-tended garden: a patch of green amid a slope of brown rocks. The garden gate is double-latched and double-bolted—not to keep strangers out, Len says, but rather to keep a clever old hound dog in.

Len knocks on a sagging wooden screen door. There is a long pause. I look at him questioningly, but he just shakes his head.

Minutes pass before a faint voice croaks from within. "I'm coming!" Finally a very old, shrunken woman stares at me through the wavy glass of the porch door. Strands of gray hair descend about her heavily freckled face. Then she sees the geologist, and her face lights up. "Well, Len! Come on in!"

Inside, the house gives me a strong feeling of vertigo. The dining room slopes woozily toward a treadle sewing machine in a corner. The window is cocked at a different angle. The door frames hump or sag to match the rickety doors. Mrs. McCaleb hobbles ahead into the living room, which slants so radically it seems about to launch itself, doilied sofa and all, through a threadbare curtain into the garden.

Len smiles at the elderly woman, and then surprises me with a fearsome shout: "How are you doing?!"

When she doesn't flinch, I realize she is hard of hearing. She also appears to be at least eighty-five and apparently lives alone, so Len's question is well chosen.

"Well now, Len, I'm all right," she says, "but since you're here, maybe you could help me cut my toenail."

"Your toenail?!" Len yells.

Mrs. McCaleb lowers herself into a swivel rocker. The coffee table beside her is littered with clippers, scissors, and pliers. "Well, yes. I dropped a wrench on my big toe, but instead of the toenail falling off, it did this." She takes off her slipper and reveals a yellow hornlike appendage sprouting straight up out of her toe. From the look of it, the toe is undergoing a metamorphosis into a rhinoceros. "It's getting hard to do all the ranch chores when it hurts so."

Len swallows hard. "I'm a geologist, Betty!" he shouts.

"No matter. See what you can do. Just don't use that hammer of yours on it."

So Len and Betty set to work, ignoring me for the moment. First

Len tries scissors, and then clippers, and then wire cutters. When all these weapons fail to cut the mighty toenail, Len unfolds the saw attachment of a pocket knife. He puts some weight into his sawing, until she winces and says, "Ooh, Len, that's hurting."

Len sits back, glaring at the thing, obviously reluctant to give up now that he's tackled it. But he finally folds the saw blade away. "Betty, I think you'd better see a foot doctor!"

She sighs. "Yes, I suppose this will be the year I have to go in."

Len looks at her, astonished. "How long has your toe been like this?!"

"Oh, I dropped the wrench back in '79 or so, I guess. It's just so hard to make doctor appointments in Cave Junction, what with the phones gone after the war."

"I thought you had a radio hookup out here!" Len shouts.

"Well, they changed systems, and the new one didn't reach anybody from here, so they came and took it out." She sighs again, and puts her slipper back on. Then she brushes back her white hair and smiles at me. "Well, so you are hiking with Len?"

I hesitate, but her intent look assures me the issue of toenail is closed. I tell her about my hike, and suggest that she must see a lot of people hiking up toward the wilderness.

"Oh my, yes," she replies. "But not as many now as back in the sixties, when the hippies would come through. I guess they were gold mining, or trying to homestead, or something back in there."

She leans back and looks out the tilting window wistfully. "You know, I kind of miss the hippies. They'd always walk in—never drive up to the trailhead. Often as not the man would be walking up front, not carrying a darn thing, while the woman would walk behind, carrying a baby and a backpack, and leading a goat or two on a rope. That always burned me up, how the women did the work."

Mrs. McCaleb wrinkles her freckled brow. She looks at me with narrowed eyes. "And you know what? There must be hundreds of unmarked graves up there." She crooks a finger toward the wilderness ominously and speaks in a harsh whisper, "*Babies'* graves!"

"How do you mean?" My shout is meant for her deafness, but it's hard to tell it from a shout of surprise.

"Well, I'd always see them hippies carrying babies on their way in, but when the hippies came back out—no baby. I often thought of reporting some of them for murder, but then I'd look at the mother and father, walking down all ragged from the woods, and I'd think, well, maybe it's best for the children the way it is."

Len shakes his head sympathetically. Then he stands up and looks at his watch. "We'll have to be going! You make sure you take care of that toe now!"

We say good-bye to the old woman and veer out through the tilting rooms. Outside, the afternoon sun and the 90-degree heat hit us like a wall.

"We'll have to make some time if you're going to get into the wilderness today," Len says. "It's eight miles over Chetco Pass to a campsite with water. Don't worry, though. My nickname's Shortcut Ramp. I'll get you to a spring near the wilderness line in an hour and a half."

He charges up a trailless slope of tough-limbed madrone trees and manzanita bushes. I heft my pack unwillingly and trudge up after him.

In the next four miles we gain two thousand feet, climbing through brush. I have no time to look at my map, and can no longer tell any directions except uphill and down. Then, in the midst of the dustiest, brushiest slope of all, Len announces, "Well, here we are."

I stare at him. This is not a good joke.

"Hey, George!" he shouts ahead.

Incredibly, a voice answers. We climb to the top of the slope and look down at Len's four-by-four pickup, waiting in a patch of shade on a Jeep track.

I stumble down after him into the miraculous little gulch. The dust on the road is three inches thick, and puffs up in big clouds with each step. "But—the spring?" I ask.

"Over here," Len says. He pushes his way through the dry brush along the bottom of the gulch. Suddenly we come upon a tiny patch of bright green grass. A clear stream of water, two feet wide and a foot deep, is flowing from a hole in one bank, rushing almost silently for ten feet, and then disappearing into another hole without a trace. The ground in all directions from this hidden oasis is perfectly dry. I look at Len with awe.

He looks at his watch. "Well, I've got to get back to the office before five. Sure enjoyed the hike. Oh, and here's something my wife sent for you."

He rummages about in one of the pockets in the back of his vest, and withdraws an insulated paper bag. Inside are four lemon cucumbers, a large bunch of table grapes, and a zucchini—all of which he has been concealing in this unbelievable vest for the entire hike. "Just something from the garden," he says.

I thank him repeatedly. I manage to stay standing as he turns to go and finds his way back out of the brush. But the moment he is out of sight, I collapse face first into the grass.

AUGUST 23

1:16 P.M. Little Chetco River. 82°F. Mileage yesterday: 19.9. So far today: 6.8. Total: 126.2.

I am taking a "slack" day today. My itinerary leaves every eighth day free, to make it more likely that I will reach my checkpoints and food drops on time. So today I have ambled only a short way through the Kalmiopsis, and stopped to wash my T-shirts and socks beside a creek. I scrubbed myself down with a bar of soap, and rinsed off over the bushes, where the suds won't hurt the fish. Now, with my cup of granola on one side of me, and a cold bottle of water on the other, I am drying in a warm beam of sun through the fir forest. A bright red crawdad crawls from rock to rock at the bottom of a clear, six-foot-deep pool. My bare feet squirm into the creekside sand. I have leisure enough to pick up yesterday's narrative in my journal.

I stayed in the grass by Len Ramp's spring for an hour—eating grapes, drinking water, and gradually reviving from the heat and the hike. It gave me time to study the oasis around the spring, which proved to be one of the Klamath Mountains' unusual botanical islands.

The oasis was shaded not by the area's usual scrawny live oak, but rather by cool, green incense cedars with drooping boughs of long, stringy leaf scales. The bushes about the miniature meadow were Labrador tea (*Ledum*), a little rhododendron-like plant with pungent, spicy leaves. The grass itself was speckled with startling

wildflowers: death camas (with the white flowers that warned the Indians not to eat its deadly bulbs), Indian paintbrush (not red, but a
pink variety I had never seen before), and gentian (with big electric-
blue cups). The boggy bank of the ten-foot-long creek sprouted with
the strangest plant of all—the carnivorous pitcher plant, *Darlingtonia*.

Darlingtonia looks like a hollow green baseball bat sticking out
of the bog—each plant with a little hood on top. A sweet honeylike
aroma wafts from a hole in the underside of the hood, luring in flies,
bees, wasps, grasshoppers, centipedes, and even snails. As insects
pursue the scent, the hollow stem becomes a one-way street. Tiny
hairs inside the tube point only downward, blocking retreat. Between
May and June, when hunting is best, the pitcher plants collect up to
eight inches of dead insects at the bottom of their stem-throats, where
enzymes soon reduce the catch to goo. In the poor soils of the
Klamaths' ultramafic rock, only *Darlingtonia* is wily enough to capture
its own fertilizer.

Most of the eccentric plants of this Klamath bog are remnants of
Ice Age populations that must have once covered the whole range,
when the world here was wetter. And before that, the species evolved
when the Klamaths were an island in the Pacific, apart from the mainland. Len's oasis seems all the more miraculous because it is a time
capsule from a lost world.

When my strength returned, I hiked five miles over a pass to
camp beside the Chetco River in the Kalmiopsis. Then this morning I
hiked over a heavily forested ridge to the Little Chetco River. On my
way I crossed a field of low, azalealike bushes, *Kalmiopsis leachiana,*
the fragment of the Klamaths' lost world that has given this wilderness
its name. The rare shrub grows only in a dozen small patches, all
close by. Alas, I have come too late in summer to see its carpet of
pink flowers.

8:15 P.M. Hawk's Rest Trail spring. 72°F. Mileage today: 10.0.
Total: 129.4.

I met no one today. I heard no motor and saw no airplane.
Wilderness is a human word for a human absence. Only when the
background noise is gone am I fully aware of the foreground.

A big male black bear was busily stripping manzanita berries from a trailside bush this evening. He squinted at me with his little near-sighted eyes, huffed an ursine "Oh my God!," and hustled up the hill.

Little puffy clouds burned red across the huge sky.

A hundred forests hushed in distant silhouettes.

My camera's rectangular box would break the spell.

I took no pictures.

AUGUST 24

12:30 P.M. Unnamed ridge southwest of Doe Gap. 87°F. Mileage so far today: 14.6. Total: 144.0.

Last night I camped beside a spring that was no more than a mossy dribble, churned by the hoofmarks of deer. I did not dare drink from it direct. I boiled water for breakfast, but it would take too much butane to boil water for the entire day's hike. Instead, I put purification tablets in a single quart bottle and set off. The tablets make the water taste so awful, I was willing to gamble on finding another source soon.

But there is no water on the Hawk's Rest Trail to Doe Gap, and none at the gap itself, despite what the map says. I must have lost three quarts to perspiration in the heat. I have only kept my tongue from swelling by eating all the hard candies I have left; they last thirteen minutes each. Now, at lunch, I set the nearly empty water bottle beside me in the dust with the utmost care.

When I fold away my map, I stare at a spot of mud. The bottle has fallen over somehow. I swallow. My throat is sandpaper. I must push on to Baldface Creek at once. The map says it will not be dry.

2:02 P.M. Baldface Creek. 87°F. Mileage so far today: 16.5. Total: 145.9.

The trail down from the ridge toward Baldface Creek is indistinct, as though no one had been to this corner of the wilderness for a decade. I lose the trail, but my tongue is now swollen and rough, so I crash headlong down through the manzanita. At 1:15 the trail is found again. At 1:40 I hear water!

And then, just fifty feet before the creek, there is a rope stretched across the trail. A bristling black Labrador dog stands guard at the rope. It curls its lip, baring yellow teeth.

I back up very slowly. I try to call, "Hello?" but my dry throat only makes a hoarse, rasping sound.

The big dog growls threateningly in reply. Now I recognize one of the bushes ahead as a camouflage shelter straight out of the jungles of Vietnam. Rifles are slung from its branches. Camouflage combat ration cans and ammo boxes are stacked in the shadows. Beer cans are heaped to knee depth behind the shelter. I back up farther, my heart beating rapidly.

When I am out of sight, I sag against a tree. Whoever built the ominous camp in the trail has left the dog as a guard. But I *must* have water. I decide to circle the camp, cross the creek, and strike the trail on the far side.

I creep through the woods, jump down the creek's ten-foot-high bank, and cross on boulders. Then I drop the pack and pour handfuls of water down my throat and over my head. I splash the glorious water over my chest and arms. I take off my boots and soak my feet until the cold makes them ache. I am just opening the pack to get my granola when a sharp voice makes me freeze.

"Hey!"

On the bluff, where I first reached the creek, is a tall, skinny, red-bearded man in combat fatigues. He wears a large pistol in an ammunition belt at his waist. Two big Labrador dogs watch me from his side. The man's hands flutter nervously between his beard and his belt.

"Hello?" My voice is back, but it cracks badly.

"Hey, I mean," the man says, shifting his weight from foot to foot. *"Who are you?"*

"I'm just hiking through."

He bounds down the bluff and walks with long, springy strides all around me and my backpack. "Shit, man, we've got to *talk* at least."

"Well, I—"

"Goddam it, Dumptruck!" He kicks a dog sniffing my food bag, and sends the animal flying. "I mean, come on up to camp. I'm gonna have lunch. I mean it." He gives me a piercing stare.

I believe he means it. "Lunch. All right."

He watches me so carefully on the way to the camp that I won-der if I am to be his guest or his prisoner. My first guess about him is not reassuring: that he's a shell-shocked vet, turned lunatic in the woods.

"Well, shit, sit down," he says, waving to some stumps around a fireplace of stacked rocks. Now I can see how very tall he is—proba-bly six feet six. His camouflage T-shirt hangs over his thin, bony frame like a sheet on a hat rack. "You want coffee? I got coffee. I got cocoa, tea, lemonade, you name it. Out of beer."

"Cocoa sounds all right."

"Jesus, cocoa? Hey, whatever, man." He lights a fire, still eyeing me warily.

I risk the question. "Uh, what are you doing, camped out here?"

"Fishing, mostly."

I nod, and look about the camp. There is no fishing pole—no fishing gear at all. But now I notice a six-foot blowgun of South American design leaning against the brush-shelter wall, below the ri-fles. I shiver.

He returns the question. "So, what are *you* doing, man, hiking around? I always walk on the rocks beside the trail, to keep track of things, you know, and when I saw your tracks, I thought, hey, wow."

"I'm backpacking the length of the Kalmiopsis." It's true and sounds more likely than my larger New Oregon Trail scheme. "I've been out seven days. You're the first person I've met for two."

"Oh, yeah?" He breaks into a toothy grin and extends a long arm to shake my hand. "Well then, it's good to meet you. My name's Ron."

"I'm Bill." We shake hands, neither of us at ease.

"You've been here a long time," I comment.

"Shit, yes," Ron says, rolling a cigarette. "I got here in May. It rained eleven days straight. That creek was six feet higher, and there was nothing I owned that was dry. Even these drums of supplies, even though I had 'em covered. That's why I built this shelter. You smoke?"

"No, thank you."

"Smoke pot?" He raises his bushy red eyebrows at me.

"Not really."

"I don't either, usually, except for one in the evening."

I am writing down all I can in the journal—which seems to be making him extremely nervous. "Why did you decide to camp clear out here?"

"Oh, hey," Ron says, suddenly smiling again. "I wanted to get as far away as I could. People said, 'Aw, you'll be back in a month'—but it's been four. Every day here I wake up in the morning and I say, 'I own my own day.' I never owned my days in the city. It's a richness."

Ron fits his cigarette onto a thin plastic tube before lighting up. "Gotta have this holder in the morning or your coffee drips down your moustache and sogs up your cigarette until it falls apart in your breakfast."

Under a tarp I can see a huge stack of Spam, sardine cans, Dinty Moore stew, and the like. I am used to carrying my food, and this collection looks awfully heavy. "How did you pack in your supplies?"

"I took five trips in with a horse and a burro. I live off the land, too. Brought my thirty-thirty, my twenty-twos, and my shotguns. Not sure I'll shoot a deer—seasons don't bother me, but I couldn't even jerk all the meat before it'd spoil. I use the blowgun to pick off mountain quail. There's a covey of about eighteen that come right into camp. The shotgun would scare them off, but with the blowgun they keep coming back."

Whatever caution Ron first felt about me seems to have been overshadowed by his obvious need to talk. However, I can't help thinking his story still has flaws. "Have you ever been in the service?" I ask.

"Shit, I joined up with the marines in '62. That was right after Kennedy's showdown with Cuba, and I figured we'd have a war down there. Damned if they didn't send me off with the first bunch to 'Nam, instead. Did two tours. When we all got off the ship in San Diego in '66, we were like a bunch of pressure cookers, all stoked up. And there on the dock were hippie kids throwing tomatoes at us. Shit, we just stared at 'em, didn't know what was going on."

He mixes up my cocoa and starts cutting up a beef sausage with a big bowie knife. "This country's full of wah-wahs, complaining all the time. Nobody's got guts anymore, they're just chickenshits. You know, Reagan's the first president we've had with *balls*? The Libyans start messing with us—he shoots down their jets. Christ, think of it—we *won* one, finally!"

I steer him away from politics. "What did you do after you got out of the marines?"

"Got a job selling cars at a Plymouth dealership in southern California. Did that five years, then put in another five years selling mechanical seals and packing for hydraulic pumps. Shit, man, I've seen it all. In '73 I bought a house, got married, had a son, and got Dumptruck here." He prods the dog in the ribs with his army boot. "Then I got rich. And I mean *rich.*"

I am about to ask, "How?" but it is unnecessary; he continues:

"I saw this ad for diamond brokers, you know, in a magazine? I thought it was crazy, but I was going crazy, too, doing what I was doing—my wife had divorced me by then—so I called them up. I tried it for a week, selling diamonds, rubies, and sapphires over the phone as investments. I made three thousand six hundred dollars that first week! I ditched my old job and started living *high!* I bought three houses I commuted between, and two tricked-out rigs. Then the diamond investment scene fell apart."

While he's talking, a skinny horse has walked up and stopped at the rope at the edge of camp. It licks a frying pan lying in the dust there. "That's Joe," Ron says with a wistful smile. "Lean and mean, just like myself."

Ron sighs, and goes on. "So I went into strategic metals. I got rich all over again for a few years. Shit, I didn't think anything of an eighth ounce of coke every Friday night. But when gold and silver crashed, too, I was back on the street. About then my folks moved to southern Oregon, and I saw this Kalmiopsis Wilderness on the map nearby. I thought about parachuting into the Alaska backcountry instead, but I didn't have the cash."

I am eating sausage on crackers. The more I hear of Ron's story, the more it seems like something he could hardly be making up. Yet I wonder. "You must have a lot of time to think out here."

"Shit, yes," Ron says. "You know, we only use ten percent of our brains. Out here, you can learn to use more. The Druids did, and they could communicate by mental telepathy with animals, plants, any living thing—that's the way. You can learn it. You can do anything if you can just flush down the toilet all the 'you can't' garbage they fill your mind with in the city. Every person I've met out here has been a neat person, but look at all the screwballs in cities! Jesus, am I glad they don't get out here."

Dumptruck snaps lazily at a fly on top of his head. No luck. Then he tries as it buzzes past, succeeds, and munches it. He lies flat again.

My writing hand is getting sore. "Have you seen many people out here since you came?"

"Just five. Truth is, all the others turned out to be marijuana growers. But I don't give a shit. They're nice folks, and they're not hurting anybody. So I say, more power to 'em. 'Course the cops see it different. *Ptrtrtrtr*"—he makes an engine sound, and his flattened palm flies in toward me—"a chopper came up the crick last night, looking for pot. First time since I've been here. It's no big deal, though. The cops come and pop the growers every so often, but not much, and no one ever gets jailed. The cops just stuff their four-wheelers with pot, drive down to the coffee shop in Cave Junction, and leave it parked there to show off. None of the growers here are big time anyway. Mostly they drive in from Eugene on weekends to check their automatic drip irrigation systems. Big-time operations? Shit, they'd rent a warehouse and put in Gro-Lites."

There is a pause—the first pause in Ron's conversation since we sat down together almost two hours ago. I wait.

"You know," Ron says, looking at me with narrowed eyes, "I don't think you're a cop after all."

"I'm not."

"Well, I'm gonna tell you something. I'm really growing a little marijuana out here."

I nod. The pieces of the puzzle are starting to fit together better. "So you were worried at first that I'd come out here to bust you."

"You're not gonna, are you?"

"No."

"And all the notes you're taking?"

"It's just my journal."

Ron leans back, laughing, and runs his hands over his face. "Jesus Christ, after that chopper came over last night, and I saw your tracks, I thought they'd dropped some weird SWAT team up on the ridge. I've been waiting for cops to jump out of the bushes. God, you had me going!"

I have a sobering thought. "But if you thought I was a cop—you could have shot me."

Ron laughs again. "You don't shoot *cops,* man, you shoot *pot pirates.* You gotta be all friendly with cops. If you'd asked about the marijuana plants up the hill, I would have shrugged. 'What plants, man? I'm just fishing.' I'm clean. This is public land."

"How did you know I wasn't a 'pot pirate'?"

"Shit, only cops would come in broad daylight. Yeah, if you'd come at night, I probably would have blown you away. There's nothing good about pirates."

"Do I look like a pirate?" The thought is frightening; I often hike at dusk.

"Not really. They look like 'Nam vets, in camouflage outfits, with shoulder forty-fives and AR fifteens or M sixteens. They've got no morals at all. They've been sitting in bars all year while the growers are out here busting their asses working. Then the pirates just sneak in at night with their faces blackened and take the whole crop. The mob's pirates are the worst. They come in big Huey choppers, with men that jump out and secure the perimeter with automatic weapons while a special team does the harvest with machetes. They're in and out in five minutes."

Now that Ron seems to trust me, his hunger for conversation is completely unchecked. My fingers ache from writing.

"You gotta understand how I got into this. I couldn't take risking other people's money all the time. You know what it's like to be a silver broker and have the price fall three dollars an ounce? A lot of people I knew, who had trusted me, lost more than they could afford. The real breaker was one old man from Brookings, Oregon, who used to chat all the time on the phone. I had to tell him he'd lost his sixty thousand dollars. The next time I called, his family said he'd died. By God, I swore right then I was through risking other people's things. With pot, it's my own neck.

"It's hard work, too. I water my plants every other day from five-gallon cans carried from the creek—no pipes or hoses to give me away. I've got five patches hidden in the woods; the biggest has twenty-eight plants. They'd be tough to spot by air. A hundred plants in all, but only forty-eight of 'em are healthy, and there's always mice and grasshoppers and deer that get a few.

"You probably think growers like me get rich. Let me tell you, the cops inflate their reports as bad as we upped body counts in 'Nam. If the cops find a hundred little sprouts—half of 'em gonna die, and half of 'em male—they'd say there's a pound of pot in each and list them at the top New York City street price of three thousand dollars a pound. That'd make a hundred plants sound like they were worth three hundred thousand dollars! Now my forty-eight good plants will get me a half pound of buds each and I'll wholesale it at fifteen hundred dollars a pound. Should clear twenty thousand dollars if I can put off the harvest until Thanksgiving."

"And then what?" I ask.

Ron looks up into the trees with a smile. "Twenty grand's almost enough. I'm gonna go one more summer, see if I can make one hundred thousand dollars, and then I'm buying me a one-way ticket to the Seychelles Islands in the Indian Ocean. I've read about what it's like there. The Creole women want light-complected children so bad they'll do anything. And a hundred grand in a tropical paradise like that—shit, it'd be enough to live like a billionaire forever."

8:30 P.M. Biscuit Hill. Mileage today: 19.0. Total: 148.4.

A fabulous golden sunset. The sun flattens into the thin line of the Pacific twenty miles to the west. I have chosen to camp on the barren rim of a bluff to photograph the event. It is a good place to think.

I have crossed the great forest of the Kalmiopsis-Wild Rogue, yet ironically the images I remember most vividly are human. It no longer seems profane to box this landscape in a camera. There would be no concept of wilderness without the frame of civilization.

The thought makes me wonder what is in the frame. Is it Ron's jungle of fortune? Is it Lou Gold's vortex of spirits? Is it Len Ramp's map of minerals?

In fact, aren't these men's definitions of wilderness really just *projections* of themselves? Or are the definitions not theirs at all, but rather my own, for how can I see these people—and the land they are in—without projecting my own preconceptions upon them? The brain stamps its imprint on every image it receives; man turns the world inside out each time he looks at it.

I set out on this hike to learn what wilderness is. Now I realize how hard it is to really see the wilderness at all. Before me is a landscape of my own making, behind which, presumably, there exist real birds, trees, rocks, and people, with purposes and powers I do not yet fully know.

My unquestioned prejudices are always ready to turn the world into a hall of mirrors, where my own image reflects from every wall and hidden door. To find a way through, I must ask, "What am I?"

AUGUST 25

12:23 P.M. Hazelview Summit, Old Redwood Highway. 94°F.
Mileage so far today: 12.3. Total: 160.7.

My aunt and uncle from Grants Pass meet me here precisely at 11:30 A.M., as arranged. I have hiked logging roads from the southern end of the Kalmiopsis, and bushwhacked the last mile to reach this old highway pass. It is very hot and very still; all the traffic of modern Highway 199 is eight hundred feet underground in a long tunnel. I have spread sweat-soaked clothes about on bushes to dry when Jack and Lucille drive up in their aged Pontiac. They set up lawn chairs, and bring out the box of trail food and supplies I mailed to them weeks ago.

What I had hoped they would bring is water. The gallon I carried from Baldface Creek is gone, and the pass is dry.

"Oh, we brought a big bottle of water," Aunt Lucille assures me. "But you'll have to share with Botchan."

I watch, dumbstruck, as she takes a bottle from the car—a single small water bottle!—and pours half of its precious contents into a dog dish for a yapping toy poodle.

I stammer, "I—I drink five quarts of water a day on the trail."

"Well, we'll save the orange juice for you, then."

"Orange juice!" I have only been in the wilderness eight days, yet already orange juice sounds impossibly lavish.

She opens a picnic basket and starts unpacking amazing foods: juicy tomatoes, fresh peaches, home-fried chicken, potato salad, and a half gallon of ice cream.

While I heap my plate with these unexpected delicacies, Uncle Jack asks, "Had any trouble with bears? I hope you've been hanging up your food in trees each night."

I nod, my mouth full. My uncle has warned me before to hang food ten feet high and five feet from the trunk. He often makes the three-day white-water trip through the Wild Rogue Wilderness, where bears routinely plague the drift-boat campgrounds.

"The tame bears are the most dangerous," he says. "They come looking for tunafish, honey, hams, margarine, and syrup. They tear open the cans with their claws and lick them out clean. We took a cooler chest on our last float trip that was advertised as 'bear proof.' I sent pictures back to the cooler company. A bear had peeled it open like an orange."

He looks at my food box, which is still sealed with packing tape. "What kind of food do you take, anyway?"

I cut it open, and he peers inside.

He takes out several little plastic bags of oatmeal and rice, and holds them between his thumb and forefingers uncertainly. "This is it?"

"Nineteen ounces a day," I say.

He frowns into the box. "To tell you the truth, I don't see anything here a bear would want."

When I have finished the chicken and thanked my aunt and uncle, I load the contents of the food box into my backpack. I swing the pack onto my shoulders with difficulty, for it is heavy again and stacked up a foot above my head. I have written out telephone messages for my wife and parents; tearing these out of my journal, I give them to my aunt and uncle.

"Oh, that reminds me," Aunt Lucille says. "There's a message for you."

"There is?"

"Yes, from an insurance agent. She wanted you to stop in at a clinic to get your height, weight, and blood pressure checked."

I throw up my hands. "A *clinic*? Out *here*?"

I think I'll let this insurance agent sweat a little, too.

AUGUST 26

1:30 P.M. Unnamed lake in High Siskiyous Wilderness. 82°F.
Mileage yesterday: 19.5. Mileage so far today: 11.6. Total: 179.5.

This morning I hike toward the looming peaks of the High Siskiyous. On the way I startle no fewer than eleven coveys of mountain
quail out of the brush beside the road. In one of the coveys I count
eighteen chicks running along like feathery chicken drumsticks, led
by an indignant turkey drumstick. This would be a good place to be a
bobcat.

As I climb, I cross an outcropping of shale that slashes the side
of the mountains. Paper-thin rocks spill across the slope like reams of
stationery. This ancient Klamath shale is just the place to look for the
fossil imprints of trilobites and sycamore leaves, since shale preserves
fossils as neatly as wildflowers pressed in the pages of a dictionary. I
flip through a few of the rock pages, but they are not thumb-indexed,
so I soon give up. I walk on, setting off a shaly clattering like a storm
in a wind chime factory.

It suits the mysterious aura of these mountains that they are best
known as the Klamaths west of here, but are the Siskiyous to the east.
Geologists and botanists call this entire are the Klamaths; travelers call
the line of higher peaks ahead of me the Siskiyous. Maps use either
name, or sometimes both.

The name "Klamath" is borrowed from the Klamath River,
whose name is borrowed from Klamath Lake (at the headwaters of
that river), whose name is borrowed from the Klamath Indian tribe.
The Klamath Indians live east of the Cascade Range, and have never
lived in the Klamath Mountains.

If that etymology seems remote, consider that Siskiyou is a Cree
Indian word meaning "spotted horse," and that the closest Cree Indians live two thousand miles away, near Hudson Bay. Apparently a
Hudson Bay trapper passing here in 1828 lost his spotted horse in the
snow; his Indian companions named the place in honor of the event.

The range is schizophrenic in more than name. The maze of
canyons and dry ridges I was hiking through yesterday is nothing like
the mountains I am seeing today. Here, the peaks are really peaks—
craggy, once-glaciated mountains, pushing timberline. Patches of

snow glint from their summits, although it is late August. Gone are the dry, gnarled madrone and canyon live oak of the Kalmiopsis. The trees are stiff, proper firs, like a forest of Christmas trees. Here and there is a droopy-topped mountain hemlock, its trunk bent into an S by the weight of winter snows.

I reach the boundary of the High Siskiyou Wilderness, and follow a trail into a broad, U-shaped valley that was carved long ago by a glacier, but now brims with a vast green, subalpine wildflower meadow. How unlike the rare little wildflower bogs of the Kalmiopsis! Here are great bunches of huge yellow-petaled composites, hardy purple asters, elegant red rock penstemon, and gentians so blue and big I feel as if I could dive in and swim.

And here's my old friend, red Indian paintbrush. It's a duplicitous old friend, perhaps, but I'm wise to its ways. Not only does it pretend its showy red leaves are flowers (the actual flowers are hidden green tubes, just suitable for a hummingbird's beak), but Indian paintbrush is secretly a parasite, for it saps other flowers' roots, given a chance.

The trail disappears into the flowers. On the far side of the meadow I scratch my head awhile, and finally launch into the woods, following the trail on my map. After two miles of maddening zigzag bushwhacking, I conclude that the trail does not exist within a half mile of its supposed location. I give up and follow the route it ought to have taken. At length, that brings me to a trail not marked on my map, and then to a pass overlooking a little, sparkling blue lake.

Fir needles are in my hair from the bushwhack, and more needles are down my sweaty shirt and pants. I am hot and sticky, and thirsty as hell. I hardly break stride as I dump the pack, kick off my clothes, and walk straight into the cold, clear water of the mountain lake.

Time seems to stop. I float naked on my back in the sun, keeping my toes just out of the water. And as I float lazily, looking up at a full circle of firs and mountain cliffs, a tension inside me finally relaxes. The heaviest weight I've carried all these miles has not been my backpack, but rather the stress of civilization. Now I feel like I am melting into the water.

Hunger brings me out of my trance. I crawl out like a lizard to dry on a sunny log. I think a hungry lizard thought: There are no mosquitoes. I come up with an ecologist's explanation: Not only is the lake alive with fish jumping two and three feet out of the water at bugs, but a fleet of blue dragonflies is policing the shore, like border-patrol helicopters of the insect world.

I have already eaten my allotment of granola at an earlier lunch stop. Now I count out the two pieces of jerky and four and a half pilot crackers I am allowed for my second lunch. I eat them slowly, sitting in the sun in the grass beside the lake, watching the breezes bring sparkles of blue to the water, then calms of khaki.

When I am done, I am still ravenous. I eat an extra half-cracker guiltily, then am suddenly afraid. I stuff the food bag away. My provisions must last six more days. I will have to pack up quickly and hike on in order to keep myself from eating more.

4:15 P.M.

I gain my first view of 14,162-foot Mount Shasta, far to the southeast, rising beyond the dark ridges of the Siskiyous like a distant, white-topped mushroom. I do not attempt a telephoto picture. I will be hiking closer to it for a week. It is not yet ripe.

7:49 P.M. An uncharted road in section 28, R. 8 W., T. 18 N. Mileage today: 22.8 Total: 200.7.

Curses! After a glorious day in the High Siskiyous, I am following a well-marked trail toward the Indian Creek campground, still three miles down a heavily forested valley, when—wham! I run smack into one of those insidious logging roads. The thing not only has clear-cut any trace of a trail into an impenetrable mess of slash and stumps, but it runs at right angles to my route, so I don't know which way to go. I have brought the Forest Service's most recent map for this area. The map shows no roads for miles.

I follow the gravel road to the right; it dead-ends in a log-truck turnaround surrounded by a big bulldozer scarp. So I hike the other way, plotting the curves of this road onto my map with compass and pedometer. It heads generally back toward the Siskiyou crest, in a roundabout, in-valley, out-ridge way. By 7:40 daylight is fading, and I realize I will not reach a campground, or a trail, or even a forest tonight. I stop at a hairpin curve in the stripped-out canyon of the west branch of Indian Creek. Tent stakes cannot be driven into this rock, so I will sleep out on the gravel. There is no tree left tall enough to hang the food bag from.

But I have a big, steaming cup of chamomile tea. And the most magnificent *Epilobium angustifolium*—fireweed—has flourished in this clear-cut. One rises four feet, with eight major flowering heads and dozens more minor shoots, all tipped with luminous violet-pink, four-petaled blooms. Like the violet evening sky, the fireweed seems to glow from within, content within itself in the midst of adversity.

I will not dwell on the death of my trail. I will sip my tea, watch my fireweed and my sky, and hold on to their glow.

AUGUST 27

6:25 A.M. Same. 51°F.

I am up before dawn to the *whoo-hoo-hoo* of a great horned owl. Venus is stealing a bow during the stars' curtain call for the night. Orion dances on throughout breakfast until finally the sun, and the owl, hoot him down.

Daylight brings back the clear-cut. It seems ironic that I should have to search for wilderness, where seventy-two years ago Joe "Nature Man" Knowles staged the greatest survival stunt of his career.

Knowles made front-page headlines in 1913 by surviving sixty days in the Maine wilderness without having brought food, clothing, or equipment. He announced he was going to attempt the same feat in an even more remote, more inhospitable place. On July 13, 1914, accompanied by dignitaries, photographers, and reporters, Knowles arrived at the edge of this Siskiyou forest. He shook hands all around, disrobed, and (in the words of a newspaper of the day) "plunged, unarmed and naked as a snake into the untamed, cougar-infested wilds of the Siskiyou Mountains of Oregon."

Knowles's manager informed the nation's media that the Nature Man intended to kill a bear and to fashion his own clothes. A University of California anthropologist would remain nearby, receiving messages from Knowles "upon bark or by other methods that employ none of the aids of civilization."

However, Knowles had hardly waved good-bye when World War I broke out in Europe. Unbeknownst to him, his reports were relegated to the back pages of the newspapers, and finally dropped altogether. He emerged, bewildered, to obscurity.

7:40 P.M. Sucker Creek Gap. Mileage today: 25.4. Total: 226.1.

I wander about on roads for thirteen miles this morning before I can find my way into the Red Buttes Wilderness. I eat my first lunch of the day on the slopes of Bolan Mountain, looking south into California, thinking of the people I have seen on those roads. There were twenty-seven in all—more than I have encountered on any single day of my trip so far—and yet not one got out of his car. None of them spoke to me; they seemed to be part of the cars themselves.

However, I have shadowy company afoot. Coyote tracks go down the middle of a dirt road and lead to a bold declaration: a prominent, centered pile of scat. At a dusty pass the smug pawprints vanish. Suddenly there are great, lordly, hand-sized cat tracks. It is *Felis concolor*—the cougar, the mountain lion, the puma. He weighs as much as I do; he stalks as far in a night as I walk in a day; he, too, follows the wilderness. I do not see Cougar or Coyote, but they have provided more conversation than Car.

I come to a trail at last. It scrambles up and down rocky slopes, following the routes laid out by gold miners more than a century ago. The miners' burros had better footing going over hills than around them, so few Klamath trails are level.

The gold miners are gone, but their names remain on the maps. My goal tonight was first dubbed "Sucker Creek" by a group of Illinois miners who staked a claim here in the early 1850s. The name did not reflect frustration, but rather pride, for Illinois is known as the "Sucker State." Likewise, the miners named the Illinois River, of which Sucker Creek is a tributary. Bolan Mountain, where I had lunch, was originally misspelled by some miners of the same heady era, who packed thirty bowling balls and twenty pins on their backs to set up a bowling alley at the foot of the remote mountain.

Toward evening I come to a shadowy valley of huge incense cedars and firs. The stillness is so deep and the woods are so gigantic, I feel like an intruder in a world of gnomes and elves. I make camp amid the great, dark trunks. The twisted shapes of purple-barked yew grope through the shadows. Strange, purple-pronged wildflowers—parrot-beak—rise from the moss. Thimbleberry bushes overhang my butane stove, eerily lit by the bluish gaslight. I pluck the red-capped berries for a tart dessert. They are delicious but then, in the dark, I regret my boldness. The berries in this fairy forest might belong to trolls.

AUGUST 28

6:39 A.M. Same. 39°F. Mileage so far today: 0. Total: 226.1.

Perhaps it is the chilly morning that has got some little red-furred Douglas squirrels into a frenzied chirping competition in the trees about my camp. One of them clutches the bark of a big fir and suddenly lets out a machine-gun rattle of chirps, at least ten a second, for thirteen seconds. His neighbor tops him by chirping fiercely for a full twenty seconds. Two others are rattling away on another tree, and then a fifth starts in, and then a sixth.

I boil water for oatmeal. The squirrels are outraged. How could I have misunderstood their complaints? Now they come right down and make an indignant pinging noise at me, jerking their bushy tails excitedly with each ping.

I have been discovered by this forest's angry little trolls: the squirrels. With a smile, I reassure them that I am hiking on, tempting as it is to stay in their enchanted woods.

By tonight I should be on the Pacific Crest Trail, midway between Mexico and Canada. It is a trail I will follow 375 miles into the Cascade Range and as far north as Mount Jefferson.

11:46 A.M. Lonesome Lake. Mileage so far today: 6.8. Total: 232.9.

With a perfectly good trail to follow, I can't resist a side trip over a rocky peak. Why go around Figurehead Mountain through forest, when there is a view waiting at the top? And this bushwhack has no bushes to whack. The feeble growth of stonecrop, heather, and kinnikinnick on these rocky ridges can be walked over like a carpet. The only trees are a few scrawny knobcone pines—with cones and needles clustered around a flagpole trunk. The mountainside is strewn with big, reddish chunks of peridotite—sub-seafloor rock—which is so rough-surfaced my boot soles stick to it like magnets, enabling me to walk up steep slopes like a human fly.

Valley by valley, the world opens up below me until, when I crawl up a nearly vertical rock cleft to the summit, the Siskiyous are strung out all around me. I peer into one valley—is there a lake there? Yes—and snoop into another—no road there either? A hawk flashing red feathers soars a quarter mile below me, slipping on the currents from ridge to ridge. With my eyes I trace the rocky up-and-down route across the wilderness I must follow next on foot: eight miles along the ridge crest of the range to the twin spires of Red Buttes, beneath the ghostlike outline of Mount Shasta on the horizon.

When I have sponged up all the view I can absorb, I amble down through the rocks and meadows to a pine-fringed lake for my first lunch.

5:12 P.M. Red Buttes. 81°F. Mileage today: 17.7 Total: 243.8.

This is supposed to be my "slack" day. But all the open ridges and beautiful trails make it hard to sit still. If I'd been serious about lounging around to wash clothes, I would have stayed at Lonesome Lake.

I packed a quart of water from Lonesome Lake, but the hot sun and a steep ridge soon make me wish I'd taken three. Now I cannot stop until I find more water. I let my tongue feel fuzzy before allowing myself a sip from the bottle. Then I come to some tall bushes drooping into the trail. As I push them aside, a big bunch of blue elderberries hits me in the face. This wetland species seems out of place here, but I accept the gift and take a few berries in passing. They are one quarter the size of peas, but have the meatiest, juiciest, sweetest flavor.

I stop, mutter, and then hike back to the drooping bush. This time I break off a whole sprig with a hand-sized cluster of the blue jewels—maybe two or three hundred. For a mile I take the sprig along like a cluster of grapes, raking off a half dozen at a time with my teeth.

The trail switchbacks over a pass on the shoulder of Rattlesnake

Mountain. A south wind whistles across the barren crags. Two black shapes soar up toward me from the California side—growing larger and larger until they bank around me with great, black six-foot wingspans. The whistling wind curls their tipfeathers. They bank again, this time just fifteen feet away, looking at me first with the bug eye on one side of their naked red heads, and then with the other.

I am being buzzed by buzzards, who must find it hard to believe I am not yet carrion out in the midday sun on this rock peak. They do not frighten me. Turkey vultures do not have the attack talons of an eagle or owl, and are unable even to kill a mouse. But no one is better adapted to disposing of carrion. Their ugly red heads are featherless, the better to probe into carcasses. Their digestive tracts are powerful enough to kill the toxic bacteria in rotten meat. If I died here, they would strip me to bones in a day and a half.

The buzzards soar away, back into California. Then I notice something flying up from the Oregon side of the mountain. It is a delicate Monarch butterfly, struggling up to this rocky crest against gale-force winds. Impossible! Yet I watch this little orange scrap of tissue paper bravely beating its tiny wings, ducking and bucking the wind, actually making headway. I am reminded of the only other Monarch I have seen on this hike—the one that followed me south along the Illinois River near Agness.

Suddenly I realize it might be the identical butterfly. Monarchs are the only species of butterfly in Oregon that does not die in the winter; instead, they migrate to the forests south of San Francisco. I saw my first Monarch nine days ago and seventy air miles away, but if it had continued flying up the Illinois, it would reach the headwaters of that river here, at this windswept Siskiyou pass. I wonder if I have unwittingly lost a race to California with a butterfly.

The fragile-looking insect crests the pass and flutters victoriously down toward the lee of the forest. No bird will bother it on its pilgrimage; the Monarch's conspicuous orange hue warns that it is poisonous. It will join the 100,000 other Monarchs converging on their crowded overwintering grounds, where it will have more than enough listeners for the tale of how it humbled a man; how it escaped a winter the fool failed to feel.

Beyond Rattlesnake Mountain there are tracks in the trail dust—not of people, but rather of a half dozen deer, two bears (such funny, fat, humanlike footprints!), and again, coyotes. I have not seen a coyote on this trip, but I have a strange feeling they are seeing me. Here again the brazen braggarts have left droppings right in the middle of the trail, as if to mark my way, or tell me who's boss, or warn me away—I don't know which.

I wonder about Coyote. In Indian legend, he is the bungling, yet immortal, trickster who created the earth, and who has been playing pranks ever since. Well, perhaps that is true; the Department of Agriculture has been doing its best to exterminate the species—killing 150,000 a year with leg traps, aircraft patrols, dogs, poisoned sheep carcasses, and cyanide landmines—yet the coyote population is steadily *increasing*.

There's no shortage of theories to explain the coyotes' success. Government trappers complain that the animals are too wily: Coyotes can run forty miles an hour, smell a trap a mile away, and have up to nineteen pups in a litter. Zoologists point out that we have virtually eliminated the coyote's predators, mountain lions and grizzly bears. Botanists say we have increased the amount of coyote prey (rabbits and rodents) by planting alfalfa everywhere.

These are all good explanations. Still, there is an elegance to the Indian theory. The Department of Agriculture would be the last to figure out it is being tricked by an immortal demigod.

I have nearly reached the Pacific Crest Trail when I come across more coyote scat in the middle of my path. There are two piles, side by side. One has been dropped in the shape of an O; the other forms a very creditable K. The message is unmistakable: "OK." I frown and hike on toward the looming rock shape of Red Buttes.

Coyote is an irreverent god. In Indian tales across North America he is acknowledged as Creator and Benefactor of Mankind. In the same tales, he is portrayed as the World's Greatest Fool: misplacing his eyeballs, falling off cliffs, or getting tricked into eating his own broiled anus. His wisdom resides in his feces (a fact missing from bowdlerized versions of the Indian tales). When Coyote gets himself into one of his usual jams, he hits his hip and calls out his feces children. Once they're out, he puts his problem to them. As soon as they come up with an answer, he slaps them back inside, saying loftily, "Oh, you're telling me what I already know. I knew the answer all along."

Now they're telling me, "OK." OK what? Perhaps it's an OK trail—I agree. Or maybe it's OK for me to trespass on Coyote's domain—but that's just what he'd say if he couldn't stop me.

So many of Coyote's messages read like upside-down question marks: little, pointy-topped squiggles, white from the fur of his rodent diet. Here, at least, is not another vague question. It is a vague answer.

At Red Buttes I camp in a meadow with a small spring, and write in my journal. It occurs to me that this is the second day of my trip I have seen no one—not even an airplane. But then suddenly I feel I am being observed.

A coyote's eerie, yipping howl echoes off the sunset-struck mountain behind the meadow.

I think: Coyote has been watching me write, and is holding his sides with laughter. Very well, trickster of the wilds, but here's my challenge: Just once before I'm through, just once, meet me fairly, man to god. Do you hear?

For a moment there is only the silence of the wilderness.

Then an insane, wavering howl from the cliffs of Red Buttes stands my hair on end.

AUGUST 29

9:10 A.M. Cook and Green Pass. 64°F. Mileage so far today: 4.2. Total: 248.0.

This morning I climb back onto the Pacific Crest Trail just as a young man is walking up. His ungainly backpack is topped by a rolled-up foam pad and an eagle feather. Pouches, wineskins, and bags are strapped around his shoulders and waist. His arms and legs are bronzed by the sun. His short beard is pale blond. He wears mirror-lensed sunglasses, a red bandanna sweatband, and a white-tailed Foreign Legion desert hat.

"Hello," I say.

"Hello." He gives the word a British accent.

"Where are you headed?" I ask.

"Mexico to Canada. You?"

"The Pacific to Idaho."

For a moment we are silent, pondering the immensity of our crossed purposes. Then I suggest, "I'm going your way for a while, though. Perhaps we could hike the morning together?"

He grins, exposing a row of perfect white teeth. "Oh, say, I could use a bit of company."

We set off together, talking. I learn that he is Chris Binns, age twenty-two, from Yorkshire, England. He explains that he spent three years earning a degree in geography from the University of Manchester—a degree that failed to provide him with a profession, but succeeded in giving him an insatiable wanderlust.

"This P.C.T., you know, is the longest trail in the world." He talks over his shoulder as we hike along. "I daydreamed about it at school when I should have been studying. As soon as I graduated I worked at a campground in the Lake District, clerked in a grocery store, and washed dishes at night in a restaurant—three jobs at once, for a full year—to save enough for this trip."

"When did you start hiking?"

He sighs. "Too late. I didn't get to the Mexican border until mid-May. The chaps who plan to do the whole trail before winter started out in April. You've got to get through the southern California desert before the summer heat hits, you know, and then get to the North Cascades in Washington before the first snow."

"Doesn't anybody hike the trail from north to south?"

He shakes his head. "I've only met two. There's probably two hundred going my way, though."

"It must be frustrating, all going the same way, so you never meet the others."

"Not at all. We all know each other. We meet at campgrounds and outfitters'. We leave notes in the trail registers, or pass word with slower hikers. A week ahead of me there's two girls packing their stuff on llamas. Two days behind me there's a lawyer who set aside his practice for five months to go hiking. One guy's already made it this year to Canada."

"How could you know that?"

"He wrote a postcard back to an outfitter near Shasta to let all the under-twenty-five-miles-a-day crowd know. Me, I don't think mileage is the main thing. I probably won't make it anyway, what with starting so late. It'll be October when I get to Washington."

I think of my own late start, and my scheduled October finish in Hells Canyon. It is troubling. I echo his words, hiding my concern. "No, mileage is not the main thing."

He waves his arm. "The main thing is all of this." Then he chuckles. "I guess it's not for everybody, though, is it? One of the two wrong-way P.C.T.ers I met was a girl who'd never been on a hike before. She'd just sold her business, bought a bunch of gear, and decided to do something wild and crazy. By the time I passed her she told me, 'You know, I don't care if I never see a tree again.'"

"Where do all the P.C.T.ers come from?" I ask.

He gives me the answer of a geography student. "About fifty percent seem to come from the eastern United States—Pennsylvania, Massachusetts, Maryland, that sort of thing. The next biggest group is Californians. Then come the New Zealanders and Australians, who, if you lump them together, probably outnumber us Britishers."

"Do you see a lot of local hikers?"

"Only on the John Muir Trail in the High Sierras. You meet armies of them there, and everywhere else, nobody. In geography we call areas like that 'honeypots.' All the bees buzz to a few choice spots. Maybe that's best. It leaves ninety-five percent of the trails to us."

We stop to rest at a pass, and trade hard candy—the essential mouth-moistener and calorie-booster of the long-range hiker. He chooses one of my butterscotch pieces. I inspect the strange Yorkshire candy he offers. It is vaguely pear-shaped, in a variety of mottled colors ranging from yellow to purple. It tastes a little to the left of watermelon, yet a little to the right of citrus. Strange, I think. This Yorkshire stuff, though good, resembles nothing I've ever seen. Perhaps it is the appropriate nonconformist fare for this nonconformist Yorkshireman. His father, he says, works in a velvet factory. His brother works in a velvet factory. But Chris? He's spending his last pound hiking the American wilderness.

"Is there," he muses, "any demand for high school geography teachers here?"

"Social studies teachers?" I shake my head. "I'm afraid there are sixty applicants for every opening."

He sighs. "It's three hundred to one back home. Sometimes I think I should try to get a work permit so I could stay on here in America. And then sometimes I'm just not sure. Everything's so big and lovely. But maybe I'm just seeing the good part of it all."

7:15 P.M. Donomore Meadows. 66°F. Mileage today: 25.3. Total: 269.1.

I leave Chris behind at lunch; I have farther to go in less time than he does.

The cairns marking the trail today are a rockhound's delight: shiny, gnarled schist; marble, white as chunks of ice; red-brown peridotite; greasy green serpentine. The Klamath rocks are an eclectic sampling of the earth's crust, rammed together by the drifting continent. But the trail crew that put together the wonderful selection in the cairns was more likely thinking: white rocks on top for visibility, flat rocks on the bottom for stability.

There are a lot of rock cairns in the eastern Siskiyous, simply because there are so many open meadows where trails cannot be marked with tree blazes. Most of these meadows date to World War I, when the price of beef went sky-high. The war left the Forest Service so understaffed it could not enforce its newly adopted grazing-permit system. Cattlemen let trainloads of Mexican steers loose in the wilderness to fatten. Other ranchers set forest fires, with the conviction that grass is more useful than trees. By 1917 the eastern Siskiyous were barren.

I am hiking through a sparse meadow when I hear a strange clang-clanging. Out from the shade of a clump of mountain hemlock come a half dozen belled cattle. They stare at me a moment, then lurch back for cover with a raucous rattle-clang. Belled Swiss milch cows may be romantic, but there is something silly about beefy Herefords wearing big tin bells.

The closer I look at the meadows, the more I think "meadow" is the wrong term. There is virtually no grass here, only cowpie-strewn rockfields, brightened by a collection of lovely wildflowers inedible to cattle. Some slopes are a sweep of brilliant yellow Klamath weed. Here and there are bursts of scarlet gilia—so amazingly red it is also called "firecracker" and "skyrocket." The green in these fields comes largely from the boat-shaped leaves and ugly, five-foot flower stalks of green hellebore, a drastic poison.

Poison hellebore root is, according to Indian lore, one of the most potent of all magic herbs. Merely carrying the root about your neck will spare you from the ravages of the terrible Land Otter People, who delight in stealing away men's minds, leaving them pitiable half-men, half-beasts. And if a sea monster rises up while you are spearing seals at night, remember to spit hellebore root at it, and the monster will vanish. Another hint: If a land monster has chewed up your neighbor's family, try rubbing some of the root on their mangled bodies. There is a good chance they'll pop back to life.

The Indians populated the wilderness with mythical bogeymen, but at least they had the sense to provide a mythical remedy. Today people have mentally filled the woods with evil bears, wolves, snakes, spiders, and Bigfeet. Where are the mental remedies to match these fears? The Land Otter People are always outside the door, and we are helpless.

Today I am in the center of the domain of Sasquatch. Sightings near here date to 1895, when a group of Chinese laborers fled their gold mine because of a "big hairy man." Since then, *Homo gigantis* has been identified much more precisely. Naturalist Buddy Mays describes this primate as eight to ten feet tall and between five hundred and one thousand pounds. The characteristic three-toed or five-toed footprints average two to three inches deep, eighteen inches long, and eight inches wide. Mays says the voice is "a series of deep-pitched grunts, squeals, and roars, Oriental in pattern, without the use of a long E."

Less than five miles from where I am hiking, North American Wildlife Research set a Bigfoot trap in 1973. The semisubterranean structure was built of steel and wooden posts. Its electronic sensing equipment was designed to alert a caretaker prowling nearby with a tranquilizer gun and a camera.

The trap was a failure. The researchers might as well have tried to capture a Land Otter Person.

A doe is leading her twin fawns across Donomore Meadows when I arrive here late in the day looking for a campsite. The little fawns do not walk or run, but bounce rubber-legged on all four legs at once—*boing!*—into the fir forest that rings this glade.

I set up camp beside a small creek and turn to my journal. As I write, a different doe walks into my camp, suddenly sees me, sneezes, and bounds back uphill. The meadows may belong to the cattle during the day, but in the evening, deer reign.

AUGUST 30

12:25 P.M. Siskiyou Gap. 56°F. Mileage so far today: 11.0. Total: 280.1.

Today Mount Shasta is just a thirty-mile arm's length away. Each writhing glacier and lava crag is cast in blue by the thin air between me and the mountain. Time and again this day I have been hiking along the dark ridges of the Klamaths and come around a corner to be stopped short at the sight of this enormous volcano. Here, suddenly, are eighty cubic miles of rock, floating effortlessly ten thousand feet above the rest of the hills, an unbelievable Antarctic island in northern California.

Shasta was sacred to the Indians, and taboo above timberline. To them, it was the great white wigwam of a spirit whose hearth fires sometimes trailed sulfurous smoke from the summit.

Those who smile at the Indian myth should, in all fairness, consider that nowadays Mount Shasta is held sacred by the Knights of the White Rose, the Rosicrucians, the Association Sananda and Sanat Kimara, the Radiant School of the Seekers and Servers, Understanding Inc., and the I AM Foundation.

How credible are the modern legends inspired by Shasta? The I AM movement was founded by a Chicago paperhanger, Guy W. Ballard, who claimed to have met a Lemurian named St. Germain high on the mountain's slopes in 1930. The Lemurians, Ballard learned, live in tunnels inside Mount Shasta, but are actually refugees from the ancient kingdom of Mu, now submerged beneath the Pacific Ocean. Like all Lemurians, St. Germain had a walnut-sized sense organ in the middle of his forehead; he also was "clad in jeweled robes, eyes sparkling with light and love."

Others moderns believe Mount Shasta is inhabited by the Secret Commonwealth, concealing the cities of Iletheleme and Yaktayvia in vast caves. The Yaktayvians are said to use the supersonic vibrations from special huge bells to hollow out caves, provide heat, and make light. Intruders are frightened away with high-pitched chimes.

O, for the days of a spirit in a great white wigwam!

I have stopped here for first lunch, but my first order of business is to take off my hot boots and air my wool socks on handy fir branches. The ants, perceiving this perhaps to be a good lunch spot too, are getting their exercise by examining my socks and bare feet in great detail. Oddly, the ants crawling on my feet do not tickle. I look closer and marvel that the soles of my feet have become mummified by yellow calluses. I tap the calluses with my finger. They are as hard and unfeeling as dried cowhide.

6:15 P.M. Atop Mount Ashland, elev. 7,512'. 40°F. Mileage today: 19.8. Total: 288.9.

I have climbed the easternmost and highest peak of the Siskiyous, and set up camp between two granite spires. The tent luffs and shivers in the south wind, but it is set in granite sand, with rocks on all the stakes. The sun has driven off the afternoon's ominous sheet of high cirrus clouds, giving this the proper lip-chapping, 360-degree blue sky feel of a mountain summit.

I have camped on the east side of the peak, just out of sight of things that would lessen the drama: a gravel road up to a grove of radio relay towers, a hulking black ski lift with gallowslike towers swinging red chairs, and a meteorological radar station topped with a white dome like a giant, malignant puffball. The radio grove hums. The radar puffball buzzes ominously. But on my side of the mountain, all is well; mountain hemlock trees clutch the granite in twisted scenic poses, just as they should.

At 7:20 P.M. I am on the summit itself, awaiting sunset. My breath flies off in the cold wind. As the sun dips lower, the ridges and mountains below become sharper—etched in deeper-shaded relief. And the shadow of Mount Ashland itself stretches farther and farther—a sharp A with a shadeless light spot at its apex, pointing toward the distant desert of the Great Basin. The route I will follow in the coming week traces the skyline to the east and north: past little Pilot Knob, over the hump of Soda Mountain, through an undulating forest, and then beside the ravine-cut, volcanic cone of dark, 9,495-foot Mount McLoughlin. Even farther north lies a dim, forested range of sudden, sharp points—the broken rim of Crater Lake. The steep volcanic tip of Mount Thielsen is the last of the Cascade peaks visible before the range flattens into a haze, one hundred miles away.

The cities of Ashland and Medford—like checkered maps in

their brown valley—sink into darkness at my feet. On a peak in the California Klamaths, a bright white speck gleams: probably the counterpart of the white puffball tower on Mount Ashland, which also shines in the sun's last orange glow. The lights of Medford turn on now, greenish-blue twinkles, while the sun is yet a finger's width from the horizon. The red haze of distance blurs the western horizon; I will only know for sure it is still the Pacific if the sun silhouettes a straight line of ocean.

I turn around. The A shadow of my own mountain has surpassed the desert, and stands against the haze like a dark, sinister rival to gleaming Mount Shasta. Mount Shasta and I are alone in the sun now. Even Mount Ashland's A-shaped shadow in the haze is being amputated from below, leaving just the peak hanging above the desert dust. An Oregon junco flies up to a rock almost within arm's reach and cheeps at me, cocking its bright eye. "Haven't seen a sunset here before?" he seems to chide. "It is my favorite hour."

The sun does not hit the ocean. Instead, it silhouettes a jagged ridge near Grassy Knob. I have come too far to see the Pacific even from a mountaintop.

Half gone. Now the cold bites. The world dims. A fiery red bead—a sudden gasp—and it is gone.

AUGUST 31

10:30 A.M. Interstate 5 at Siskiyou Pass. Mileage today: 11.9. Total: 300.8.

I am worried about the shortening days. While I had fourteen hours of daylight at the beginning of my trip, I now have barely thirteen. Each night has eleven hours of darkness, but I do not need eleven hours of sleep. Against all expectations, I seem to need less sleep on this arduous trek than I do living in the city. Evidently rest is less important for weary muscles than for a weary brain.

I awake this morning at five A.M., an hour and a half before sunrise, and can sleep no more. I lie in bed, my hands behind my head. At 5:35 I dress and begin breakfast. A full moon silvers the land. I watch the sky turn from black to magenta.

At dawn I set out. Near the dry, windy summit I see the first sagebrush of my hike, but as I hike down the 3,400 feet to Siskiyou Pass, I return to the moister land of cedars. There are big-leaf maples, the stately native shade tree of western Oregon towns. There is Oregon grape, the state flower, which now has lost its yellow sprays of blossoms and offers instead tough but edible blue berries. And there are the first snowberry bushes I have encountered on my hike.

Snowberry is a misunderstood bush. Nowadays it is cursed by loggers and cattlemen for choking clear-cuts and pastures with persistent, woody brush. But Lewis and Clark recognized its beauty, noting that its white berries give it a festive look all winter. They carefully brought back snowberry seeds to President Jefferson, who was so delighted with the "handsome little shrub" that he presented some plants to the Marquis of Lafayette's aunt in France as a gift from the United States.

As I hike through the snowberry bushes in the peaceful forest near Siskiyou Pass, it seems impossible that a train robbery could have taken place just four hundred feet from here. Even harder to imagine is that it happened four hundred feet *underground*. But it is true. The most violent robbery in Oregon history began directly below me, in the railroad tunnel that connects Oregon with California.

On October 11, 1923, the Southern Pacific express stopped just before entering the Siskiyou tunnel, its crewmen checking the brakes as usual, and allowing the passengers a last breather before going on into California. The train carried a mail car, filled with payroll and valuable express. But when the train pulled into the tunnel, it was carrying three new passengers: the D'Autremont brothers.

The youngest D'Autremont, Hugh, nineteen, ordered the engineer to stop the train with just the locomotive and mail car out of the tunnel. Then the other two D'Autremonts—twins Ray and Roy, both twenty-three—blew open the mail car with dynamite. The charge was far too large. It killed the mail clerk inside. It reduced the contents to debris. It jammed the car's brakes. While the D'Autremonts argued about what to do, the whistle of an approaching train sounded. Quickly they shot the only three trainmen to have witnessed the crime. They dipped their shoes in creosote and sprinkled pepper on their footprints to throw the police hound dogs off their track, and ran into the wilderness to hide out from the law. The D'Autremonts camped just three miles from the pass near the route of the present-day Pacific Crest Trail. When I camp there tomorrow night, I'll write how they eluded the biggest manhunt in Oregon history.

Around a curve of trail I hear the drone of big diesel tractor-trailer rigs grinding up Interstate 5. I had seen this highway the night before—incredible cuts and fills in duplicate across the rounded brown foothills of both states—with tiny, silver-flashing specks that moved. From Mexico to Canada, this freeway parallels the Pacific Crest Trail, yet seems to traverse a different world.

Here is a gas station, and a restaurant, and the telephone that will let my family know I have arrived this far in safety. I myself do not know how, but I am a day ahead of schedule.

II.

THE CASCADES

Climb the mountains and get their good tidings. Nature's peace will flow into you as sunshine flows into trees. The winds will blow their own freshness into you, and the storms their energy . . .

—JOHN MUIR

7:56 P.M. Pilot Rock. Drizzling, 50°F. Mileage today: 7.3. Total: 308.1.

After a day at the Medford home of my aunt Nancy and uncle Bob—eating everything I could, washing clothes, unpacking my second box of trail food—I return to the Pacific Crest Trail at Siskiyou Pass. Ever since seeing high clouds two days ago, I have been expecting a rainstorm; now it has arrived. I am wearing rain gear from head to toe, and my pack is protected by a bright red nylon cover. My uncle shakes his head as I set off up the steep, muddy trail.

The carpet of snowberry bushes is spangled with silver water beads—crystal berries to match the white ones. At the foot of the firs along the misty trail I discover a giant puffball mushroom, *Calvatia gigantea,* which looks like some rare albino basketball. I cut a wedge from its twenty pounds of edible white flesh just to breathe the musty aroma of autumn.

The trail passes below the fogbound cliffs of Pilot Rock. This remnant of an ancient volcano earned its name by guiding pioneers to Siskiyou Pass. Since the railroad came through three miles away, Pilot Rock has been a landmark only to backpackers and train robbers.

I pitch my tent near where the D'Autremont brothers camped sixty-two years ago. While the D'Autremonts hid out, detectives learned their identity by tracing a crumpled money-order receipt found in some abandoned clothing near the train. Four million wanted posters, in seven languages, were distributed from Canada to Latin America, and from Europe to the Orient, offering a reward for the capture of the D'Autremonts. Hundreds of deputies with dogs began searching the Siskiyou wilderness. But the wilderness was simply too vast.

After ten days the outlaws ran low on food, and still had no money, so Ray ventured out. He went back to the scene of the crime, hopped a freight to the first town on the Oregon side of the pass, and ordered a cup of coffee in the depot. There he bought a newspaper and was alarmed to see a picture of himself on the front page. He went back to warn his brothers to devise aliases.

The brothers weren't discovered and brought to justice until four years later, when Hugh was an army private in the Philippines, and Ray and Roy were steelworkers in Ohio.

They needn't have scattered around the globe to hide. They were safer here in the wilderness, just three miles from the scene of their crime.

SEPTEMBER 2

9:50 A.M. Soda Mountain. Raining, 44°F. Mileage so far today: 4.2. Total: 312.3.

The Pacific Crest Trail crosses a small dirt road high on the shoulder of Soda Mountain. I had arranged for someone from a local conservation group to meet me here at ten o'clock. However, this morning a cold rain gusts across the forested ridge. The trees are faint gray silhouettes. I am shivering. My hands are almost too stiff and wet to write.

I do not really expect anyone to show up now. The group was only going to fill me in on its campaign to have the Bureau of Land Management designate Soda Mountain as Wilderness.

I drop my pack and walk up the road a way, trying to keep warm while I wait. But when I return, a Jeep has appeared at the trail crossing and sits there, dripping in the storm.

A rain-streaked window rolls down, and a red-bearded, blue-eyed man about my age blinks at me, as if he had been interrupted in the midst of faraway thoughts.

"Are you from the Soda Mountain Wilderness Council?" I ask.

"Yes." He thinks a moment more. Then he says, "Why don't you get in?"

As soon as I have closed the door, the windows fog, and we are in a space capsule in the clouds. He is wearing a rakish English sport cap, a blue chamois shirt, a down vest, snow pants, and running shoes.

"I'm Bill."

He nods. "I am Roger Murray."

"I guess it's not a day to hike around for views."

"No. But I can tell you about Soda Mountain here."

And so Roger tells me about this small, forested mountain standing at the junction of three botanical regions. It does not really belong
to the Siskiyous, although its valleys are filled with the Siskiyous'
characteristic cedar, scrub oak, and manzanita. It is not quite in the
Cascades, although its summit is a subalpine fir forest, such as one
might expect in the Cascades. Nor does it belong to the fault-block
steppes of the Great Basin, although its southern ridges host sagebrush, rabbit brush, and gnarled juniper. Soda Mountain is the transi-
tion point, in the middle of the three zones.

"I show most people the ecosystems," Roger says, "by taking
them on a bushwhack from the ridgetop to the canyon bottom. It's a
forty-five-hundred-foot vertical drop, past rock outcroppings, manzanita chaparral, and maple brush."

"Sounds awfully rough," I say.

"I don't intend for them to want to come back. That is not my
duty."

"Your duty? Do you have some kind of paid job with your conversation group?"

"No, no. I'm self-employed. I run a mail-order bicycle parts
business."

I think of other motivations. "Then, do you own property
nearby?"

"Actually, I do live on forty acres at the foot of the mountain.
But it would be wrong to think I am merely trying to protect my
property value."

"Oh?"

"I built my house by myself for three thousand dollars, with
lumber salvaged from an old motel. There is no electricity. I use kerosene and candles for light. I live alone. I spend most of my time
reading in my three thousand-volume library, and thinking. That is
the source of my duty."

Now I am more puzzled than ever. "What do you read?"

"Many things." He pauses. "The Bible."

The rain taps on the metal roof. The fog of our breath keeps the
windows of the spacecraft white. I wait, uncertain how delicate this
new subject will prove to be.

Roger continues, speaking as though he were weighing every

word. "You see, I spent eleven years studying philosophy and the-
ology—at the University of California, in a Chicago seminary, and in
London. But my goal was never to become a minister, a professional
Christian. I came to Soda Mountain to continue my spiritual study
alone."

"And what do you study?"

"Various misunderstood issues. Earth domination."

The rain beats harder on the roof. I realize I have encountered a
new species of wilderness animal: the wilderness theologian. I might
not see his type on this hike again. "Earth domination is misunderstood? I thought the Bible made a point of saying God gave man
dominion over the earth."

Roger knits his brow. "Yes, in Genesis. But look more closely at
the creation myth. What did God create first? Man? No, the earth and
the beasts were God's first creations. Man was created *last,* and then
given 'dominion.'"

He leans back, his brow still knit. "It's a problematical word,
'dominion.' Does it mean to destroy? Some Fundamentalist Christians
believe in *consuming* resources. But it seems improbable that Adam
was put in the garden to use up God's creation. Adam's dominion
gave him the duties of a caretaker. In the same way, I have dominion
over the apple trees in my yard—I prune them, help them flourish,
and only then can enjoy the fruit."

"But, for the sake of argument," I say, "couldn't a good caretaker
harvest and replant these forests, like any other crop?"

He shakes his head. "I would not pick apples if I could only do
so by destroying the orchard forever. The forests around Soda Mountain are too dry and steep to be profitably replanted. Each clear-cut
here requires thousands of dollars an acre if new trees are to live. It
takes fertilizer for the poor soil, shade cards to protect seedlings from
the sun, herbicides to keep down brush, and seedling cages to keep
deer from eating new shoots. The Bureau of Land Management loses
money with each timber sale, yet the sales continue. People do not
want to accept that the elimination of the low-elevation old-growth
forests has doomed most local sawmills. The temptation is to put off
the inevitable decline of the timber industry by consuming resources
that can never be replenished. The temptation is to be masters rather
than caretakers: reckless masters of the earth."

Roger's deep, thoughtful blue eyes stare out the white wind-shield. He sighs and says, almost to himself, "Man's duty is to take care of the land where he lives. That is the essence of loving thy neighbor—for God's earth is our most cherished neighbor. And that is why I must protect Soda Mountain."

7:47 P.M. Hyatt Reservoir. Overcast, 54°F. Mileage today: 25.7. Total: 333.8.

I descend Soda Mountain as the rain lifts, and come to a long, rolling upland. This is the Dead Indian Country, named for a wickiup of corpses found here in pioneer days. A group of white hunters at-tempting to force a passage here in 1869 described this five thousand-foot-high plain as "one continuous forest of standing timber, almost impossible for horses and adapted, mainly, to the production of yel-lowjackets."

Now it is a checkerboard of BLM and private land, adapted, mainly, to clear-cuts, cattle, and reservoirs.

I look at the dark hump of Soda Mountain; an island of wilder-ness in a mastered land. It seems a challenging task for a caretaker, to decide to do nothing.

SEPTEMBER 3

12 noon. Burton Butte. Clear, 64°F. Mileage so far today: 12.1. Total: 345.9.

The rainstorm is past, but the forest still revels in moisture. Wet bushes beside the trail keep boots and pants legs dripping until my first lunch; then I spread everything out to dry. Today I am hiking through fields of chinkapin, thistle, and weedy, green mullein—failed attempts to regenerate clear-cut forests. At times the trail slices through rolling forests of grand fir and white fir. I am puzzled by thudding sounds in the woods until I see a five-pound white-fir cone fall. Then I see the squirrel that felled the cone spring down after it, eager to tear it apart for the seeds.

There is other wildlife. I collect several reddish feathers from the trail, thinking to save them for my daughter, who will delight to hear they are from woodpeckers—the red-brown flickers that swoop from tree to tree. I pass a dozen groups of deer this morning; they hardly look up from their browse at a silent backpacker on a windless day.

The Pacific Crest Trail map tells me to get water at Big Springs before heading on across sixteen miles of dry lava lands. So I let my water supply run out, in anticipation of Big Springs. At last I come to a trail sign, SPRING, and follow the arrow to an oily bog churned by cow hoofprints. I open the lid of a corrugated-metal spring box, and find to my horror that the water in "Big Springs" is stagnant. Suspended beneath its filmy surface are the moldy remains of a mouse.

There is no alternative. Holding the dead mouse back with a stick, I fill my bottles and add a heavy dose of water-purification tablets.

Big, tan-colored blocks of lava now line the trail, for I have entered the blast zone of the intermittently violent, volcanic Cascade Range. Behind me, Mount Shasta raises its head above Soda Mountain in a final, cloudlike farewell. The day of cold rain has left Shasta's great cone a dreamy white, covered with the first snow of the coming winter.

I hike into the first stand of lodgepole pine I have seen since Cape Blanco. At Cape Blanco the pines formed a contorted mat that justified their scientific name, Pinus contorta. Here, however, they live up to their common name, and grow in stands of nearly limbless, perfectly straight poles, suitable either for Indian lodges or small log cabins. Scattered underneath the lodgepole pines are smug little white firs, which seem to be gloating that one day they will grow taller than the lodgepoles, shade them out, and form a climax forest. But the lodgepoles are sanguine. They are counting on a forest fire to sweep through this dry land before the white firs win out, leaving only the lodgepole pines' fireproof cones to reseed the burnt earth.

I have just finished my second and final lunch of the day, and am still ravenous. What is even more troublesome is that I have been assaulted with daydreams of food much of the morning. In one of the vivid food fantasies, I prepared a sumptuous spinach quiche dinner, with French bread, corn on the cob, a large garden salad, and a big beaker of white wine. In another I assembled an enormous hamburger, item by item. It hung before me on the trail, a waking nightmare.

My trail diet ought to be sufficient. I take vitamin pills to make up any deficiency. Yet I had never dreamed I would hike more than twenty miles a day. I began this trip weighing a very lean 145 pounds. I cannot afford to be losing weight.

SEPTEMBER 4

8:44 A.M. Beside Mt. McLoughlin. Clear, 55°F. Mileage yesterday; 32.8. So far today: 2.8. Total: 369.4.

How different the Cascades are from the Klamaths! After my hungry lunch stop yesterday, I hiked all afternoon across a great field of black lava. Mile after mile, jumbled, man-sized blocks of basalt formed a terrain so wondrously inhospitable that the Pacific Crest Trail had had to be blasted out of the rock on level ground. Here and there little islands of stunted firs survived between the rock flows, but in the rock itself there was no grass or flowers—only an occasional diehard quaking aspen fluttering its silver-green leaves like a distress signal. There was nothing so stark and raw in the Klamaths.

I have crossed from one of America's oldest mountain ranges to America's youngest. The Klamaths' schist and shale predate the dinosaurs, but lava was still oozing out of Mount McLoughlin when Rome was being sacked by the Vandals. The peaks of the High Cascades are the tallest in Oregon, but a mere million years ago they did not exist.

The basalt lava is more than half silica, and cuts boot soles like glass. When I finally reached a forest floor of spongy duff near Mount McLoughlin, I sprawled out with relief. The snow-bent pines and blue huckleberry bushes told me I had come to the forests of the High Cascades at last. The map said I had entered the newly designated Sky Lakes Wilderness, the first of a string of seven wildernesses that stretch, almost uninterrupted, for 250 miles along the Cascade crest, past Crater Lake National Park to Mount Jefferson.

A porcupine waddled up into a nearby bush to welcome me. I looked at the spiny, two-and-a-half-foot-long beast and laughed. He glared at me with his beady eyes, bristled his yellow-tipped quills, and set to chewing the bush's bark. Here, I thought, was a fellow who will never be hungry in the woods. When he runs out of his favorite skunk cabbage (a plant avoided by other animals because of its smell) and lupine (a source of selenium poisoning for other animals), there's always plenty of bark. He kept on eating even though I was just five feet away. Porcupines have no serious enemies. One good whack of their tail leaves coyotes and mountain lions blinded, or with crippled tongues.

Porcupines are protected by law in many western states—as a source of survival food for lost campers. A sharp blow with a stick on a porcupine's nose will kill it quite easily, and make it suitable for skinning and roasting. I was not yet that hungry.

When night began to fall, I looked around for the creek promised by my map. I'd hiked twenty-eight miles and had to camp soon. Instead of a creek, however, I found a dry, rocky ravine. The only water left in my bottles was a half cup of sludge from the dead-mouse spring. Wearily, I looked at the map. The next water shown was a lake five miles away, and 1,200 feet up, on the shoulder of Mount McLoughlin.

For a moment, I felt defeated. I'd come too far to go five more miles uphill. But then my legs took over. I stood up, put on my pack, and fairly catapulted up the trail. The darkness deepened, but my legs kept springing, without pain or particular effort. By moonrise, I was sitting beside the high mountain lake, musing that I had somehow traveled 32.8 miles that day—despite two lunches, a stop to dry rain gear, a dozen stops to take photographs, and an hour of writing in my journal. Across the dark lake rose the snowless, 9,495-foot cone of Mount McLoughlin.

In my sleeping bag, I flexed my legs over and over, working out the kinks; my thighs were so thick with strange new muscles, they felt like frog's legs. I wondered: What is the limit of a man? Is the limit after all not the body, but rather the will? Perhaps the body is like a clever old horse that acts lame when it is eager to turn back to the hay in the barn. On this trip I have suffered sore feet, and aching shoulders, and pains in my hips from the pack belt—but only one malady at a time, as if my body parts were taking turns, crying out for me to stop this eternal hiking. The body reveals its hidden reserves only under protest. A "lame" horse can do some pretty astonishing tricks when it is finally saddled by a rodeo rider wearing spurs.

In the morning I am besieged by camp robbers. "Camp robber"

is the local name of the Clark's nutcracker, the constant camp com-
panion of these mountains. I scoop out my cup and a half of breakfast
oats and hear a feathery *swish*! as one of the crow-sized, blue-and-gray
birds sails past, its tail feathers fanned for the attack. There are camp
robbers so bold they snatch sandwiches from picnickers' hands. Even
in midwinter, when I've been cross-country skiing in the Cascades,
the nutcrackers are still up here, hungrier than ever. And the music
they make! Caws of the most raucous sort, whistles, and all manner of
demanding, scolding chatter.

I have seen no person for a day and a half—forty miles—but
there's company aplenty with these rambunctious thieves in the High
Cascades woods.

3:53 P.M. Trail in Sky Lakes Wilderness. Wispy cirrus clouds, 67°F.
Mileage so far today: 18.5. Total: 385.1.

Today I hike the Cascade crest through a viewless, flat forest of
mountain hemlocks, pines, and huckleberry bushes. On and on the
forest stretches, until its length becomes a wonder in itself.

With no landmarks to hike toward, it is difficult to decide when
to stop to rest or eat. Each tree and log seems as inviting as the next,
regardless of how far I have come. So I set up stops by the pedometer
I wear at my waist: rest at miles 4 and 8, first lunch at mile 11, rest at
14½, second lunch at 17½.

How grudgingly such a system makes the miles go by! But at
mile 14½, the trail climbs up a rock pile and all my calculations are
for naught. How can I stop before I reach the view this ridge promises?

I climb on, accompanied by the *meep*! of the rock pile's native
pikas. I spot one of these little, round-eared rock rabbits; it stands on
its haunches to *meep*! at me, and then scurries off. It has to be busy,
for it must spend the short summer storing bushels of cut grass in its
burrow. Remarkably, although pikas live in a habitat higher than that
of any other North American mammal, they spend long winters under
the snow without hibernating. Without the grass they stockpile in the
crannies of rockslides they would soon starve and freeze.

Finally my ridge yields up its view across the forests. It's the first
good look I've had at Mount McLoughlin since I camped beside it last

night. It doesn't look as smooth and barren from here. This shadier north-facing side still has snow, and is deformed by a deep gouge—evidence of an Ice Age glacier.

I look eastward and get my first glimpse of eastern Oregon—the half of the state lying in the rain shadow of the Cascades. Forests roll across the mountain crest, slide a half dozen miles down the canyons on the east slope of the range, and crash-land into a flat brown plateau. In the distance, low, forbidding brown hills stretch toward the deserts of the Great Basin. Before my hike is over, I will have to cross that arid land, too.

7:15 P.M. Seven Lakes Basin. Mileage today: 26.7. Total: 393.3.

I am sitting in the grassy margin of a broad, breeze-rippled lake at sunset. Above the firs on the far shore is a long, pink-lit ridge, cresting in the pinnacles of Devils Peak. This 7,582-foot-tall mountain is often overlooked in the procession of taller Cascade peaks, but from the Seven Lakes Basin its grandeur is unrivaled. The breeze dapples its reflection into diminishing bars of forest green, sky blue, and cloud pink. A stand of reeds sails out into the reflection, masts against the breeze.

I remember backpacking to this lake basin as a six-year-old boy, proudly carrying my little wooden-frame backpack, struggling to keep up with my older cousins. It was in July and the mosquitoes nearly carried us all away. After a frantic night of swatting, we fled. But now it is September, and the year's brood is gone. The evening is nearly silent.

There is a *plip* from the lakeshore—perhaps a fish, more likely a frog. Millions of these tiny frogs, each no bigger than a fingernail, populate the lakeside grasses. Even to sit down I had to help two or three of the bumbling little innocents hop through the grass forest and out of the way—and then I couldn't sit in that spot anyway, for I found a host of delicate, trumpet-shaped yellow flowers peering up from the grass as well.

The lake basin before me is a two-mile-wide amphitheater: yet another elegant project financed by the Ice Age. A glacier began right in front of me, with the snows that clung to Devils Peak's shady north cliffs. When the snow had packed to ice on that slope, its weight sent the whole mass crawling down across the lake beds. The ice spilled out downstream over a lip, creating a deep, broad, U-shaped valley below—now the home of the Rogue River.

The Rogue! I've hiked in a great arc around this river in the past two weeks, from Agness, near its mouth, to Devils Peak, where I drank straight from a tumbling, bemeadowed brook at the Rogue's very beginning. Tomorrow, at Crater Lake, I will finally leave the Rogue's watershed. Crater Lake is the never-never land of Oregon's rivers—a lake without inlet or outlet, surrounded by drainages of the state's great rivers: Rogue, Umpqua, Deschutes-Columbia, and Klamath.

The clouds have thinned to three stripes, which now all catch sudden fire, branding sky and lake in a chevron of scarlet backed with deepest blue. A first star shines above one cottony bar, like a newborn sun amid a glowing nebula deep in the galaxy. A flat white mist begins to slide out from the lake's cool edge, smothering the few colored water bars left from the evening breeze.

A solemn silence. Not a cricket. Then there is a single chuckle from an impious nutcracker. And just as the stillness of sleep should close the lake's weary eye beneath the sheet of soft mist, *all* the crazy nutcrackers begin to chuckle. Then to laugh. A dozen of them, around the lake, all squawking with fits of cheeps and chatter. What is it they know, the scoundrels, that turns them monkey at the point of the sermon? Thinking of it makes me smile, too. Even I cannot explain; but then why should a sunset be melancholy?

The first of the bats begin their erratic, silent flutters over the lake. Two ducks whistle over the dark lake's mirror and disappear among the stars. And then even the nutcrackers are still.

SEPTEMBER 5

9:11 A.M. Trail in Sky Lakes Wilderness. Damp fog, 55°F. Mileage so far today: 6.7. Total: 400.0.

I wake to a half-moon overhead in a dawnless sky. I check my digital watch by matchlight: 5:09 A.M. I can sleep no more, so I pack my tent in the silvery darkness. I eat oatmeal and cocoa by the lakeshore, waiting for day to happen. Low clouds hide Devils Peak and fuzz the moon to a big hazy ball. At 6:12 A.M. I set off on the trail, while daylight-softened clouds descend.

> *2:00 P.M. Highway shoulder in Crater Lake National Park. Blustery, 48°F. Mileage so far today: 23.1. Total: 416.4.*

In the forest, in the fog, I watch the rocks and trees change as I hike toward ground zero of one of the greatest explosions ever to shake the planet Earth. I am approaching what was until recently the tallest mountain in Oregon—twelve-thousand-foot Mount Mazama. In a single hour, 6,600 years ago, the top mile of Mazama was blown into the sky, leaving a caldera seven miles wide. The cloud of pumice and ash that boomed into the air blanketed the earth as far away as Saskatchewan. Then—even more terrifying to the Indians who lived here then, and whose legends recall the event—a glowing avalanche of frothing magma raced down the slopes on a cushion of hot gas. So powerful was this avalanche that it carried six-foot pumice boulders twenty miles over flat ground. It sailed right over four-mile-wide Diamond Lake, and descended the Rogue River for forty miles, destroying all life in its path. In that one hour Mount Mazama blew up fourteen cubic miles of rock—fifty times more than Mazama's Cascade sister, Mount St. Helens, puffed into the air in 1980.

The first change I notice in the forest is the abrupt loss of the lovely carpet of huckleberries—all those round green-and-autumn-red leaves. Under the increasingly sparse lodgepole pines and mountain hemlocks there is now only a campground-clean expanse of pine-needle duff, strewn with yellow, and then red, pumice cinders. The soil here is buried under six feet of ash.

However, even pine needles on cinder provide fodder enough for September mushrooms. So, while clouds drag the ground, mushroom watching is my amusement of the morning. Big purple-domed russulas loom white-stalked, white-gilled, and edible, but often already tasted by squirrels or kicked apart by probing deer hooves to reveal a network of worm canals. Clumps of little tan collybia cluster about a stump. And everywhere there are slippery jacks—huge, slimy-topped, yellow-pored boletes shoving up bark and twigs or, where they lie under heavier fallen wood, oozing up in contorted shapes through the chinks, like sourdough loaves on the rise.

When I reach the highway, I find station wagons with out-of-state plates and roof racks full of tarp-wrapped bundles fleeing the National Park, windshield wipers slapping.

8:27 P.M. Mountain Lounge, Crater Lake Rim Village. Mileage today: 27.4. Total: 420.7.

"There's a bug in my water," says the little girl at the next table, but no one pays her any attention except me. I am writing in my journal and drinking a glass of Blitz Weinhard beer.

I arrived at the rim of Crater Lake three hours ago, in a cold, wind-swept fog that turned the lake into a howling gray void. The ranger at the hikers' station informed me the rim campground I had come to find was dismantled several years ago. At the lodge I paid $23.56 for a two-bed cottage, and set out, bracing myself against the gusts of wet cloud, to find it.

As I write this in the restaurant, the little girl is still talking to the hamburger in her paper-lined wickerwork tray. "There's a *bug* in my water." Her dad has a pitcher of beer; her mom is eating fries.

My cottage turned out to be a low, nine- by twelve-foot plank shack. Inside, a single bare bulb lit a single room lined with institutional green quarter-inch plywood. The windows were four small panes of glass hung with dishtowel curtains. A lightless closet in the corner contained a crooked white toilet and nothing else. I spread out the wet gear from my backpack on one of the twin beds, since there was no table. Above the cold-water laundry-style sink I found a small wall heater. Even when the heater was glowing red, I could see my breath, for the wind blew in through an inch-wide crack under the cottage's plank door. I thought: Chipmunks are as likely to get into my food here as at any of my forest camps.

Now, in the Mountain Lounge, the little girl's dad is rolling his Naugahyde chair back on its casters. He sets his beer on the Formica and smiles down at his daughter. "Can I ask you some questions, honey?"
  "Awright."

"What's been the best part of your vacation? You like San Francisco?"

The girl's mom joins in. "You like the big redwood trees?"

Dad asks, "Lake Tahoe? The lighthouse? Remember the house with the light? Remember we used the stakes to put our tent up? Come on, honey, what do you say was the best part of the whole vacation?"

The girl wrinkles her brow, still staring at the table. "The bug in my water," she says.

In the cottage I quickly set up my camp stove, made a two-man freeze-dried dinner, and ate it greedily. But then I thought: I am a day ahead of schedule again because I've hiked through the fog without dawdling. So I decided to heat another teapot of water and fix a second two-man dinner. When it, too, was gone, I was still hungry. And then I had another thought: Tomorrow I expect to reach the next food drop at Diamond Lake, where the emergency rations I am carrying will be replenished. I opened my emergency potato-flake dinner, mixed it into a white goo, and astonished myself by eating it all. I stared out the window, wondering more than ever about my diet. I went to the Mountain Lounge.

The girl's dad is studying her carefully. "I didn't know you liked bugs that much, honey." He looks at his wife. "What do you think? Maybe we ought to get her some books about bugs."

When my beer glass is empty, I go back outside to feel the cloud. Even from there the modern restaurant looks like any other such place in America, set in an asphalt parking lot.

Then I walk past the dark cars toward the old Crater Lake Lodge—a long, hunkered-down-for-winter, small-windowed, barn-shaped building. It squeezes four stories into the height needed for two. Yet the lobby is roomy and warm, with varnished log banisters and log-bark walls. Silver and china glint from red tablecloths in the restaurant. In a side room as narrow as a hallway is the Caldera Lounge: appropriately, a smoky hole. I go back to the lobby to sit and write.

The mood of the guests is one of relaxed boredom. A group of six is gathered at a table to watch a two-person backgammon game. Two elderly women are shuffling cards for gin rummy on the arms of their overstuffed chairs. There are no hamburgers here.

The lodge clerk repeats: "No rooms have showers, ma'am. There are no showering facilities in the park."

Two men with reading glasses hold up the *Oregonian,* exposing banner headlines of hurricanes in Mississippi. The men are sitting bolt upright, earnest about each article.

"This time of year? You could—gosh, I don't know," an elderly man tells a young woman in the next chair. "Everything's cold. You could head towards Reno and see the balloon races."

"We have to be back to work on Tuesday," the woman explains.

The voices start to merge: "In fact, we were supposed to go back to Tampa." "It's raining in L.A." "Oh, OK, then you'll have to head back soon." "Two sixty! My God, I'm getting skunked!"

I walk outside again. Cassiopeia gleams a moment over the dark clouds in the lake, and is gone. The storm sweeps up Mount Mazama's slopes, finds no summit, and, in angry disappointment, howls into the depths.

SEPTEMBER 6

7:15 A.M. Crater Lake cottage. 38°F. inside.

I toss and turn miserably on the soft motel mattress. When I am finally convinced dawn must be coming, I turn on the light to start packing, but it is 1:15 A.M., and I sag back onto the bed. At three A.M. the wind, which had been making the walls shudder all night, finally breaks into a deluge of rain, rattling the shake roof and sending pinecones and snow shutters banging.

When a feeble gray dawn finally lights the downpour outside, I lay out my rain pants, raincoat, and waterproof pack cover. Out the windowpane I catch a glimpse of the little girl from the Mountain Lounge. She and her mother are running from the next cottage to a Volvo. The father rushes from cabin door to car and back, carrying their things through a gusty wall of rain.

7:32 P.M. Diamond Lake. Mileage today: 23.5. Total: 444.2.

I hike the rim of Crater Lake, with a white wind blowing sheets of rain horizontally across the ground. To keep from being blasted off the craggy cliffs, I lean so far into the wind that each pause in its force sends me staggering to my knees. I wonder why my left hand has grown numb in my waterproof coat pocket, and discover that the driving rain has filled my left pocket with ice water. I dump out the water, but in five minutes the pocket is full again.

I have seen this lake's amazingly blue waters before; now that I cannot, I feel the abyss and watch huge, gnarled whitebark pines loom up through the storm on the rim. These are trees so used to such weather that their supple branches can literally be tied in knots. Then I follow the highway north, watching the infrequent cars pull into the viewpoint turnouts to read the National Park markers through rain-streaked windows, as though the directional arrows to Union Peak and Mount Thielsen had significance in such a storm.

Watching the ground as I hike down Mount Mazama's flanks, I compare random square meters of roadside. In the Pumice Desert, where cinders fell two hundred feet deep 6,600 years ago, there are still no more than two struggling plants per meter: yellowed bunchgrass and dwarf lupine. Then the first scrawny lodgepole pines appear, and their height increases until, a dozen miles from the lake, they form an even fifty-foot stand. The forest is a giant's lawn, with a straight lawnmower swath cut by the highway.

A pair of touring bicyclists pass me, pumping hard, cursing. And I think: Why should such weather make one miserable? Clouds are much more common to these mountains than sunshine, so why not learn to enjoy the storms? It is far too easy to complain of being cold, wet, hungry, sore, and tired. By my own reckoning, I am only about 20 percent cold, as long as I keep walking, and still no more than 15 percent wet, 35 percent hungry, 20 percent sore, and 25 percent tired.

John Muir, while living in Yosemite Valley in the 1860s, would rush outside during blizzards, rainstorms, and earthquakes, so as not to miss any part of nature's varied beauty. In a rainy windstorm like this one, he climbed a tall fir and whipped back and forth near its top, listening to the wind songs of the different tree limbs. How much one misses by not daring to get 20 percent cold and 15 percent wet!

When I hike down from the clouds I can see Diamond Lake ahead—a gray steppingstone in the broad lawn of lodgepole pines. Surprisingly, Diamond Lake draws twice as many visitors each year as

the more famous Crater Lake. A quarter million people visit Crater
Lake in a year—three quarters of them from out of state—but Diamond Lake hosts half a million annual visits, almost entirely by
Oregonians. The reason? Cold, cliff-rimmed Crater Lake is all but
useless to swimmers and fishermen. Diamond Lake is full of trout and
averages just twenty feet deep, so it is warm enough in summer to
make swimming enjoyable.

Even in the rain, the campgrounds I hike past are filled with
trailers and pickups. Families peer at me sullenly from the windows.

A food package is supposed to be waiting for me at my great-
aunt Elsie's vacation cabin, in the lakeshore pines a mile past the last
of the campgrounds. By now I am 45 percent wet—including my
patent "waterproof" boots—and 90 percent tired, so I am thinking a
great deal about this cabin. I have not visited it since I was a child.

The cabin is the legacy of my late great-uncle Arnel, who designed and built it fifty years ago. I remember Uncle Arnel, a sensitive, quiet man, who got to know the Douglas squirrels and gray
jays about his cabin so well that he gave them all names. He con-
founded his numerous in-laws, who found it hard to believe a man
would build a cabin at a mountain lake, and then never hunt or fish
there. They understood even less why he refused to replace the icebox
with a refrigerator or the kerosene lamps with light bulbs after electricity arrived at Diamond Lake in the fifties.

Arnel's attitude about work was different, too. Instead of pursu-
ing a "proper" career, he took a job in the basement of the Medford
courthouse microfilming legal records, because he was allowed to finish a week's work at his own pace. He microfilmed almost continu-
ously for half of each week and spent the other half feeding gray jays
at Diamond Lake.

It is hard to picture a more peaceful man than Uncle Arnel. So it
came as a shock when he gave a fifteen-year-old hitchhiker a lift near
Diamond Lake in 1978, and the boy followed him to his cabin,
stabbed him to death, and stole his van.

When I finally spot the rustic, steep-roofed chalet, it is much
smaller than I remember. I open the door with the key I have carried
for more than four hundred miles. A prominent switch in the en-
tryway makes the electric lights jump on and the refrigerator hum—
innovations since Uncle Arnel's death. I make my way past piles of

skis, boots, ice skates, inner tubes, and firewood to the tiny kitchen, dark behind heavily shuttered windows.

In a moment I've unshuttered the windows, torn off my wet clothes, and built a crackling pine fire in the kitchen box stove. I pour a tumbler from the big brandy bottle under the sink and let the liquor burn my insides, the way frostbitten fingers burn when they thaw. Then up goes my wet gear on the hooks and strings above the stove. The water pump has to be primed with a bucketful from the choppy lake outside the door, but then it gushes crystal water. I put two big kettles on the wood stove to steam, and soon am downing a dinner of hot noodles.

Great-Aunt Elsie has left my food package on the kitchen table, along with an unexpected bag of fresh fruit. I eat an apple while I load the trail food into my backpack. Then I start to think about breakfast. Why not pancakes? But as soon as I locate the pancake mix and syrup, there's no stopping me. I cook and eat a dozen syrupy pancakes on the spot.

Finally I stretch out on a sofa, listening to the radio station of choice here. I don't believe in fiddling with tuning dials on other people's radios. Only the owner's choice sounds right. And so I hear KBGG—K-Big—playing Big Band hits of the forties. Thirty percent chance of rain, says the station, and slips into a 1950 radio show about an innocent girl turned mad by gambling.

Doped with heat, brandy, and pancakes, I fog about the cabin, taking in the dark walls' dense decor: eighteen-inch-long sugar-pine cones, six-point elk antlers, and five hundred different kinds of beer cans nailed in rows around the edge of the ceiling. The curtains are all counterweighted with great masses of fishing tackle, salvaged from lakeside snags by a man who never fished.

"'Enjoy yourself, it's later than you think,'" croons the raspy radio. "Pop! Crack!" The pinewood snaps red sparks while my boots and socks steam.

Uncle Arnel's presence is everywhere. Above the kitchen drainboard is a penciled list of the gray jays he banded and watched year after year; one bird returned six years before the records end. Arnel was another spirit of the wilderness.

SEPTEMBER 7

6:00 A.M. Diamond Lake cabin.

At the break of dawn I take the key hanging on the elk antlers and hike out to the shingled shed labeled POTTY-O. A slot-topped soda-pop can nailed behind the seat bears a metal sign borrowed from some ancient parking meter: 30 MINS. 5¢, 60 MINS. 10¢. On the wall: NO GARBAGE DOWN THE HOLE. THIS IS THE LAST OUTHOUSE WE'RE GOING TO DIG.

By the kitchen stove again, I breakfast on more pancakes, hot chocolate, and a real orange. It is a little tempting just to stay here— burning firewood and eating pancakes all day in the still half-shut-tered-up cabin, sipping cups of fiery brandy, coaxing orange-bellied Douglas squirrels onto the porch, counting the ceiling's beer cans by firelight each evening. But there's too much inertia in such a life for me, too passive a contact with the wilds.

6:45 P.M. Maidu Lake Shelter. Overcast, 45°F. Mileage today: 19.4. Total: 463.6.

I set off around Diamond Lake on the kind of misty, cool Satur-day morning that fishermen dream of. Diamond Lake is not named for its shape, but rather for a fisherman, Mr. Diamond, who first stocked this lake a century ago, carrying a bucket of trout fifty miles.

Through wisps of fog I hear a voice across the water and a *putt-putt-putt.* Small waves lap the shore, bringing the smell of outboard motor fuel, and memories. Suddenly I am thirteen, on an uncle's powerboat, wind whipping back my hair, shouting in vain over the whining roar of the racing motor; I am seven, chilled fingers fumbling with bait in the oily water below a wooden boat's floor slats.

Smells bring more sudden, vivid memories than any number of old photographs. If only it were possible to compile smell-albums of childhood, instead of mere photograph albums. I would shut my eyes and turn the pages, reliving warm haylofts, gunpowder fireworks on the beach, Grandpa's sweet pipe tobacco, and the perfume Mother wore when she was young.

The fishermen drift out of the fog, all in a cluster: a hundred different skiffs and dinghies. Three hundred hooks in one foggy bay of this shallow lake! Perhaps there really are that many fish in the water beneath this silent, motionless fleet. How many Saturdays can the boats be there, though, and there still be fish?

A two thousand-foot climb up past Tipsoo Butte regains the Pacific Crest Trail in the Mount Thielsen Wilderness. In the fog the mushrooms are vaulting up the duff more furiously than ever. But this dark, wet forest is really ruled by the lichens.

Lichens are everywhere I look. Some resemble green beards caught in the tree limbs, others are warty gray seaweed on the bark, and still others encrust the rocks with bright orange and yellow hieroglyphs. Each one is a clever fungus, which, instead of trying to sap its host tree or rock, has captured a speck of algae to cultivate and parasitize. The trees are not victims, but rather disinterested hosts for these enterprising algae farmers.

A cousin of mine once spent two summers in the Cascades climbing trees to collect lichen samples for a government-subsidized research program. That research showed lichens to be the most inexpensive and sensitive pollution monitors known to science. They extract their nutrients from the air and rainwater, and quickly overdose on any impurities. Fifty to a hundred species thrive in the forest canopy of the Cascades. Only ten can live in downtown Eugene; only eight in a city as large as Portland; and only one in a metropolis like Stockholm.

Two shaggy green lichens in particular catch my fancy. The first is *Letharia,* a stunning, fluorescent, Day-Glo–green growth that absolutely electrifies otherwise gloomy snags on dry ridge crests. This lichen's Latin name sounds lethal, because it is. In fact, it is so poisonous, pioneer sheepherders who could not afford to use strychnine against coyotes laced sheep carcasses with *Letharia* instead.

My other favorite lichen of the day is old-man's-beard (*Usnea*), whose drooping, gray-green fibers festoon nearly every limb and trunk on north-facing slopes. I would vote to rechristen it the "toilet paper" lichen, if I were not afraid some huckster would then strip the woods of it and market it under the name Hemorrhoid-Eze. The stuff only grows above the trees' winter snow line, a line that the lichens demarcate as clearly as the high-water line on a flooded riverbank is marked by mud. By this gauge, the winter snowpack at Diamond Lake is five feet deep. However, the depth increases to ten feet near the Cascade crest, putting this lichen out of reach even for my humble purposes.

I think more of winter the higher I go. The trail is blazed with blue diamond-shaped markers a full fifteen feet off the ground; these markers are not there for hikers, but rather for the Nordic skiers who will be here in less than three months. The temperature takes a dive as I reach the meadows along Tipsoo Butte. The cloud I am in begins to move sideways over the ground, takes sudden shape, and bursts into white bloom.

Snow! It is early September. My route ahead lies through mountains I can scarcely cross in snow. Yet the flakes fly and my hands grow numb. The beautiful white meadow raises ugly doubts: Could I even find my way back to Diamond Lake in a whiteout? Should I go on?

Then, as soon as I hike a hundred yards onto the eastern side of the Cascade ridge crest, the temperature jumps ten degrees, and the sun makes the snow seem like a silly dream. To dispel my fears I try thinking about Indian summer, the sunny weather that brightens many autumns. But I know these mountains divide the state's weather like a knife. I can hardly expect Indian summer until I leave the High Cascades and hike east.

A glance at the map shows that if I wish to drink water tonight I must hike into the western clouds to camp at little Maidu Lake, the headwaters of the North Umpqua River. The area is known for its miserable weather. The research notes in the front of my notebook include an excerpt from the journal of David Douglas, the Scottish botanist who camped in almost the identical spot in 1826 while tracking down rumors of an enormous species of pine trees with sixteen-inch cones. Rereading Douglas's adventure gives it a startling immediacy:

> *October 25th, 1826.* Last night was one of the most dreadful I ever witnessed. The rain, driven by the violence of the wind, rendered it impossible for me to keep any fire, and to add misery to my affliction, my tent was blown down at midnight, when I lay among bracken rolled in my wet blanket and tent till morning. Sleep of course was not to be had, every ten or fifteen minutes immense trees falling producing a crash as if the earth was cleaving asunder. . . .
>
> I hope I find my pine.

The following day Douglas not only identified the sugar pine for science, he nearly lost his life in the process. After marveling at a monstrous sugar pine, 215 feet tall and 57 feet in circumference at the base, he concluded the only way he could get sample cones from the lofty branches was by shooting them down with his rifle. Unfortunately, the rifle's booming report also brought him eight unfriendly Indians, painted with red earth and armed with bows, arrows, bone spears, and flint knives. Only by tricking them into searching for pinecones with the promise of some tobacco did Douglas escape, pistols drawn, and live to spend another night shivering in the wilderness.

The headwaters of the Umpqua are tamer now, even though their wilderness has since been sanctioned by Congress. I arrive at Maidu Lake and find a three-sided log shelter facing the lake and the reflected clouds. After cooking my dinner on my butane camp stove, I think about the very long and very dark night approaching. I have avoided campfires on the hike so far, for I dislike leaving blackened fire rings in the wilderness, but now I need one for the same reason Douglas's journal mentions—for light to write by.

There is an art to starting a fire without paper in a very wet forest. A handful of "toilet paper" lichen from the dry side of a large treetrunk is the first step. Next, I gather "squaw wood"—the small, dead branches hanging underneath trees, sheltered from rain by the live branches above. I take only the branches that snap with a *crack!* when bent; more supple ones are surely damp or green. Then I prowl back into the forest for some sturdier fuel. A large fallen log, trussed up off the wet ground, has the answer. Underneath it, the loose rotten chunks are dry. I break off some nice pieces and hear a buzz: Bees have found the log bottom is a dry spot for a home. After a second's indecision, I grab the wood and run.

The campfire is mesmerizing. Flames hang silently above the dry wood. It occurs to me that fire is another of Coyote's gifts, according to Indian legend. And since a campfire demands a tale, I will tell it, as well as I can remember.

In the days when only the animal people lived on earth, no one really believed Coyote could get fire, despite all his trickery and power. The only fire in those early days was at the top of one of these Cascade peaks, jealously guarded day and night by the three Skookum sisters—powerful, tireless demigods. But Coyote thought it was silly that everyone was cold and ate their food raw, so he hit his hip and called out his feces children, and asked their advice. No sooner had they suggested a plan than Coyote slapped them back inside and said, "Oh, I knew that all along."

The next day Coyote positioned some animals on the mountain-side and sneaked up to the Skookums' camp in disguise. When the sisters were changing guard by the fire, he raced out, grabbed a flaming brand, and ran down the mountain.

The Skookum sisters were right behind him, and since they never grew tired, they eventually closed his lead. But Coyote passed the burning brand at the last moment to Cougar, who ran until he, too, was exhausted, and passed it to Fox. Just as the Skookums were about to grab Fox, he passed it to Squirrel, who ran through the treetops. At the end of the forest, the Skookums were about to catch Squirrel, but he passed the burning brand to Antelope. Antelope ran swiftly, but the Skookum sisters were just as fast. At a river Antelope had to stop, and gave the only remaining ember of the fire to Frog, who swallowed it and swam under the river.

The Skookums swam, too, but when Frog came out the other side, he spat out the ember to Wood. Wood absorbed the fire without a trace.

The Skookums sat there a long time, puzzling about this. Wood was not on fire, but it now had the *potential* for fire. Frustrated, the Skookums finally went back to their mountain. Only Coyote knew that rubbing two sticks of Wood together would release the flames.

Tonight, then, I praise Coyote.

SEPTEMBER 8

6:22 P.M. Summit Lake campground. Overcast, 45°F. Mileage today: 27.8. Total: 491.4.

At dawn in the Maidu Lake shelter it is 33°F. My numb fingers go through breakfast preparation in slow motion: carefully grasping the wire clasp on the oatmeal bag. Untwisting it once, twice, three times. Dropping it. Picking it up twice.

The joints in my feet are so sore and stiff I stand up with pain. It is a result of being on my feet every daylight hour. In a damp, cold forest, sitting down means getting chilled and wet.

By noon it is still close to freezing. The Pacific Crest Trail crosses a small road with a single parked car. Two miles up the trail to 7,664-foot Cowhorn Mountain I stop to unpack rain gear. The first flakes of another snowstorm are falling. The three people from the car hike down past me, practically jogging back to the road.

The man in front says, "Getting ready for snow, eh? You'll find it, I bet."

The second man gloats. "You're heading into the land of sunshine, pal."

The third, a girl, puts in, "And if you believe that, I've got a bridge in Brooklyn you'll want to buy."

They tramp toward the road, smirking. Yet, as I hike on, the gentle white snow shower is the most beautiful part of the entire day. And on the far side of Cowhorn Mountain I find an unexpected culinary treasure: King Boletus.

Boletus edulis is the king of edible mushrooms. Chefs from the world's greatest cities wish in vain for a reliable supply. Now I, half starved in the wilderness, can pick armloads. Tender young ones line the trail. I pick one off its pudgy stem and cut open the smooth tan cap, just to check. It is positively in the bolete family, since there are little pore tubes under the cap instead of gills. The pore mouths are a satisfactory white; only the poisonous boletes have red pore mouths. And the white flesh does not stain purple when cut—another trait that sets King Boletus apart from most other boletes.

I pop three of the fist-sized mushrooms in my backpack and hike on, plotting their fate in a dish of Oriental noodles. When I reach the remote Summit Lake Campground, where my trail crosses a little-used dirt road, there is only one other camper. I greedily set to cooking dinner. The mushrooms have very little flavor. Perhaps they are too young. Perhaps I did not cook them enough. I don't care. After the day's twenty-seven-mile hike I am so hungry I eat everything and lick the bowl. Only then do I sigh and look up at the man at the next site.

He has been watching me eating and writing. Now he calls over to me, "Come on and share my fire if you want."

I come and share. My neighbor is Ed Kaiser, a stocky man in his sixties. He's wearing a camouflage baseball cap and a puffy down vest. The vest is open enough to reveal a red T-shirt emblazoned with a black, double-headed eagle over the word "Ruger." His new pickup has a chain saw under the bed, a fiberglass toolbox in the back, and an aluminum powerboat on a trailer behind. There is no tent in his campsite, only a rumpled sleeping bag under a big blue tarp. At the edge of the gray, forest-rimmed lake there's a fishing pole stuck upright among some rocks.

"The High Cascades buck season opened Saturday," he says, "but I been here since Thursday, so I could get the best campsite, cut some firewood, and scout things out. Been out every morning at six; haven't seen a thing. Four, five elk, but that's no good now. Oh, and a mink and a cottontail. Would've shot the mink, too, if I could've got my shotgun. First one I've seen up here."

I find it disconcerting that this deer hunter is so willing to shoot rare nongame wildlife. On the other hand, he has a crackling fire that is gradually warming my fingers. I ask, "Then you come up here often?"

"Hunt here every year. Want some coffee?" When I nod he puts on gloves and fills two mugs from a black pot that's been sitting on the fire for hours, boiling. "Whoa," he says to himself, "might melt the cup." The mugs read: OREGON CITY 7 ELEVEN COFFEE CLUB. I sip from mine cautiously, and my stomach gives a kind of nervous quiver at the tarry liquid.

Ed gulps the scalding brew thoughtfully. "I camped up here once for a month, years ago. I was still married then, and was getting over an accident. My wife was giving me such a rough way to go, I just said, 'To hell with it, you'll see me when I get back.' I just jumped in the pickup and took off, went up to Taylor Burn—you know where that's at? I stayed thirty-two days, fished, watched the deer walking around. Ran low on food, hadn't planned on staying that long. Killed a porcupine, rabbit. Finally ran out of coffee, that's the only reason I came back."

Ed pours himself another mug of the thick coffee and swallows it in two or three drafts. When I ask if he's ever bothered by drinking so much strong coffee, he laughs. "Hah! An old truck driver like me? Hell, the battery acid they give you at some of these truck stops—I can take anything."

Then he catches sight of the fishing pole on the shore and shakes his head. "That poor worm must be 'bout drowned by now. I put him on there yesterday, 'bout one o'clock. Took him out this morning, put some anise on him. It's a fish attractant. Least it's supposed to be. Hasn't attracted nothing here yet."

He muses a moment, then turns to me. "So what's this hike you're on?"

I tell him of my plan to cross the state, and of my hope to find Indian summer when I reach the Blue Mountains in October.

"Is that so?" Ed lifts his eyebrows. "I had a pal in my veterans' organization went elk hunting out in the Blue Mountains last year in October. He thought he'd tough out a freak storm. Got six, eight feet of snow, wind came up, tree fell over, nailed him. They couldn't even get his trailer out of there till the next June. I'm pretty good friends with his widow now."

The story leaves me pretty badly shaken.

Ed slowly walks down to the shore and reels in his exhausted worm. On the way back he takes a bottle-sized brown paper bag out of his pickup. "You take any of this?"

"Uh, yeah, thanks." I find myself hoping it is strong.

He pours whiskey into the coffee in our cups. "Some do and some don't. Makes a good nightcap." He drinks and smacks his lips. "Hoo, that do taste good."

I sample the powerful drink and have to take a deep breath.

"God, I wish they had this hunt in regular summer," he says, putting a pinch of chewing tobacco inside his cheek. I shudder to watch him drink the spiked coffee again with tobacco still in his mouth. "I hate the cold mornings so much I sleep in my full clothes. If it's real bad I go straight from the sleeping bag to the pickup and drive twenty miles to a café for breakfast."

"How much longer does hunting season last up here?"

He leans back in his folding chair. "I got another week unless there's rain and snow so bad I can't stand it. Or unless I get a deer between now and then. I tell you, the hunt boundary's a mile and a half away, but if something walked down that hill"—he points to a dark shape behind the firelit trees—"it'd be dead. Got a big garbage bag. I'd put all the innards in it, dump 'em somewhere, take 'em home. I don't care."

Ed lights a big cigar and puffs thick smoke into the night air. There is a long silence as we watch the fire, thinking. Finally he stubs out the cigar.

"Gotta hit the hay," he says. "Sleep well."

SEPTEMBER 9

9:14 A.M. Same. Snowing, 33°F.

I have been violently ill all night. Now, for the first time on this hike, I am afraid death is watching my every move.

When I left the deer hunter's campfire last night, I blamed my uneasy stomach on his spiked coffee. But after vomiting out the opening of my tent from ten P.M. until four A.M., down to the gruesome, wrenching cramps of dry heaves, I know it is not just the coffee. I have poisoned myself with mushrooms.

For ten years I have gathered and eaten wild mushrooms, checking each specimen against the descriptions in a field guide. Yesterday, hungry and tired, I trusted my memory. Through the night I have been visualizing those mushrooms again with horrifying clarity. How could they possibly have been King Boletus when they lacked flavor? Weren't they really too young to identify well? Weren't they instead an immature form of the enormous ugly, red-capped boletes I've seen along the trail for days? And just what exactly *are* those red-capped boletes?

I have ransacked my memory for all I know about mushroom poisons. But there are so many different toxins. Without knowing which I have eaten, I cannot predict what symptoms might follow nausea. Might I still suffer convulsions? Hallucinations? A sudden, fatal seizure? Or, worst of all, gradual cellular deterioration of my body's organs, leaving me two grim days till death?

After finally collapsing for four hours of sleep, I awaken, weak and trembling, to the sound of a motor in a strangely bright morning. With great effort, I raise myself to my elbow and peer out the tent opening.

The ground and trees are covered with an inch of snow. More snow is falling fast.

Worst of all, the increasingly distant motor is from Ed's pickup. I can just make out the blue tarp and lawn chairs tossed in the boat hitched behind. Ed, the only other person in this remote campground, has pulled out before the snow can strand him in the High Cascades for the winter.

If I'd thought to crawl to him in the night—if I hadn't slept while he packed up—I might be riding with him, toward a hospital.

I am on my own.

I must organize my thoughts. The nearest plowed road is seventeen miles away, across the wilderness. The trail there climbs 1,700 feet over the shoulder of Diamond Peak. There may be so much snow at that elevation that the trail cannot be found. And even if I could find it, how could I hike seventeen miles when I hardly have energy to sit up?

I have been cheating my body of calories for weeks. Now I have lost an entire day's food and can eat nothing to replace it. The thought of my breakfast oatmeal mush makes me shudder.

If I wait here for help, the storm may bring subzero temperatures and feet of snow. And, by my own strict instructions, my wife will send no search party until forty-eight hours after I miss the next checkpoint—which is still four days away.

At the earliest, I would not be found for a week.

Noon. Diamond Peak Wilderness. Snowing, 28°F. Mileage so far today: 5.7. Total: 497.1.

For "breakfast" I make chamomile tea and manage to keep down a few sips. I swallow broken bits of hard candy like pills, knowing I must have sugar. With numb hands I shake the snow from my gear and pack up. Then I try to lift the pack onto my back—and collapse when my knees buckle. Finally, setting the pack on a snowy picnic table, I slip on the straps and stagger toward the trailhead. I puff cold air through gritted teeth, commanding my legs to lift and move each horrible step.

Beautiful flocked trees. Squirrel tracks. The cold snow crunch of boots. Five elk look up, as big as shaggy cows, and thump away. The musty smell of mushrooms, white-capped with snow along the trail, brings my stomach to my throat. My body is nothing but gelatin and will.

I see on my map that I am at Emigrant Pass—where the "Lost Wagon Train" of 1853 attempted to find a shortcut between the Old Oregon Trail and the Willamette Valley. Six hundred and fifty covered wagons foundered here in the timber and the cold at just this time of year. When a rescue party finally led the fifteen hundred settlers to Eugene, they doubled the population of Lane County. But there is no one looking for me.

The trail climbs sharply and the snowflakes fall more thickly until a three-inch layer of smooth white fluff makes every gap between the trees seem as if it might be the true trail. Holding the topographic map in my left hand and the compass in my right, I compare the small area of ground visible through the snowstorm with the lines on the map. Time and time again I realize I have lost the trail and must backtrack to where I last saw one of the trail's infrequent tree blazes.

When I finally climb beyond timberline, every muscle crying mutiny, there are no more blazes. There are only endless white clouds and endless white slopes.

I could be anywhere. Suddenly everything seems pointless. I drop my pack and collapse against it. I have forced myself to a bleak and desolate dead end.

I swallow more pieces of hard candy and write in my journal, holding the pen in my numb fist, as the snow gently covers my legs.

Then a brief, fluffy hole opens in the clouds. There is a brilliant blue, and an enormous, ice-crusted mountain peak appears almost directly above me. When the wind swirls again, the incredible Himalayan dream is gone. But I know it must be Diamond Peak.

I have not lost my way. I have reached the highest point of the trail to the highway.

6:03 P.M. Willamette Pass. Raining, 40°F. Mileage today: 17.8. Total: 509.2.

I swing my slack-kneed legs one after the other down from Diamond Peak. The warmer, lower forests exult, dripping snowmelt along the path of my escape. Friendly plants of the Willamette foothills appear from the slush to cheer me on: rhododendron, bunchberry, and vanilla leaf. Little lakes pop out of the forests along the path, and then disappear back into the rain. I start whistling "I've Got Sixpence," believing that I am really rolling home. From the pass our Eugene apartment, and Janell, and the children, will be just a seventy-mile hitchhike away.

Finally I hear cars. I reach the pavement too weak to celebrate. I just put out my thumb.

For forty minutes I stand in the rain, grinning stupidly at the occasional headlights and frantic windshield wipers, then wait again, watching the empty gray road disappear into clouds. I had simply wanted to show up at home, like a soldier returned from the wars. But the trucks and campers do not know my need, and spray sheets of ice water at me.

I walk the highway shoulder to a ski lodge that should be closed for the summer. Miraculously, it is open. There is a telephone in its cavernous lobby.

Janell must hear the tiredness in my voice, for I have hardly told her where I am when she announces she is dispatching a friend's car to pick me up. "Just stay where you are," she tells me.

Suddenly so sore-footed I cannot stand straight, I limp into a huge, urinal-lined washroom designed for crowds of winter skiers. I stare into the mirror at a red-nosed, wet, stringy-haired wild man with black-lined fingernails and a drooping neck. The strange man's hollow cheeks are gray and skeletal. It is no wonder no one stopped to pick up this hitchhiker.

I wash my face in the hottest water, and tingle, but look no better. I do not have the energy to change into my other smelly shirt—the "clean" one I save for encounters with civilization. I unfold a twenty-dollar bill from my camera-case pocket and go upstairs to order a hamburger at the lodge's white-tableclothed restaurant. Having eaten nothing but hard candy all day, I chew each bite a long, long time, testing. But it goes down. And now I write, waiting for the friends to come.

SEPTEMBER 12

8:05 P.M. Waldo Lake. Overcast, 47°F. Mileage today: 10.6. Total: 519.8.

Three days at home have refilled me with food, strength, and love. It was late at night, and I was half dead, when I lugged my backpack into our Eugene apartment and put my arms around Janell. I was surprised by how tired *she* seemed, too.

Little Ian was asleep, but Karen had overheard my phone call and now sprang out of bed, where she had been feigning sleep, and climbed to my shoulders, giving me desperate hugs. Janell had baked an apple crisp. I ate, soaked in a hot bathtub, and collapsed into bed.

I woke up at daybreak as usual, an hour ahead of my family, and could sleep no more. So I researched boletus mushrooms in a field guide. I had remembered the general rules of the boletes correctly. The variety I had eaten, *Leccinium,* was not listed as poisonous, but then it was not rated as edible either. Seventeen miles deep in the wilderness, in the face of a snowstorm, I was lucky my carelessness had not cost me my life.

I thought: This too is part of what wilderness is. Congress defined wilderness as a place offering "outstanding opportunities for solitude." But to be truly wild, an area must also offer outstanding opportunities for death.

My first day home was Karen's first day of kindergarten. I walked her to the bus stop, limping but otherwise like the other parents who came to see their children off. She clung to me tightly and only climbed the bus stairs when I promised I would not leave home again that day.

Ian treated me differently. He climbed on Janell's lap and eyed me suspiciously. Could he, at age two, have forgotten his father in a single month? Or did he remember, and was jealous? I had to win back his trust slowly, like a dentist cajoling a child with a toothache.

Janell had spent the mornings at her part-time job teaching twelve preschool children, then came home, exhausted, to care for our own two kids. What she had missed most, she said, was the company of adults. Each night while I was gone before putting them to bed, she had shown the children on a map where I was supposed to be camped. Then she had had an hour of complete silence before falling asleep herself.

She confessed that, out of suppressed resentment, she had looked through some mail-order catalogs and had sent for a handful of completely unnecessary items. I raised my eyebrows at the ten-and twenty-dollar gadgets she had bought, but said nothing. It could have been worse.

When I announced I was strong enough to hike again, Janell tried to heft my pack, failed, and asked, "Does your pack feel as heavy to you as it does to me?"

I shrugged. "I guess I've gotten used to carrying fifty or sixty pounds."

"Good, because I won't let you leave without taking more food." She made me add 50 percent to all the meal packages. Then she baked up a three-pound bag of chocolate chip cookies and stuffed them on top of the huge pack.

As we were riding back up to the ski lodge at Willamette Pass, Janell snapped her fingers. "I almost forgot to tell you about the insurance agent."

I sighed. "Do they *still* want to check my height, weight, and blood pressure?"

"Oh, that, sure. I didn't remind you about that stuff because I didn't want to lose any time with you at home. What I meant was about mountain climbing."

"Mountain climbing?"

"As long as the agent kept calling, I decided to pin her down on whether your policy's void if you hike over a mountain. It turns out you're only 'mountain climbing' if you have special mountain-climbing gear and training."

"Which I don't." I thought about the absurdity of this. "In other words, the life insurance policy will cover me for all the rock climbing I want to do, as long as I'm completely unprepared for it."

"Well, yes," Janell said, and gave me a gentle look. "But please don't do any climbing. And try to keep yourself dry."

We both knew the forecast was for rain. "Don't worry," I told her, "I've got it planned so I'll be staying at shelters the next three nights." The Forest Service had built quite a few remote log shelters in the High Cascades before the Wilderness Act discouraged permanent structures. I intended to seek out those that remained.

At Willamette Pass it is still cold, overcast, and hunting season. After I embrace Janell and the children one last time, I hike ten miles very quickly into the Waldo Wilderness to where the map promises my first shelter.

But when I approach the log lean-to, I hear a radio. A man comes out. His eyes cross and uncross at me. He opens his fly and pisses on a huckleberry bush.

"Pardon me," I say. "Hello."

He stares at me blankly, and then weaves his way around the corner. I think: Perhaps he *is* miserably drunk and inhospitable, but should that rule out my sharing a shelter with him in threatening weather?

I follow him around the corner. Inside, the shelter has been outfitted like a vacation cabin, with food and spices on the shelves, lamps hanging on the walls, a gas stove up on logs, and a nearly empty bottle of Jack Daniels on the ground. Pistols lie on a board. Deer-hunting rifles hang from the rafters. Another man, a woman, and a boy come back from tending a half dozen horses tethered in a meadow. The shelter is too full to share.

With a sigh I leave the shelter behind. A mile farther down the trail I build a fire on Waldo Lake's narrow beach and put up my tent.

I have escaped a crowded, unfriendly shelter and discovered a far superior evening: rainless, by a cheerful fire, on the shore of a huge and amazingly clear lake. Waldo Lake is eight miles long—the second largest natural body of water in Oregon—and the purest lake its size in the world.

The clouds drift gray along the lake horizon. The moonless night gradually darkens the water until it joins the starless sky. Firelight turns the trees behind me into a flickering, yellow shelter of my own. I heat a cup of tea and eat a chocolate memory from home.

SEPTEMBER 13

8:19 P.M. Island Lake. Raining, 41°F. Mileage today: 28.3. Total: 548.1.

By dawn, rain has settled in over the High Cascades. I put on my rain gear, thinking brightly that I will be able to dry out tonight at Cliff Lake Shelter. It is twenty-eight miles away, deep enough into the Three Sisters Wilderness that I do not expect to be outflanked by deer hunters.

I am surprised that the tendon in my right shin is so sore from yesterday's short hike. By mile 8 today, the tendon alarms me by sending out shooting pains. I have to limp heavily to my left. Still, I suspect this new pain is another of my body's little hoaxes. I can't recall straining that particular tendon more than any other.

So I limp on, past rain-spattered lakes and rolling forests, waiting for the pedometer hanging from my belt to register "28," which is when I expect to be at my shelter. For two hours I walk through a perfectly even stand of forty-foot-tall lodgepole pines, the "Taylor Burn" area where Ed, the deer hunter, had once camped. The place is named for a shepherd who ranged his flock here in the nineteenth century, and who burned off the virgin forests for pasture. The result, evidently, was not more grass, but only a stand of fireproof trees.

When my pedometer is still reading "27," two backpackers appear out of of the mist, hiking toward me. The man and woman are dressed in rain gear and boots much like my own. He is young. She is pretty. They carry identical long walking sticks.

"Hello," I say.

The woman smiles disarmingly. "Hi. Where are you headed?"

The question is apt, for it is late in the day and we are deep in the wilderness.

"Cliff Lake Shelter," I say. "And you?"

The young man behind the woman frowns. "We're going to Cliff Lake Shelter, too."

"Haven't you passed it?" I ask.

"Are you sure *you* haven't passed it?"

All the maps come out, but Cliff Lake is right on the edge between our two maps, and this rather adds to our mutual consternation. Still, I am positive I could not have missed a large lake and a trailside shelter. And my pedometer shows Cliff Lake is still a mile away. I feel a little sorry for the two backpackers.

I console them. "Maybe it was hidden in the trees."

The young man frowns again and studies me. "Yes, I suppose you could have missed it that way." He is relentless.

I smile. "No, really. The shelter can't be far ahead. Why don't you come on with me and we can all camp together and talk."

The young man looks at the woman, who shakes her head and says, "We really wouldn't want to backtrack. Still, it's a shame we can't talk. We haven't met a backpacker for days."

Gear for the trip

Jim Rogers and Carrie Osborne, Audubon birders, on Coast Guard property atop Cape Blanco

W. L. SULLIVAN

Safely across the Elk River, near Cape Blanco

William O'Sullivan's tombstone at Cape Blanco
Pioneer Cemetery

Bob Keefer, reporter for the Eugene *Register-
Guard*, rests on the Illinois River Trail

Lou Gold, Earth First! watchdog, camped atop
Bald Mountain with his prayer sticks

Len Ramp talks with a gold prospector on the edge of the Kalmiopsis Wilderness.

Emily Cabin, the gold miner's cabin deep in the Kalmiopsis Wilderness

Green Hellebore, the poisonous weed of Indian legend

Sunset into the Pacific Ocean from Biscuit Hill,
in the south Kalmiopsis

Ron, the Kalmiopsis marijuana grower, warily
prepares my cocoa.

W. L. SULLIVAN

W. L. SULLIVAN

A rainbow morning in the Kalmiopsis Wilderness,
the largest and wildest roadless forest in Oregon

I hike the Pacific Crest Trail around Shale
Mountain, in the Sky Lakes Wilderness with
Mount McLoughlin in the background.

The James Creek shelter, Three Sisters Wilderness, before the snow

Camp at Island Lake in the Three Sisters Wilderness,
the night I missed the shelter

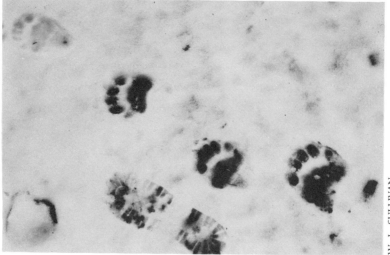

Snow in the Three Sisters Wilderness shows
bear tracks—and my own tracks—on the Pacific
Crest Trail.

Dead Whitebark Pines and lava at McKenzie Pass

Camp at the climber
bivouac area of Smith
Rock State Park, in
central Oregon.

My parents, Wes and
Elsie Sullivan

Conservationist and former log truck driver Tim Lillebo,
in Prairie City, with the Strawberry Mountains behind him

W. L. SULLIVAN

W. L. SULLIVAN

Ranger Tyler Groo splashes off in Rock Creek.

Del Stevens, camouflaged elk hunter, in the Strawberry Mountain Wilderness

"Pinky" gesticulates while building a bridge over the North Fork John Day River

I arrive at Anthony
Lake in 19°F. weather.

The "Bigfoot Hilton" in the North Fork John Day Wilderness

Anthony Lake and
Gunsight Mountain

LOREN HUGHES

Atop Hat Point, I look back at the Snake River
and the end of this 1,360-mile hike.

So we talk, standing there in the rain with our packs on, neither willing to back up an inch.

The gangly young man is Bob Bagley, age twenty-five, until recently employed as an electronics engineer for a company in Hillsboro. Debbie Demming, age thirty-one, was a data processor for ten years at the same Hillsboro company.

Under Debbie's dripping rainhood, her blond hair is neatly brushed and her light makeup is remarkably fresh. "You just can't believe how burned out you can get," she says, "typing numbers into a computer and staring into video display terminals right into your thirties. A month ago we just decided to quit our jobs. We went to the northern Oregon coast and started hiking across America."

Bob nods agreement, yet I suspect the trip is Debbie's idea. She seems pretty enough, and strong-willed enough, to persuade a young electronics engineer to do almost anything.

"After ten years I just *had* to do something different," Debbie says, wiping a raindrop from her delicate nose. "And this is sure different."

Bob explains that their trek could take years; they will find winter work in Nevada, and then face Utah and the Rockies in the spring. After I tell them of my own hike, we briefly discuss backpacking technique. Debbie will not walk more than twelve miles a day, and marvels that I can be on the trail by seven A.M. Bob seems relieved to learn that my boots, like his own, are damp inside despite the manufacturer's watertight guarantees.

Finally we say good-bye and go off our separate ways, each sorry the other doesn't have the sense to go back to the shelter they must have just passed, each pitying the other for a night out in the rain.

But to my tremendous surprise, I am the one who must have overlooked the shelter, for half a mile later I come to a trail crossing that is unmistakably past Cliff Lake.

At first I am angry. Then I am jealous. Still, I can't bring myself to hike back two miles, especially not if I have to face the sympathy of Bob and Debbie, and admit my grand goof.

Grimly I go on a mile to Island Lake, a green thing with a boggy little island. The rain pelts the surface into choppy rings. I put my pack down glumly at a barren, camped-out spot, and let the rain drip off my hood awhile.

Then I think: Can't I somehow make the best of this?

I scout around and find a dense cluster of big mountain hemlocks. Under their thick boughs, by the trunks, the ground is not wet. That will serve as my dining fly. Previous campers have gleaned this forest for firewood, but they've overlooked the dry bark on the south side of a leaning snag. A little lichen and a few twigs from the dry hemlocks starts flames to work on chunks of bark I've gathered.

Then for the next two hours I am busy with all kinds of warm and cozy chores: I change to dry socks and shoes, and put my damp boots to steam by the fire. I boil a potful of lake water for drinking. Then I sit back, with my journal and tea and two precious chocolate chip cookies. I think: What a pity that in past years I have quit camping trips on account of rain, run out of the woods to a car, and tossed my gear and clothes into a dryer.

Bob and Debbie can have their shelter tonight; I've got the satisfaction of knowing I can stay warm and dry in a world of wet.

SEPTEMBER 14

10:10 A.M. Trail in the Three Sisters Wilderness. Overcast, 46°F. Mileage so far today: 7.3. Total: 555.4.

Intense pain in my right shin tendon has brought me to a halt. The Three Sisters, the three 10,000-foot volcanoes that give this area its name, lie just ahead, lost in masses of clouds.

While I am resting, a striped chipmunk scampers over some jagged boulders, stops at the base of a lodgepole pine, stares at me, and says quite distinctly, "Skwisskwiss."

His statement sets me to thinking. *Skwisskwiss* is in fact the word for chipmunk in Chinook jargon, the long-dead trade language of the old Oregon frontier.

Or is Chinook dead after all?

A glance at my wilderness map shows a landscape teeming with the old jargon. If I chose, I could cross Skookum (big, powerful) Creek, camp in Olallie (berry) Meadows, climb Talapus (Coyote) Butte, and get a good view of Tipsoo (grassy) Butte and Cultus (worthless) Lake.

Not to mention all the *kah-kah* (crows), and *haht-haht* (ducks), and *chee-chee* (little birds) that keep me company out here in the *sticks* (trees, woods).

In the 1870s, the jargon was a vital second language for one hundred thousand people between the Rockies and the Pacific, from California to Alaska. In an area with more than one hundred mutually unintelligible Indian languages—as well as the white man's English, French, Russian, and Spanish—Chinook was the only sure lingua franca.

Since those frontier days, the Oregon Country's wilderness has retreated up to its mountain strongholds. Now, looking at the names on my map, I'd say the old frontier's trade language has retreated up here, too.

No one knows just how old Chinook jargon is. It was well established when Lewis and Clark reached the mouth of the Columbia in 1805 and were greeted by an Indian chief who replied to their questions, "Waket commatux (no understand)," in the language he assumed every foreigner should know.

The coming of white men changed the language rapidly. The *Kingchautschman* ("King George men," or Englishmen) and the *Boston* (Americans) contributed words for things the Indians did not have: *ship, bed, house, lum* (rum), *pusspuss* (cat), *glease* (grease), and even *tatoosh glease* ("breast" grease, or butter).

The French trappers donated the word for "barter," *huyhuy* (from "oui! oui!"), as well as *siwash* (from "sauvage"), *lebiskwee* (biscuit), and *lesak* (sack).

It is not just the Chinook jargon's eclectic charm that makes it easy to learn. Its grammar is so simple, it makes Esperanto look like Sanskrit. There are no verb tenses, no conjugations, no possessives, no plurals, no inflections of any kind. There is only one preposition, *kopa,* which does duty as "with," "for," "to," "from," and all the rest. In fact, there are only five hundred words altogether.

With only five hundred words to express the entire range of human experience, thought, and emotion, Chinook jargon can be challenging in other ways. A truly adept speaker must think like a poet and gesticulate like a thespian.

Consider that *tipsoo* means not only "grass," but also "leaf," "fringe," "fur," "feathers," "hair," or "beard." The precise meaning depends entirely on whatever demonstrative hand motions the speaker can come up with.

Clever compound words help stretch the vocabulary, if the listener is quick enough to decipher them. *Chuck* means "water," so the compound word *salt chuck* means "ocean." *Cole chuck* is "ice." A *skookum chuck* ("powerful" + "water") is a rapids. And *muckamuck chuck* ("food" + "water") means "to drink water."

Flipping through my research notes about Chinook jargon in the front pages of my journal, I feel as if I'm getting the hang of this old language. What else could a *skookum house* be than a jail? A *ship stick* is a mast! And of course a *muckamuck house* must be an inn.

But enough of this *wawa* (talk). I've finished my noontime *muckamuck,* and my *tumtum* (heart, feelings) tells me it is time to go.

Much as I dislike walking sticks, I am going to have to whittle one now to take the weight off my lame leg. But then, as I limp onward into the Three Sisters Wilderness, I'll be listening more carefully than ever to the language even the birds and chipmunks here seem to know.

4:26 P.M. James Creek. Overcast, 40°F. Mileage today: 15.4. Total: 563.5.

This tendon in my shin! I've been limping heavily all day, following the Pacific Crest Trail up and over the shoulder of ten-thousand-foot South Sister. Clouds drag the ground up here, concealing the top of that glacier-clad volcano.

The trail becomes rockier and more barren. I pass a string of gray lakes at timberline, among alpine fields of struggling, autumn-red huckleberry. Finally, just as snow materializes from the low clouds, I walk out onto a moonscape of pumice—a barren plain extending for miles, bounded by the abrupt two-hundred-foot face of the Rock Mesa rhyolite lava flow. This is a land just up from the interior of the planet, and not yet fully acquainted with our gentle ways.

By four P.M. the snow flurry has ceased and I am in need of a second lunch. Humbled by my map-reading failure yesterday, I am fearful I've missed the proper cutoff, and suspect I am up on some high and stormy trail instead of descending toward a promising-looking square symbol shown on the map—perhaps a structure?

Up here the trail has been churned into a bog of mud and manure by the passage of innumerable horses. Finally a cold drizzle sets in, and I sit beneath a hemlock, shivering and eating. After a half hour I raise myself painfully onto my sore leg, walk fifteen feet farther down the trail, and come face to face with a large, soundly built, and wholly unoccupied shelter.

Incredibly, I can search for this kind of thing all day and get nothing; but when I've given up hope, *then* one turns up. It's a clear sign to stop limping and set up camp.

The previous tenants were apparently the horsemen whose stock so damaged the trail. Every tree near the shelter is girdled by chafe marks from tether ropes, and each tree has a circular mud pit around it from the hooves. The horsemen's diet is obvious enough from the potato peelings, corn shucks, and candy wrappers on the ground. A burlap bag hung on a nail contains food they didn't want to pack out: a can of tomato paste, an onion, two potatoes, a plastic container of pancake flour, some bread, a bottle of syrup, and two sticks of margarine. The horsemen have also left a fresh deer hide, a set of hooves, and a pile of ghastly viscera beside the trail at the meadow's edge.

After I have finished my own dinner of instant rice and soy bacon bits, I begin to think about this burlap bag hanging over my head. It seems a shame, really, to leave the food out where it will only attract bears. What's more, if bears did come and eat if, then it wouldn't be here when some underweight backpacker shows up on a cold and stormy night.

As I'm thinking this, the rain turns into a thick, beautiful snow, silently covering the meadow. For some reason, the snow makes it seem all the more imperative not to let the unexpected food bag go to waste.

Surely, I think, as I take down the bag and peer into it, this is not my intellect searching for the syrup, but rather some primitive Winnie-the-Pooh stomach. In fact, I am aghast at what my stomach, in its search for cold-weather calories, is making me create. The recipe, for those who find themselves under similar pressures someday, follows:

CARDIAC ARREST FRENCH TOAST

(à la James Creek Shelter)

4   slices whole wheat bread (week old)
½   stick margarine
6 oz.   orange juice bottles filled with imitation maple syrup

Slice the margarine into patties and arrange these so as to completely
cover all 4 untoasted slices of bread. Place the bread, one piece at a
time, into a flat-bottomed, orange plastic bowl and submerge under 1
oz. (⅛ C.) syrup. Allow to stand 10 seconds at 40°F, or until the syrup
congeals into the bread and the margarine gets quite stiff. Eat with a
tablespoon. Serves 1. Provides a heart-quickening buzz, followed by
general stupor.

SEPTEMBER 15

8:20 P.M. Toe of lava flow in Mt. Washington Wilderness. Starry,
48°F. Mileage today: 25.9. Total: 589.4.

Hiking this morning, I am bombarded with all four seasons in
rapid succession. First the long tunnel of autumn storm clouds begins
to break up, opening views of the Three Sisters so astonishing I drop
my pack and run back and forth madly photographing the three volcanoes' glaciers and icy crags. Then winter suddenly rolls in, with silent
snow falling everywhere in a world of white grass, rocks, and trees.
Then, over a ridge, I hike into the spring thaw, with the snow everywhere pitted by drips from slush on the branches of the big hemlocks.
Hiking farther, I pass spring meadows still wet and matted from recently melted drifts. Around another bend the world freshens into
summer, with Indian paintbrush, asters, and pearly everlasting bloom-
ing beside a sun-sparkled, meandering brook. Up another hill and it's
fall again, where I began, in musty-smelling woods full of big round
mushrooms and bright red huckleberry leaves. On this day, when a too
early fall storm is backing out of the mountains, mumbling apologies, I
am treated to all the Cascade Mountains' moods at once.

The most remarkable thing about these three big volcanoes is that they stand in a row less than ten miles long. They're lined up like scoops in the world's biggest sundae.

The South Sister, the tallest by a few hundred feet, is also the youngest. Since the Ice Age it has added a very fresh-looking crater to its summit, which fills each summer, becoming Oregon's highest lake. The Middle Sister is the shy one of the trio, frequently hiding behind its siblings, perhaps because it is so plain—just a big half-dome of cinders. North Sister, the oldest and once the tallest, has lost one thousand feet of its height and one third of its bulk to the grinding of glaciers. Still, it wears on its summit a proud crown of crags.

These volcano triplets are also closely surrounded by a family of lesser snow-capped peaks: the Brother, the Husband, the Wife, and Broken Top (I wonder which relative that might be). In the 1920s an Oregon geologist declared that all these mountains were just remnants of an exploded supervolcano, Mount Multnomah, which had been so huge it made Crater Lake's ancestral Mount Mazama look puny. It was an attractive theory for Oregon geologists, since it gave the state one of those monstrous, world-class mountains like Denali or Kilimanjaro—if only in retrospect. But, alas, recent work shows that the Three Sisters are really just three separate volcanoes that sprouted up along the same fault line, and that most of the nearby "family" are parasitic side vents.

I despise finding litter in the woods, so I shake my head when I find shattered black glass along the trail. Then I notice there is black glass everywhere *off* the trail, too. I pick up a piece. It is fractured into a smooth, shiny curve of black. Then I realize it is obsidian, the silica-rich, gasless kind of lava that attracted Indians to this area in years past. By lunchtime I come to an entire cliff of the stuff—a mountain of shining black glass!

The Indians of the Oregon Country had no flint for making arrowheads, so they became adept at using antler points to chip away flakes of obsidian, shaping the black glass into fragile arrowheads, knives, and scrapers. In this season of the year, tribes would camp around the Three Sisters, and while the women picked huckleberries the men would gather obsidian to trade with faraway tribes.

Beyond the obsidian cliff I hike into a huge region at the foot of North Sister where the work of the volcanoes is still in progress. It could not be more clear if I had come across a sign, PARDON OUR MESS WHILE WE BUILD A NEW MOUNTAIN HERE FOR YOUR ENJOYMENT.

Red cinder cones dot the horizon. Lava flows snake between them like streams of molasses poured on a sandpile. The lava's surface is jumbled into a chaos of grotesque, chunky shapes. Forests end abruptly in the rubble of fresh black walls. Creeks detour or disappear.

In the thick of this no-man's-land is the Sergeant York of cinder cones: Collier Cone, the little volcano that dared erupt in the path of the biggest glacier in the state.

The battle began fifteen thousand years ago when the cinder cone blasted a one-mile-square plain of desolation right in the path of massive Collier Glacier. The glacier charged back during the Ice Age, tearing away a good-sized chunk of the cinder cone. The little cone retaliated by melting back the glacier with eight and a half miles of lava flows. As soon as the lava cooled, however, the glacier rode up the cone's side and filled its crater with outwash. Now the glacier has retreated and the cone lies dormant. But the war of fire and ice is not over. The near geologic future promises both another eruption and another Ice Age.

In Oregon almost every city tries to lay claim to some mountain or another as its own private symbol. Portland, being the largest city, grabbed Mount Hood first. Salem, the capital, seems to think it owns the next tallest peak, Mount Jefferson. The Three Sisters, however, are a triple prize so enticing they are still being fought over. The city of Bend, to the east, has by far the best view of them. But Eugene, nearly out of sight to the west, has staked an insidious claim up here in the form of geographic names. Collier, Renfrew, Diller, and Chambers glaciers were all named after nineteenth-century Eugene merchants and professors.

And then there's Yapoah Butte, the little red pile of cinders crowded among the other cones at the foot of North Sister. In the language of a defunct Eugene-area Indian tribe, its name means "isolated hill." Since Yapoah Butte is not at all isolated, this name seems odd.

In fact, Yapoah originally was the name applied to a little hill in the Willamette Valley. But when settler Eugene Skinner founded Eugene City beside the hill in 1850, he renamed Yapoah "Skinner's

Butte." Three quarters of a century later, a Eugene professor proposed that the old Indian name, Yapoah, be preserved up in the wilderness, where many Chinook jargon appellations had already collected.

No wonder the Indians call the white men relentless; even the Indian place names seem to have been sent to uninhabitable reservations.

From Yapoah Butte I limp along with my stick toward a scenic, winding state highway at McKenzie Pass, passing more and more day hikers who are here to catch glimpses of the icy mountain trio. First I meet two pleasant Portland CPAs in red-checked shirts. Then I spot an army-green pup tent beside a small lake. Finally a family of bespectacled Eugene teachers stops me in a sudden 40-degree hailstorm to discuss whether my weatherproof rain gear, despite its alleged breathability, doesn't make me overheated.

McKenzie Pass itself is a sea of lava. I cross the narrow highway and follow the Pacific Crest Trail up toward Belknap Crater, the source of most of this rock. For four miles I pass no plants except a few dozen scattered whitebark pines. None are are taller than fifteen feet. All but two or three are dead.

I am climbing a river of rock. Yet the surface is so rough and jumbled it's hard to imagine it was liquid just 1,500 years ago. The only sure sign of its ancient liquidity is the elongated air bubbles frozen everywhere into the rock. The lava looks so rugged because the surface of the flowing rock cooled first, and as the molten lava below kept moving, the crust jumbled and ripped apart or was left behind as hollow tubes. I am hiking on the mess of the lava's old crust.

The cinders crunch and clatter underfoot, as though I were climbing this four-mile hill on broken bottles. When I stop to rest, I see my boot treads—already worn thin from nearly six hundred miles of hiking—have been badly hacked by the lava. It is good that I have arranged to trade boots at my food pickup point tomorrow. The boots are scheduled to be resoled and traded back at the following food drop.

Over Belknap Crater the trail descends to the base of the frosty spire of Mount Washington, the ancient plug of the next Cascade volcano to the north. Pioneers originally gave this little crag the descriptive handle "Squawtit Butte." It was rechristened in 1839 as part of an attempt to bill the Cascades as a Presidential Range, like the one in New Hampshire. After all, the Cascades already had a Mount Jefferson, named in 1806 by Lewis and Clark.

I'll bet the promoters of the Presidential Range would have liked to honor the Father of Our Country with something nobler than Squawtit Butte, but the names for the loftier peaks—Shasta, Rainier, and Hood—were already too well established to change. Perhaps that's why, after Mount Washington was announced, the Presidential Range idea fizzled out.

SEPTEMBER 16

8:50 P.M. Wasco Lake. Drizzling, 40°F. Today's mileage: 25.7. Total: 615.1.

This morning, Mount Washington and North Sister gleam brilliantly white against a blue sky. The past weeks' storms have turned the mountains into ice sculptures, glistening from peak to base. But as I hike down to 4,500-foot Santiam Pass, where my checkpoint is, the wind picks up and a fresh batch of high clouds slips in, promising more treacherous weather. If I can hold out just one more day in the High Cascades, my route will take me into the dry, hot lands east of the mountains.

Ahead at the pass I can see the Santiam Highway climbing around the base of Hogg Rock, an enormous basalt mesa guarding the pass. Partway up the mesa's sheer cliffs, chiseled into them, is a narrow ledge—certainly an unlikely-looking place for a trail. But that narrow upper path nearly brought a transcontinental railroad across the wilderness mountains.

The railroad scheme was the brainchild of Colonel T. Egenton Hogg, a former Confederate officer and released political prisoner from Alcatraz. In 1872 Colonel Hogg announced that Newport, a tiny town on the Oregon coast, was destined to be the Pacific's new San Francisco. He plotted a grand railway over the Cascades and across the continent. However, the London investors he approached to finance the project were skeptical that a Cascade crossing was feasible.

Undaunted, Colonel Hogg hired an army of Chinese coolies, packed a disassembled boxcar through the wilderness to Santiam

Pass, built eleven miles of track there, and pulled his one-car train back and forth with mules. Then, with a straight face, he told the doubters in London that the line was complete across the summit of the Cascades—two scheduled crossings a week.

He got the investors' money, but the track from Newport never did reach the pass. Now the abandoned eleven-mile grade forms part of the southern boundary of the Mount Jefferson Wilderness.

I am still limping, and my leg has begun to swell alarmingly, but I am an hour early to my checkpoint at the pass. My mother arrives, bringing much appreciated conversation, concern, and family news. She also brings a very heavy load of food. It seems everyone sends their love in the form of food. My sister wants me to have cashews. My wife sends two heavy bags of chocolate chip cookies, although the next food drop is just four days away. My mother has brought unrequested bananas, peaches, cherry tomatoes, and apples. Did she really imagine I could carry a fifteen-pound produce display? I eat what I can on the spot, toss the rest in the pack, and stagger to my feet under a sixty-pound load.

"Do you have to leave already?" my mother asks.

I look up at the approaching dark clouds. My escape route out of the High Cascades is twenty miles away, and it's getting dangerously late in the day. "I'm afraid I've got to beat a storm."

She hugs me, pack and all. "Take care."

The Pacific Crest Trail climbs relentlessly toward Three Fingered Jack—another craggy volcanic plug of the High Cascades. This peak resisted being named for one of the presidents because its three-pronged summit reminded people not of Polk or Monroe, but rather of a well-known, mutilated Mexican bandit who terrorized central California during the gold rush.

The trail does all but climb the rocky peak, skirting steep scree slopes, while the summit's red-black–banded lava spires tower right overhead, frosted with ice. The clouds lower as I near the 6,500-foot shoulder of the mountain, and hit just as I arrive. I slip around the leeside just as thirty-mile-per-hour winds hurl clouds of cold, wet air behind me, whistling and whipping the stunted mountain hemlocks until I am afraid they will be torn to shreds.

The mountain itself is taking a terrific beating. The winds blast every cornice and ridge, sucking insane-looking clouds over the top in writhing, fingered nebulae. Once past the peak the clouds slowly become calm and sail on at the higher elevation into a more peaceful sky, allowing patches of sunlight and rainbows to dapple the dry pine forests stretching off into central Oregon. The clouds resemble the frothing waters in the wake of a powerboat, boiling at the mountain propeller, then calming again. The wonder is that the mountain has survived it as long as it has.

I, however, do not want to try to survive the gale at that elevation. And here I differ from John Muir, who might well have climbed up in one of the whistling hemlocks at the crest just to feel the storm. Once he became so engrossed watching an approaching storm from the summit of Mount Shasta that he was obliged to spend the night up there at fourteen thousand feet, without tent or sleeping bag, rolling in the shallow, sulfurous hot springs of the crater while a howling blizzard covered him with three feet of snow.

So I hoof it down a cold trail three miles to drizzly Wasco Lake, set up camp under a fairly dry hemlock, and gather firewood. Surprisingly, every scrap of wood here is so wet that I fail in three tries to light my evening fire. The rain grows colder and harder. It is 8:20 P.M., and so dark I can hardly see my way across camp, but I do not intend to be driven to bed this early. I turn to my last resort—something recommended in no Boy Scout manual—and light the butane stove. Holding the stove sideways toward the smoldering, charred twigs for sixty seconds finally starts a weak, smoky fire.

There is light enough to write, but to keep my journal dry I am forced to pen these lines while kneeling under my raincoat before the little flames, like a penitent before an altar to Warmth.

I think now of the several hikers I met today near Three Fingered Jack, six miles into the wilderness, wearing day packs and tennis shoes. They all greeted me so merrily. The storm had not yet closed in.

Wilderness is marvelous that way. It is possible for people who lead city lives to walk for two hours and put themselves on the side of a snow-frosted mountain, exposed to the genuine danger of being surprised by rain or snow or mud or rocks or animals—or themselves.

I recall environmentalist Edward Abbey writing that every Boy Scout troop deserves a forest to get lost, miserable, and starving in.

Without risk, adventure is an empty word.

III.

THE OCHOCOS

It must be a poor life that achieves freedom from fear.

—ALDO LEOPOLD

SEPTEMBER 17

9:01 P.M. Metolius River. Starry, 43°F. Today's mileage: 32.6. Total: 647.7.

After a night of torrential downpours and thirty-mile-per-hour winds at my camp beside Wasco Lake, the cold daylight reveals an inch of snow decorating all the trees. It is as though the High Cascades know I am leaving them today and ordered the trees to put on their fanciest dress whites to see me off.

I worried during the night that my sleeping bag might get wet for the first time of the trip. But it didn't. To camp dry, one must go against a simple instinct: Do not pitch the tent in a hollow. When a person thinks of bed, it is true, he thinks first of a snug, cradlelike, hammock-shaped hollow between the trees. It's likely to be the flattest spot, too. But think of that hollow as the bottom of a rowboat in a rainstorm. No matter how good a tent floor is, it will leak if it's in a lake.

From my Boy Scout years I remember getting out of my tent at two A.M. in my underwear, wet and numb in the rain, fumbling with an army folding trench shovel, and making a godawful mess as I dug mud ditches desperately trying to divert a dozen creeklets from the lakelet under my sleeping bag. Since then, I've concluded this kind of late-night engineering lacks foresight. So now I go against instinct and pitch my tent on a hummock.

The only positively joyless routine I've found on this hike has been packing up my tent when it is wet and cold. The tent instructions say this is a forty-five-second job. Yet today I spend ten minutes attempting to poke the icy, slush-covered fabric into its stuff sack. My numb fingers are as unresponsive as so many half-frozen Vienna sausages.

With the tent stowed away—a full pound heavier than it would be dry—I use my fingers as a windscreen for the camp stove, hoping to thaw them. As the snowy gusts blow the little blue flame back and forth, I observe that the blond hairs on my knuckles are shriveling up with an unpleasant smell. I pull them back reluctantly, make oatmeal, and am tempted to plunge my hands straight into the steaming mush.

However, I know that heating my fingers too rapidly would only make them hurt more. The fingers do not fully come to life again until they swing along as I hike the Pacific Crest Trail above Wasco Lake.

I inspect the ranks of white trees at attention along the trail for my farewell salute to the High Cascades. Where the snow has been very dry the mountain hemlock needles are little clusters of perfect white stars. The dry snow has drifted across the trail rut, leveling it as neatly as a knife levels a cup of powdered sugar. Where the snow is wetter the pine-needle clusters hang like Christmas tree ornaments— white balls rayed with green spikes.

My boots crunch softly. All else is silent—until an outraged Douglas squirrel claws about on a tree, scolding and inspecting me upside down.

In the valleys of western Oregon, where I grew up, many winters pass with no snow at all. For six months of cold rain, the children wish for white. And at the first sign of snow, school closes and couples go for romantic walks to watch it drift down. Today I have the wonder all to myself, in mid-September.

Junction Lake, where I turn east from the Pacific Crest Trail, is a forlorn slush puddle in a timberline lava barren. It makes parting with the Cascades easier to bear. So I head down Sugarpine Ridge—a spur running east from unseen Mount Jefferson—and hike into a whole new world.

The trail dives four thousand feet into central Oregon, a dizzying descent through a biological time tunnel. It is as startling as falling for two hours down a rabbit hole.

I had not realized how similar the last two hundred miles along the Cascade crest had been, how much I'd gotten used to mountain hemlock and huckleberries in the snow. Here, within eight miles, the flora reels from alpine to lowland forest to semiarid steppe.

The pains in my swollen shin are temporarily forgotten as I romp downward, exclaiming every minute over new plants: "Alder! Sword fern! Chinkapin—haven't seen you since the Siskiyous. Thimbleberry! Yew again?" Then I walk into an entire old-growth Douglas fir forest, complete with palm moss, wild ginger, and faded bleeding heart. And, just as suddenly, it's gone.

"Ponderosa pine! Wild rose hips!" Nothing lasts for more than a moment. Every Oregon species seems jumbled together somewhere on Sugarpine Ridge—except, strangely enough, for sugar pine. Then, just as I arrive at a lush understory of Oregon grape and snowberry, I walk out from under the clouds of the High Cascades into warm sunshine.

Behind me, the gray clouds form a line along the summit of the Cascades. Before me, the blue sky has only a few fluffy white clouds. It's as though this tall mountain range were being paid to keep central Oregon dry. The annual precipitation on this side of the Cascades is five times less than at the summit. And though I roll up my rain gear and strip to a T-shirt, it might well be snowing up there right now.

Finally the trail bottoms out in a dry, sparse forest of big, orange-trunked ponderosa pine and larch, with only a sporadic ground cover of bunchgrasses and desert bitterbrush. Four miles across this arid plain, however, I suddenly come to a clear, swift river—a summery oasis at the edge of the desert.

The Metolius is the most magical of all Oregon rivers. Without warning, it emerges fully grown from a single enormous spring at the dry base of a black cinder cone. From the bank where I am resting, eating both second and third lunches at once, I can see the snowless butte ten miles to the south where the Metolius begins.

How on earth could such a pile of cinders really be producing fifty thousand gallons of water a minute, winter and summer without variation, at a constant temperature of precisely 46°F? And yet here is the river, sixty feet wide, deep right to the edge, racing along at a white-capped ten miles per hour even at the bank, where it nearly sweeps a water bottle out of my hand.

After much puzzling, geologists decided the cinder cone was not creating the river, not even by magic. Instead, they said, the cinder cone has been trying to destroy the river for several thousand years, by erupting right on top of its traditional channel. What's more, the geologists pointed out, the vast lava flows around Mount Washington covered up all trace of the poor river's ancient headwaters.

The Metolius River was decapitated, and then buried. But the river refused to die. The melting snows of the eastern slope of the Cascades went underground instead, slowly percolating through the lava until the water found its old riverbed at Metolius Springs. There the river emerges victoriously and splashes on as ever.

I hike along the river until dusk, following it into a deeper and deeper canyon. The banks are aflame with autumn-colored vine maple, like scarlet bunting hung out for white-water parade.

SEPTEMBER 18

7:15 A.M. Same. 35°F.

Before sunrise the air is as cold as it was yesterday morning at Wasco Lake. But this is not the wet, wintry cold of a mountain blizzard. It is the pleasant autumn chill of the desert on a clear blue morning. The air is so dry that my wet tent dried during the night. It seems anything could burn here. Last night I gathered a handful of twigs off the ground, put one match to them, and the evening fire leaped into life.

In the night, with the river by my bed, I dreamed of roaring gutters, canals, and waterfalls. But this river does not merely make the usual "white" river sound—the usual rushing *shh*—it also has unexpected bass notes as boulders rumble forward underwater, dislodged by the tremendous push.

Fish must grow strong in such a current. Through the glassy water I can see them, dark, and then silver. They are so close and so beautiful. The urge to catch them is powerful, like the urge to possess a briefly glimpsed beautiful woman. But it is the agony of longing that is the true joy. And I will not play the only angling game allowed on this fragile, wild river: catch-and-release.

9:33 P.M. Deschutes River Arm, Chinook Reservoir. 51°F. Mileage today: 33.7. Total: 681.4.

Before setting out this morning I wrap my stubbornly lame shin in a tight elastic bandage. With some alarm, I have calculated that I have to hike sixty miles in just two days to reach my next checkpoint, where I'm scheduled to spend a rest day with Janell and the children. I have yet to cross the Lower Desert and the Deschutes River.

As I start out along the rushing Metolius, its dry, V-shaped canyon grows still deeper, and finally becomes topped with cliffs of black basalt rimrock. I often peer across the river. Here the Metolius is the boundary of the vast Warm Springs Indian Reservation—one thousand square miles inhabited by fewer than one thousand people, the descendants of eight different central Oregon tribes. In fifteen miles of walking along the reservation border, I have seen no road, camp, or structure of any kind over there. White men are only permitted to cross the reservation on a few major highways. I wonder what is there.

Then, as suddenly as the Metolius began, it stops. At one bend the river is still splashing, as clear and swift as ever, but at the next bend the river is dead. The red rock slopes and basalt cliffs plunge straight into the silent surface of the Billy Chinook Reservoir. The vine maples and ponderosa pines that made the river a linear oasis are gone, submerged by a 440-foot-high dam fourteen miles away.

After bushwacking awhile around the steep-sided reservoir, I decide to short-cut a bend by scrambling up to the plateau bordering the canyon.

So I climb, into a still drier region—the high desert steppe.

The only trees are some occasional gnarled junipers, seldom even twenty feet tall. Their sun-bleached limbs are twisted like wrung-out dishrags and speckled with growths of fluorescent green *Letharia* lichen. Some of the junipers in central Oregon have ring counts proving they are over one thousand years old. Even the oldest are too small to use for lumber, but ranchers sometimes cut them, making each tree into just one fence post. They say the wood is so tough the posts "outlast two fence post holes."

The desert exudes a pungent, intoxicating smell. Partly it is the juniper, whose berries are in fact the flavoring in gin. But mostly it is the sage: *Artemisia tridentata,* the queen of the American West. I pick a clump of the slender gray leaves and crush them in my fingers, releasing a heady dose of spice. Distilled to an oil, the leaves of one species of *Artemisia* flavor the knockout liquor absinthe; boiled, sagebrush leaves provide a potent liquid that is variously recommended as a prompt head cold remedy or as a hair tonic.

I cross a flat of hot, bare rock, turn, and am surprised by a huge pyramid of snow: Mount Jefferson, the 10,497-foot Cascade peak that hid itself in clouds when I was much closer to it. Now, rising above the sagebrush, its frozen splendor seems as unlikely as a cold beer, or a hot shower, or all the other things this desert makes me miss.

Cross-countrying is delightfully easy up on this tableland—until I come to the edge of the table. Ahead is the reservoir again, caroming between canyon walls toward the still invisible dam. But at my feet is a sheer fifty-foot basalt cliff. There is no cliff shown on my topographic map. The map's contour lines are at eighty-foot intervals. I will simply have to backtrack . . . unless . . .

Prowling along the lip of the cliff, I find a broken spot where the talus slope below is only thirty feet down. Even at this cove in the cliff, part of the rock face is overhanging.

For a moment I think of Janell's request that I take no chances. For safety's sake, I decide to lower my backpack down the thirty feet on a nylon cord, leaving the upper end of the cord tied to a small, loose lava rock. That way I can pull the pack back up if I can't climb down after all. Then I toss my walking stick over the edge.

As soon as I've dropped the stick, I regret it. Of course, I dislike lugging around walking sticks. But now I realize that after having to carry this particular one 135 miles because of my tendonitis, I've grown attached to the darn thing. It is incredible how people can get fond of anything familiar. I'd always wondered about the garish mementoes that some people treasure on living room shelves, or the ratty little lapdogs they claim to cherish, yet I now find myself worried about a stupid stick lying at the bottom of a cliff.

I start out by chimneying down a crack. There are no footholds or handholds in the basalt. Only the pressure of my feet and hands on the rock on either side of the crack keeps me from falling. After ten feet the crack ends, and I am clinging to a ledge on the cliff's face. I think suddenly of broken legs, and then of the $100,000 life insurance policy my father took out on me, which is redeemable only after accidental death.

At this point I turn my head and see a tiny cluster of beautiful pink flowers growing out of a small chink—a handhold at my side. It is rock penstemon, a rare wildflower that often hides in such frightening places, as if to cheer on the faint of heart. I share its handhold in the rock. Then I discover a lower ledge, and am soon at the bottom of the cliff, reunited with my silly walking stick. I pull merrily on the cord attached to my pack, but by then I have naturally forgotten about the lava rock tied on the upper end, and it nearly brains me for good.

Stick in hand, I pick my way down the talus slope and skirt a bend in the lakeshore, hoping for no more surprise obstacles this day. The map promises only more uninhabited desert range, with only a few bleak-looking gray squares of private land.

So my jaw drops open when I round the bend and find an enormous marina. Yachts and powerboats fill the slips in front of a floating gas station and snack bar. A row of shiny aluminum, mobile-home–style houseboats hugs an Astroturf-covered dock where people in sunglasses and loud-patterned shirts sit at redwood picnic tables.

I hesitate, then walk self-consciously to the road, past a flock of gleaming conversion vans. But the people on the dock do not hail me. Walking out of the wilderness seems to make me invisible to them.

I follow the broad gravel road up the canyon's slope, hoping it leads toward the Lower Desert and my night's camp on the Deschutes River. The arid hillside is now dotted with cedar-and-glass A-frames, like the rubble of some urban eruption. Cars drive past me, and I give each an embarrassed half-salute, the standard acknowledgment of a nonhitchhiking neighbor on a country road. I feel dirty and disheveled, as incongruous here as Sasquatch. I'm painfully aware of my suspicious limp, and I see I have a bloody scratch on my arm from the climb.

The drivers stare, but as long as I give the half-salute they do not slow, presumably thinking, "God knows why he's out there, but if he waved, it must be OK."

Then a cherry-red Corvette convertible swerves over. A stunning redhead, with bright red lipstick and an iced drink in one hand, leans toward me, smiles, and asks, "Did a blue van pass you in the last few minutes?"

She is beautiful and cool and casual. She seems to embody every attractive quality of civilization. When her question finally registers, I rack my memory for blue vans. I'd do anything to please this miraculous woman, but I've been paying attention to everything *except* vehicles.

Finally I mumble like an idiot, "I guess there were some vans, but I'm not sure they were blue."

She smiles again, and I think: Now she will say, "Oh, come on, you smelly old dear, hop in—you look like you need a Jacuzzi and a cold beer."

But no.

I have hours to think about the girl in the red Corvette, for this road has me wandering off through a tract of private developments where I have no choice but to walk the hastily bulldozed roads. And for a time the girl's memory imbues the endless procession of "5-Acre View Lots" with more glamour than they deserve. After all, every lot in central Oregon's vast tableland has a view of the snowy Cascade volcanoes.

I come to my senses when I pass a real estate sign asking four thousand dollars an acre for a hillside that has been overswept by a range fire. The sagebrush is in ashes. The few junipers are black snags. The agent listed on the sign is Joan Frisbee. Instead of her phone number, the sign notes: CB CHANNEL 3—HANDLE: "SWINGER."

Of course there is no water at this site or any other. The fire hydrants planted so prominently at a few road intersections are miles apart, and not near any buildings. I'll wager if I kicked one of those hydrants it would fall over.

Away from the few reservoir-front lots the vacation homes are shabbier, too. There are mobile homes like big aluminum breadboxes. There are campers on jacks, Sears metal outbuildings, and TV satellite dishes. A big, yellow diamond-shaped highway sign by the driveway of a rundown trailer reads: WARNING: RUBBER TIRE BUMS BOB + EV. A silhouette on the sign depicts a car with a domineering woman gesticulating at a man cringing in the driver's seat.

The roads peter out at the edge of the Lower Desert. Before setting off cross-country for the Deschutes River Canyon, I decide to ask directions from two men working in the yard of what appears to be the last house.

The two men grab my maps and turn them all different ways. They point to the horizon and argue about the highway intersections and roadside taverns for twenty, thirty miles around. It seems they are only able to give me car directions.

Finally the older man has an idea. "Get in, I'll drive you there, show you."

I shake my head. "I want to *walk* the ten miles to the Deschutes." As I look ahead at the hot, black-rock-and-sagebrush desert, I have to stand crooked under my heavy backpack in order to shift weight off my painful shin. My words don't seem to be impressing him as sincere, so I add, "I'm trying to make it from the Cascades to the Ochocos on foot, you see."

"Oh? How far you come today?"

I am too tired to do anything more than pull out my pedometer and tell the truth. "Twenty-four miles."

The old man studies me guardedly. The younger man, too, is strangely silent.

I thank the two men anyway, walk down the remnant of a dirt road, and get out my compass for the trek ahead. I've only gone a quarter mile into the desert, however, when I hear a motorcycle behind me. The younger of the two directionless men is roaring up on a big yellow bike.

"Hey, mind if I walk with you to the Deschutes bridge road?" he asks. He can't describe the route, but he can show me the way with his own two feet.

I grin. "Sure, come on. My name's Bill."

He leaves the bike where it stands and pulls two cans out of his hip pockets. "I'm Mark. Have a cold beer."

It's almost as though my daydream were coming true. Except, of course, that Mark is hardly the girl in the red Corvette. He's stocky, with an eager, round face and a crewcut. His red T-shirt is emblazoned at navel height with a realistic picture of a .45 revolver, as though the handgun were casually stuck in his belt.

He directs a businesslike frown across the sagebrush to the horizon. "Hell, I bet it's only half, maybe three-quarters mile to the paved road. I'll get you there." He strides off purposefully, beer in hand.

"This is sure good of you—" I begin, but he breaks in.

"Aw, hell. You know, I've been up in Alaska, took my journeyman cruise on a research vessel, they were studying the oceans up there. I tell you, that's the life. Started out in the engine room as a wiper, worked my way up to junior engineer."

The connection between Alaska and the Lower Desert leaves me puzzled, but I'm drinking Mark's beer and it tastes good, so I'm not critical. "It's really something that you're willing to just hike off across the desert like this."

"Aw, it's *nothing*. I was out waterskiing all morning, then put in some new solar panels with my father-in-law all afternoon, till I saw you. I used to take my cycle all over the back roads, finding old rundown homesteads, as many as sixty head of deer a day, never a buck in season, though. You know, one guy's got three buffalo on the range out here. And last night a coyote came right in the yard, teasing my bulldogs. Saw a porcupine in the gulch last weekend."

We've already hiked a mile with no sign of a road across the dried mud flats and black rock, yet his enthusiasm continues. I try to focus his obvious need to talk. "So you've been putting in solar panels? I bet you can heat water fast in this sun."

"Oh, hey. We've had solar hot water for years. I just put two hundred-and-fifty-dollar twelve-volt panels on the roof, with a big truck battery for storage. We were running the lights, the TV, the stereo, and still had the battery acid boiling from the charge. The stove and fridge run on gas, so we've pulled the plug on the power company, told them to shove it."

There is a pause. We are still hiking, dodging sagebrush. I glance at my pedometer: two miles.

Trying to keep spirits up, I say, "I suppose your summer house has a well, then."

Mark frowns, looking a little tired now. "Naw, a neighbor had to drill five hundred feet through solid rock before he hit any water. So we buy a six-hundred-gallon truckload every summer from him for twenty bucks." He hangs his head. "Besides, it's really my father-in-law's place. He's had it fifteen years, I guess. And you know, it's funny"—he looks up at me almost hopefully—"you're only the second guy he's seen hike by in all that time."

The wistfulness in his tone makes me wonder. "Then you mostly work up in Alaska?"

Mark sighs. "I guess I only did that for part of a year, after I got out of trade school. I've been married now for eleven years—God, I was drunk on my wedding night, bashed the old Chevy's side against a telephone pole. Haven't put a scratch on her since. Then along came the kids, and it's no more wandering."

"Where do you work now?"

"Aw, I'm a millwright at a big Portland steel mill, running lathes. I don't want to talk about it. Course I've got to take my damn summer vacation in September, 'cause I've only got eight years' seniority, and all the old guys get July and August when their kids are out of school. A goddam week, and it's half gone."

The paved road takes me by surprise. It is 6:30 P.M. Mark's "half, three-quarters mile" turned out to have been fully three.

Far down the perfectly straight highway gleam the headlights of a single car. Mark watches it silently. Then he sighs again and pours out the remainder of his warm beer on the pavement.

"It's them," he says.

The car seems to grow as it drones toward us on the desert road. When it slows I can see it is an old Chevrolet with a single large dent on the driver's side door. A youngish woman with her hair in curlers smiles in embarrassment from behind the steering wheel. There is a child in a car seat next to her.

"Thank God," a voice says from the backseat. The back door opens and a heavy-set older woman leans out, holding a baby in a blanket.

Mark motions toward me. "This is Bill."

The heavy-set woman gives me a pained smile. "Well, I tell you, we found his motorcycle with the engine cold, and then dinner was on the table, and no boy. We were getting a little worried."

The woman scoots over to make room, and Mark gets in without a word. The car backs and drones off in the direction it came, slowly getting smaller.

Alone again, I face the empty road. I cannot camp without water, and water is seven more miles down this road at the Deschutes bridge. The hard pavement makes the soles of my tired feet flame with each step.

The sun sets across the tops of the Cascade peaks to the west, silhouetting them in red and gold. A thin crescent moon rises above the sagebrush plain. Birds I do not recognize flit through the dusk singing lonesome evening songs. The smell of sage seems even stronger in the dark.

A billion stars have lit the sky when the road begins to wind down into a great dark canyon. For this last downhill mile, the unavoidable jolting of my strained shin tendon makes me wince so badly I sing "Frosty the Snowman" through fiercely gritted teeth, so as not to cry out with each step. Tears are running down my cheeks when, after 33.7 miles, my day's hike across the desert ends beside the dark curves of a one-lane suspension bridge.

I fumble among the dark clumps of sagebrush finding sticks by touch, then heap them in a flat spot and light a fire. I go for water, and discover the Deschutes is not a river here; it is another stagnant arm of the same enormous reservoir. The water is warm and smells like boat bilge, even though it must once have come from the cold, crystal-clear Deschutes and Metolius.

At my little fire I gently unwrap the elastic bandage on my shin. The leg is streaked a ghastly purple and bulges out between the folds of the bandage like bread dough. I have limped on this leg for 160 miles. Now I wonder if I can go on, if I have already gone too far.

The constant lapping of the shore sounds like distant rain. A single car rattles across the suspension bridge. Far up the reservoir, the lights from a boat go out. A shooting star leaves a sudden streak across the sky.

I think of Mark, lying in his bed, watching this same sky. He folds his hands behind his head. A sliver of moon hangs among the stars. And he thinks again: Alaska!

SEPTEMBER 19

8:33 P.M. Smith Rock State Park. 57°F. Mileage today: 27.4. Total: 708.8.

I awake to the eerie call of a coyote echoing off tall basalt cliffs. I shiver, feeling I am being watched. But when I am dressed, all is quiet. I try out my ruined shin with great caution. Miraculously, it appears to be much better.

Knowing a hard day lies ahead, I rest a bit before starting out, studying maps and photographing. Then I cross the suspension bridge over the Deschutes River arm of the reservoir. On the far side, the road angles left toward the dam, but I go to the right, scrambling over boulders on the steep scree slope between the tall cliffs and the shore. An hour and a half of this hard hiking brings me to where the river runs free again—green, white-capped, and flanked by ponderosa pines.

This is a part of the Deschutes Canyon people rarely see. Fishermen stop at the end of the reservoir. White-water boaters, who float the rapids on almost every other part of this river, are blocked here by two major waterfalls ten miles upstream. Four-wheelers are stymied by the cliffs, which rise in tiers seven hundred feet on either side.

Deer and coyotes must hike here a lot, though. Hoof trails meander through the purple sage and yellow rabbit brush. Deer bones litter the rock clefts where coyotes have lurked. A jackrabbit casually lippity-lips away from me toward some junipers, the veins standing out on his huge ears. His big leg muscles put little effort into the escape, since I am obviously no coyote.

The layered cliffs rimming the canyon are a cutaway view of a stack of lava flows. And though the stack looks like a huge pile of lava from here, its true size is staggering. These flows are part of the Columbia River basalt flows, which between sixteen and twelve million years ago covered 250,000 square miles of land under an average of two thousand feet of rock. Virtually everything between the Cascades and the Rocky Mountains—from Canada to Nevada—was buried flow by flow, in some places as deep as a mile.

All this lava resulted when North America crunched its way over one thousand miles of Pacific plate and the buried seafloor basalt melted. Sixteen million years ago that molten Pacific rock bubbled up to the surface near Hells Canyon, and for another four million years it poured out intermittently, wreaking its revenge on the continent that had tried to bury it. The big basalt cliffs above me represent just a tiny backwater from those great rock floods.

I suspect it will be easier to hike along the rim of this canyon, so I decide to climb out, if possible. I look for breaks in the cliff layers above me, see some promising gaps, and start out.

Now I am grateful for the nonbasalt slopes separating the lava flows. Since often one hundred thousand years elapsed between basalt outpourings, there was plenty of time for river gravels and forest soils to build up a relatively friendly landscape before the next flow wiped the slate clean again. Here occasional volcanic ash deposits trapped between flows have eroded into gargoyle-like formations striped pink, white, and yellow.

Close up, the cliffs themselves look like the broken edge of a monstrous black honeycomb. Molten basalt tends to crack into hexagonal pillars as it cools and shrinks. Since the pillars form at right angles to the underlying cooling surface, flows that have overridden ridges have their columnar basalt twisted sideways or splayed like folding fans. Brave red penstemon spangle the fiercest of the basalt pillars with cheery little blooms.

I follow a prominent deer trail around the cliffs, hoping the deer know where they're going. Sure enough, the track leads through a hidden gap in the rock up to the canyon rim. On top I strike out cross-country toward the distant blue curves of the Ochoco Mountains through a flat sagebrush steppe. The land here differs from the Lower Desert only in that it has a few stray tufts of grass.

Looking at this steppe, it's hard to imagine that most of central Oregon was a grass prairie just 120 years ago. Up until the mid-1800s the military insisted that white settlers stay west of the Cascades and that Indians stay east of the range. But when gold was discovered in the Blue Mountains in 1861, the miners poured through central Oregon, and saw the grasslands. When the gold rush died out in the 1870s, the disillusioned miners turned to ranching. They brought in millions of cattle and sheep. Within a decade the grass was gone, and instead sagebrush and juniper began to spread across the barren steppe.

I don't see many clumps of the original prairie bunchgrasses here. The dry, bristly stuff that forms a yellow haze over the ground is cheatgrass, a European import the ranchers brought in to stop erosion. Now that it has spread, the ranchers curse it. Except for a few weeks in spring, cheat is so tough and inedible it gives cattle "cheat sores" in their mouths. And the stuff gets so dry that "cheat fires" run through the range in the fall. Sagebrush and bitterbrush are both better browse, and they space themselves out across the steppe to protect themselves from ordinary range fires. But cheat fires burn everything.

By afternoon the first craggy ocher rock formations of the Ochoco Mountain foothills are rising above the sagebrush and cheat plain like ships in the desert. As I hike nearer to the crags of Smith Rock State Park, I come to dirt roads, and then to asphalt. Weathered barns and sleek Arabian horses stand in startlingly green, sprinkler-irrigated hayfields. And the roads are lined with tumbleweed.

I recall learning the hard way why the locals call tumbleweed "puncture weed." It was on a bicycle tour I took with my wife ten years ago. We hadn't gone far across the high desert steppe when our tires went flat. The problem was that tumbleweed spreads its spiny seeds by drying up in the summer, breaking loose from the ground, and rolling along highways and fields with the wind.

I used up all our inner-tube patches covering seven holes. Then we rode on, this time watching for tumbleweed seeds as carefully as if they were broken glass. But in five minutes the tires were flat again.

I cursed all Eurasia, the original home of this alien tumbleweed plague. I cursed road ditches and fencelines for giving the awful plant the kind of disturbed soil conditions it thrives on.

Then I realized the second set of flat tires was my own fault. After patching the first flats, I had forgotten to pull out the tumbleweed seed spikes imbedded in the tires before putting the inner tubes back on. With seven new, unpatchable holes, we rode sullenly on the rims fifteen miles to the nearest service station.

This afternoon, as my pedometer needle climbs into the twenties, I am not thinking of the looming, mysterious Ochoco Mountains, which I have never visited before, but rather of a tiny, remote gift shop I remember at the edge of Smith Rock State Park. The shop sells a marvelous ice cream made from genuine wild huckleberries.

Finally I see the store, with an Old West false front of weathered planks, a hitch rail and water trough in front, and a broad porch with a Hires root beer thermometer. But the door's locked. It's closed.

Disappointed, and very thirsty, I look around back to see if I can just get my water bottles filled. An older woman bustles out from somewhere, sizes me up, and says, "Come on, we'll open up and get you some ice cream."

"That'd be great." On our way around front I can't help adding, "Are you the same one who's always run this store?" Though the woman must be at least sixty, her platinum-blond hair is as long and dramatic as a teenager's. She wears big-framed, modern glasses and a white sweatshirt decorated with splashy motifs of Paris. It seems I would have remembered her.

"I used to own the place right at the foot of the Rocks," she says, jerking her thumb toward the ocher crags jutting out of the desert down the road, "but the state condemned it for the park seventeen years ago, and I've had the store since."

She unlocks the door, leads the way through the dark displays, and turns on a small light at the ice cream counter. Somehow she looks more familiar in here. I say, "It's such a remote place for a store."

She shrugs. "It's never been the kind of place to make money hand over fist, but I don't care. At the trade shows, salesmen show off their gimcrack doodad junk and say, 'This is what's selling this year—you'll make a million.' But I won't buy it. I only buy things I like."

While she scoops out blue ice cream, I look around the dimly lit store: imported candy, Ansel Adams photograph postcards. "I think it's very nice."

"Oh, we have a few tourist things. The plates with 'Oregon' written on them, the Indian beadwork, the twenty-cent postcards with 'Greetings from Central Oregon.'"

I take the cone and am immediately lost in a cool, creamy world of huckleberries.

"I never did care much about money out here," she says. "I'm just happy to be near the Rocks and to run things my own way. In the city there'd be all these officious busybodies with nothing else to do but come in and tell me I can't stay open certain hours, or that my parking area's too shallow, or that I need to pay for licenses and fees and tax districts and parking campaigns. I've only had one guy like that the whole time I've been here—just one. He comes in and tells me if I serve ice cream I've got to have three sinks. One to rinse in, one to do something else in, and a third for something else again. You seen them? Aren't they pretty?"

I finish my cone and sigh. "That was wonderful."

She smiles. "Did you say you were on a long hike?"

I tell her briefly about my trip as we go back through the dark display racks.

She locks the door. "You know, you're doing the same thing I am in a way—just going out to be away from it all, and who cares about money. Isn't that right?"

I nod, and for a moment we both look toward the sheer face of Smith Rock, which now glows orange in the twilight.

"Have a good night out there," she says. "On a Thursday like this you'll about have it to yourself. Watch out for Friday morning, though."

"Why's that?"

She shakes her head. "You'll see."

I shoulder my pack, wondering.

As I hike through the park's day use area there is only a single small cluster of bored teenagers from Prineville, watching a flickering gray-blue TV set and laughing even more often than the canned laughter.

The park has no regular campground, but only a little field of sagebrush with a sign: CLIMBER BIVOUAC AREA. There is an old Datsun station wagon in the parking lot. The man beside it is so intent on unloading piles of complicated, jangling gear by flashlight that he does not even answer my hello.

From the sagebrush where I finally pitch my tent, the pinnacles of Smith Rock tower against the orange sunset sky in jagged, Andean silhouettes. The crescent moon slices into the horizon between the dimples of distant Cascade peaks.

Then, just as I'm about to crawl into the tent, a long, slow fireball drifts across the sky. For a full minute the strange light burns southward from Mount Jefferson to Mount Washington, leaving three yellow novas along a glowing orange streak.

Is it a sign, or a dream? Meteors are much faster; burning planes much smaller. The light is either hundreds of miles away, or in my head.

Coyote, if you are playing with lights for me, come explain them!

SEPTEMBER 20

8:23 P.M. Warm Springs Indian Reservation. Mileage today: 18.0. Total: 726.8.

When I wake up from long, stormy dreams, late in the morning, the parking lot is already full. Puzzled, I walk along the row of recently arrived, beat-up, dusty little foreign cars. Toyotas, Datsuns, VWs with bicycles and kayaks tied on top. License plates from California, British Columbia, Colorado, even Alaska.

Up go the hatchbacks, trunk lids, and doors, like the wings on a fleet of ladybugs. Then a colorful collection of ropes, interior-frame backpacks, and little pickaxes begins to line the sidewalk. A stern, broad-chested man in knickers and a crash helmet is sitting on the curb, methodically covering his face with white warpaint that is probably intended as sunscreen.

"These cliffs must be pretty good for rock climbing," I say.

"Uh." He paints his nose white.

"Seems to me it'd be more interesting to climb mountains in the Cascades, though. They're a lot taller."

He glares at me, like a Zulu warrior about to throw a spear. "Climb that crummy lava shit? The rock here's welded rhyolite tuff, guy. The best climbing this side of Yosemite. I'm trying Monkeyface—it's a four-hundred-foot pillar, smooth and overhanging on all sides."

I look down the row of cars. "Looks like you'll have a crowd up there."

"Hey, guy, there's two miles of cliffs with routes." He yells over his shoulder to a man who has crawled halfway into the trunk in search of gear. "Say, B.J., are you going for the Crack of Dawn or the Moonshine Dihedral?"

A voice resounds from the trunk. "Thought I'd try the Wombat."

"The Wombat? Geez, man, don't do the Wombat. Take Godzilla, then."

In front of the next car a sinewy little woman with bulging arm muscles is wearing a white helmet. The blue-yellow-red braided rope slung across her chest looks like a colorful python trying to strangle her diagonally. Unconcerned, she is strapping big, puffy chunks of foam rubber onto her elbows.

"Hi, what's the foam rubber for?"

She is too busy to look up. "Banged up my arms pretty bad last time on Wartley's Revenge. Need some protection."

Beyond this woman a clean-shaven young man is studying a pile of hardware heaped beside his pack on the sidewalk. I recognize the three-inch, O-shaped clips as carabiners, but a pile of spring-loaded aluminum doohickies has me baffled.

"Pardon me, what are those?"

"Friends," he answers.

"Friends?"

"Yeah, that's their name. They're designed to expand inside cracks and hold like anchors."

"Handy gadgets."

The young man starts loading the hardware into his pack. "The best thing about them is they pull out when you're done. Used to be, climbers would just hammer in pitons and bolts everywhere. They'd leave the face cluttered with junk and make it too easy to climb. They don't allow that here anymore."

I walk back to my own camp to pack up, thinking about the crowds of climbers that have made it necessary to protect even sheer cliffs from development.

By the time I hike off toward Prineville, where I'll start my weekend of rest, the orange cliffs of Smith Rock are already dotted with colored spots of helmets and backpacks—strange Technicolor flies caught on the cobweb lines strung across the rock.

Walking the highway shoulder, I am accompanied by black-and-white, long-tailed magpies that swoop ahead to watch me from the telephone wires. Blackbirds sing from fence posts, then flash their red armbands as they dip across the sprinklered hayfields.

In the afternoon my father drives up, and suddenly I am whooshed away at astonishing speed across the hills into the Warm Springs Indian Reservation. For my weekend off, my father has rented a suite at a luxury resort in the middle of the reservation. It is the only place there where white men are allowed to stay uninvited.

The state highway crosses the reservation through some of central Oregon's driest and most picturesque badlands. Bold red and yellow lava layers jut out here and there from the dry, rolling hills, like toys peeking out of piles in a child's sandbox. Occasionally, dark junipers dot the slopes. I have to admit the reservation looks as empty from the inside as it did from the outside when I hiked along it for thirty-five miles.

The resort is a different matter. We drive past a guard booth toward a modern motel and an enormous hot springs swimming pool set amid manicured, glowing green lawns. In the motel room, I can tell I am immersed in Indian culture, and not in a Holiday Inn, only because of the angular Navajo patterns on the chairs' upholstery. Outside, there's a row of thirty-foot tepees set up on concrete pads that can be rented for half the rate of a motel unit. Beyond, where the lawns end and the sagebrush hills begin, is a sign: DO NOT CLIMB. STAY OFF TRAILS.

The sign might as well have said: STAY IN YOUR BUBBLE, WHITE MAN. DREAM ON, AND PAY.

With a day of rest ahead of me, I am suddenly so tired I can hardly move. I come back to life when Janell arrives with the children. We embrace and talk as though it had been years instead of weeks since we were last together. Karen and Ian delight in the colored pebbles and feathers I have collected for them. Janell and I laugh as she tells me how an overflowing bathtub poured water into a neighbor's bedroom in Eugene.

Then I start to fade again. Karen is allowed to celebrate her fifth birthday several days early, but I am lost in a daze. When I unwrap the bandage about my swollen, purple-streaked leg, I distantly hear voices crying out in alarm. But I alone know the inflamed shin is better. It is going to get well despite all I have done to it. I will be able to go on.

SEPTEMBER 21

7:15 P.M. Same.

Today Janell and I drive back to the state highway to see if we can't find more Indian culture in the reservation town of Warm Springs, population 500.

On the edge of town, looking out of place among the desert hills, is a sawmill with a large stack of logs. The trees come from tribal lands in the High Cascades, for the tribe owns the entire eastern half of Mount Jefferson and does not hesitate to harvest old-growth forests next to the white man's designated Wilderness Areas.

The center of town has no business district. Instead, the uniform white clapboard houses of government officials from the Bureau of Indian Affairs stand in evenly spaced rows. Near these, where a gravel and a dirt street cross, amid a large, dusty parking lot, is the store.

There is only one store in town—a legacy of the government's trading monopoly with Indian tribes. It is a functional, worn building that looks rather like a small, twenty-year-old supermarket. On the bulletin board inside the door are posters telling of tribal dances, deer-hunting regulations, and touring country-music groups. The ceiling beams are decorated with local cattle brands.

All manner of groceries, hardware, and supplies manage to squeeze onto the little store's shelves. Just beyond the nails and kerosene lamps is the transmission fluid. Cloth is for sale, but only in plaid wools. A large case has craft materials: beads, bear claws, jingle bells, plastic dentalia shells, genuine dentalia shells, and belt buckles. A few finished craft pieces are for sale on commission. Two giggling grade school girls are trying on beadwork earrings against their long black hair.

In the back of the store, unannounced by any sign, is a kind of museum. One of the dusty glass cases displays arrowheads and basketry, and a photocopy of President James Buchanan's treaty authorizing the reservation. The next display case, however, contains ordinary-looking trophies made of little brass columns and marble tiers. Each trophy is topped by a silver angel holding aloft a Greek laurel wreath of victory. One inscription reads: BEST FANCY WAR DANCE, 1973. At the checkout counter, muscled Indian boys in red net football jerseys are buying Sno-Kones and Slurpees.

I can't figure out just what seems wrong here until we leave the store and Janell finds Owenuma Blue Sky. Owenuma is a barrel-chested Indian man of about thirty, with a single black braid down his back. He has set up a folding table at the back of his beat-up pickup truck in the dusty lot across the street from the store. Surrounded by a jostling crowd of schoolchildren, he is baking fry bread.

Owenuma kneads a ball of plain white bread dough into a disk the size of a pie pan. Then he slips the disk into a tray of oil kept hot by a small butane burner. As soon as the bread is crisp and brown, he fishes it up. The first kid in line grabs it and sprinkles it with one of the two shakers on the table: salt, or sugar and cinnamon.

There is no sign. Owenuma's customers know what he sells, and that it costs a dollar. When I ask, he admits the bread is not a traditional Indian food, since the Indians had no flour, but that does not prevent him from going on to tell the story he has memorized for curious white tourists—that the fry bread recipe dates from Kit Carson's defeat of the Navajos.

Then Owenuma sees Janell's T-shirt with a picture of a wildflower and the inscription NATIVE PLANT SOCIETY OF OREGON. Immediately he changes gears. This big Indian man, with his hands full of dough, begs Janell to tell him how he can join her society. He says he has sent repeatedly to the Prineville library for books on the local wildflowers, but none has been satisfactory. None even had color pictures. Yet he desperately wants to learn the names of the flowers that grow on the reservation. Couldn't she plan a field trip from Eugene with her society to help him learn?

Then I know what is wrong. It is my own assumption that Native Americans belong to a race that is genetically closer to the land. The people here in Warm Springs are just as able as people elsewhere to cut down the wilderness forests and forget the flowers. And the luxury resort where I will sleep tonight is not really a bubble built by the Indians to cage white men from their world. The whites have put the Native Americans in a larger bubble, in which the resort is a decoy, hiding the truth that Owenuma sees.

The ancient closeness with the land has been lost. And so Mr. Blue Sky bakes fry bread year after year, and he tells the tourists stories. But he, too, craves the knowledge of wildness that still beckons from the flowers.

SEPTEMBER 22

9:22 P.M. Green Mountain Trail. Starry, 48°F. Mileage today: 15.0. Total: 741.8.

This morning my father drives me back to Prineville, where I left off hiking two days ago.

This town is the legacy of one Barney Prine, who, in a single day in 1870, built the first house, store, saloon, and blacksmith shop, all under the same rickety roof. The town grew up rougher than Dodge City. In the 1880s, when a single sheriff served all of central Oregon, masked vigilantes handled Prineville's legal affairs by hanging nine men, several of them guilty.

Behind Prineville the brown hills of the Ochoco Mountains look disappointingly drab and low. And yet, the closer I get to them, the more rugged and interesting they become.

At the edge of town there is a brief rim of suburbs with here and there a steer picketed in a front yard. Then, where the road turns to dust and the sagebrush turns to pines, I hike into the Old West.

Ahead is the headquarters for the Circle H Bar O Corporation— a weathered ranch house and silo in a dry gulch. I've already gotten the OK from the ranch boss to short-cut across their cattle spread to the Ochoco National Forest lands. I'm hardly past the barbed-wire fence and clanging cattle guard when a couple of cowboys approach to size me up.

The Old West atmosphere vanishes amid the din of their three-wheeled all-terrain vehicles.

The cowboys prove to be Lindsey and Brett Corklin, sons of the cattle corporation's hired resident managers. Brett, a teenager, climbs off and spits tobacco juice over his beardless chin. Lindsey, in his upper twenties, squirms on his ATV, fidgeting with the brakes and lights, and wrestling his legs nervously around the seat. His stubbly yellow beard bristles when he grins, which is often. He has no moustache to soften the remarkably white glare of his teeth.

"So you're hiking, huh?" Flick, flick go the brake handles. Lindsey's eyes are lost behind the shiny disks of his dark glasses.

"Yeah. Have you been up to the Green Mountain Trail? That's where I'm heading."

He gives a big white flash of a grin. "I was up there about noon today, driving thirty cow-calf pairs back up to the Forest Service land we got summer permits on."

"Do you always take them up there in the fall?"

Lindsey squirms. "Aw, no. We take 'em up in spring, but by now they've cleaned out all the graze up there. Maybe they can smell us cutting the hayfields in the valley, 'cause they've been bustin' down the fencelines trying to come down."

"Do you—do you herd cattle on an ATV?" I hesitate to have this part of my image of the American cowboy destroyed, but I have to know.

"Don't think I haven't tried. But when a cow dives off into the juniper over the rocks, your ATV has to pick its way through, you know? Cows get away. Now a horse, it just *goes*. Anywhere a cow can think of going, a horse will, too."

Relieved, I ask for directions to my trail. Lindsey draws a map in the dusty road. When I observe that his map and mine disagree violently, he points out several roads on my map that do not exist, and adds a few trails that do.

Finally he says, "Well, you just follow the road you're on until it gives out. Then you keep right on going. But don't follow any side trails or they'll really take you to heck and gone."

An hour later, after my road has become a many-forked cow-path, I'm wondering how I am to recognize the dangerous "side trails." Finally I take out my compass and prove to myself I'm at least a mile astray. Dark falls as I climb out of a forest of twisted juniper into a zone of stately ponderosa pines. And there, coming guiltily down the hill, are fifteen white-faced Herefords with their calves.

They look as sheepish as it is possible for a cow to look. They shy away, expecting me to herd them back up to the grassless National Forest. But I just hike past, and soon find the trampled fence where they have escaped. Lindsey will be up here on horseback to-morrow.

The sun sets, and a gibbous moon begins casting sharp silver shadows through the woods, but I hike on, not yet tired. Today is the autumnal equinox. I have twelve hours of night ahead. I will only need seven for sleep.

At last, I stop on a high, bare ridgetop. No need for a fire. I can write by moonlight and cook dinner by camp stove.

The cool air is still. The forested hills below me are a rumpled, silver-tipped fur robe. Behind me, from the starless silhouette of Green Mountain, resounds a coyote's howl.

These arid mountains must be Coyote's true home—where he plays his games best. When he stops his yipping song, the intense silence rings in my ears.

Below the moon shimmers a distant strip of orange light; it is almost like the fireball I saw from Smith Rock. This time the light does not move. It is Prineville, on the plain fifteen miles below.

This weekend I was told that the fireball I saw at Smith Rock was an abandoned Soyuz spaceship burning up in the atmosphere.

From here in the wilderness, Soyuz and Prineville cast the same glow: the dazzling incandescence of the white man's amazing civilization slowly disintegrating—burning up on reentry to Coyote's magic planet.

SEPTEMBER 23

11:07 A.M. Wildcat campground. Lovely day, 66°F. Mileage so far today: 14.5. Total: 756.3.

By the light of day, the Green Mountain Trail looks like the Chisholm Trail—a wide, dusty route of interweaving cowpaths. I find the forest delightful, though. Above five thousand feet it changes to Douglas fir, watered by creeks and springs I would not have believed existed in these dry-looking hills. I could hike anywhere here; there is no underbrush, save for sparse bunchgrasses, a few autumn-red wild-strawberry leaves, and the withered leaves of what must have been spring wildflowers.

I reach Wildcat campground a half hour ahead of my scheduled rendezvous with a staff environmentalist for the Oregon Natural Resources Council. I quickly write a letter to Janell, knowing the ONRC's paid mountain man will be able to mail it.

6:41 P.M. Mill Creek Wilderness. 56°F. Mileage today: 21.9. Total: 763.7.

Don Tryon arrives at 12:40 P.M. in a battered pickup. Far from looking like a wizened mountain man, however, he is a clean-shaven thirty-seven-year-old businessman with trim brown hair and friendly blue eyes. He trades his dress shirt for a T-shirt, laces up a pair of high-topped hiking boots, shoulders an aged backpack, and says, "Well, let's go see one of my favorite wildernesses."

We cross a fenceline and follow a path along a pine-rimmed valley meadow. The trail crosses and recrosses sparkling Mill Creek on rustic log footbridges.

It is so lovely, and Don is obviously so content hiking along, that we do not talk for a mile. Then I notice a closet-sized wire frame in a meadow. Since it is the only man-made object I have seen in this newly designated Wilderness Area other than the bridges, I ask what it is.

Don stops, giving a sigh that is suddenly weary. "It's the botanical preserve."

I look skeptically at the chicken-wire fence. "It's too small to be a botanical preserve."

He nods. "One square meter protected from the cattle. In a twenty-four-square-mile Wilderness Area."

Now I know he's putting me on. There were cattle all over Green Mountain, but this is wilderness. "Cattle, here?" I am about to add, "It doesn't even look grazed," when I notice that the grass inside the frame is two feet taller than the rest of the meadow. Could it be true?

"Mill Creek's recovered a bit since they improved the grazing management, but I'm afraid you'll still find cattle in all the eastern Oregon Wilderness Areas. We had the clout to lock out the loggers but not the cattlemen. They rent the wilderness at a dollar thirty-five per animal per month, even though the range out here's so rugged it costs the government ten dollars a month per head just to keep up the fences and all."

I object again. "But why would the government put up with losing money like that?"

He shrugs. "Tradition. Each Wilderness Area has been grazed by this or that ranch, probably for generations. Of course, the Wilderness Act was supposed to protect native plants from being wiped out by grazing—sort of a genetic storehouse, you know. But just about the only botanical preserves are these little range-monitoring enclosures."

We look together at the little sagging fence. Don says, "It's like fencing an acre as a grizzly-bear preserve to see if .005 grizzlies will live there."

As we hike on, I can't help thinking the forest-rimmed valley is beautiful anyway. I try to cheer Don up. "At least the cattle haven't eaten the trees."

He looks more disgruntled than ever. "But they have."

"What?"

"Look at those big cottonwoods by the creek."

I look, skeptically. The three towering poplars certainly appear uneaten.

"Do you see any little cottonwoods?" Don asks.

"No."

"That's because the cattle browse off any little broadleaf trees that try to sprout. In all of eastern Oregon, creekbank alders, willows, and cottonwoods are dying out. My own theory is that that's why we've got so many insect plagues."

I've heard of the various tussock-moth, pine-beetle, and spruce-budworm infestations that have ravaged eastern Oregon's conifer forests for decades, but the connection with browsed cottonwoods is beyond me. "How could that be?"

"Cottonwoods have big, soft trunks that are easily hollowed out by birds. Since most of the cottonwoods are gone, and most of the conifer snags are logged out, the cavity-nesting birds that keep down insect populations are gone, too."

He waves his hand toward the trees. "This forest should be full of woodpeckers and owls. Sometimes it's the things we *don't* see that should worry us most."

As we hike on through the afternoon, I can tell Don's personal concern for this wilderness valley is greater than even his job as staff person for an environmental group can explain.

At the evening's campfire in a starry ponderosa glade, he turns sizzling elk steaks in the cast-iron frying pan he's carried all day in his pack. The firelight flickers on his T-shirt; it has the words HYDRO BUSTERS below a red, slashed circle on a picture of a dam.

When I ask about the T-shirt, he tells me his organization has successfully opposed thirty-seven dam projects proposed for the Deschutes River, including the canyon where I hiked last week. "It's funny, though," he adds thoughtfully. "My father used to build dams. He started out as a technician when they built Hoover on the Colorado."

The comment gives me a suspicion of how Don himself got started in conservationism. "Sounds like you were one of the rebellious kids of the sixties—the generation gap, you know."

"No, not at all. I didn't question what my dad was doing back then, even when he was working on the high dam at Oroville, in northern California."

He turns the elk steaks again. Then he takes a Tupperware container marked SALT and pours some in his hand. "Goddam it!"

"What's wrong?"

"I put the Wesson Oil in the wrong container." He shakes oil off his hand. "Probably should just burn it off, like they do in the circus."

"I wouldn't risk it."

He grumbles and wipes off his hand with a cloth. "Anyway, I wasn't even a conservationist after getting out of college. I worked eight years in central Oregon as a timber cruiser for the Forest Service." He stares into the fire. "That's when I first saw Mill Creek. It was ten years ago this week. I had a free weekend, and asked my supervisor about this blank spot on the map of the Ochocos. He said,

'Go see it.' So I went. It was very badly overgrazed then, but still beautiful."

"Is that when you got interested in environmentalism?"

He shakes his head. "I guess conservation had been growing on me. But my real conversion came in Canada."

I give him a questioning glance, but he just stabs the elk steaks onto tin plates with a bowie knife. "These are going to be chewy. It was a tough old bull."

"That's all right." For a moment all is quiet as we chew. Then he continues his story.

"I'd been talking with a friend about the old fur traders and how they used to canoe from the Rockies to Hudson Bay. I wondered if it could still be done. He said, 'Let's try.' So we did. We took a train to the Canadian Rockies and put our canoe into the headwaters of the Athabasca River."

I look up. "Maybe I've got my geography wrong, but doesn't the Athabasca go to the Arctic Ocean?"

"Right. So after five hundred miles we portaged to the Churchill River drainage, and were still two thousand miles from Hudson Bay. Two months later we came to South Indian Lake, a lake so big it shows up on world globes. The only people there were families of Cree Indians, spaced a day's voyage apart on the lakeshore. Like us, they were living on nothing but fish. We asked directions to the Churchill River outlet. In broken English, the Indians said the outlet was a bad spot. They said Manitoba Hydro was building a dam there that would stop the fish runs and ruin them.

"Another week of paddling brought us to the outlet. We were welcomed as guests of the dam supervisor. He said the dam would raise the lake level just fifteen feet, but that would suffice to send the lake waters spilling out a new outlet, into the less wild Nelson River, where Manitoba Hydro already had powerhouses. He told us the dam was nearly complete. When we explained our plans, he said, 'You'd better make it to Hudson Bay in two weeks, because that's when the floodgates close. You two will be the last ever to run the lower Churchill.'"

Don knits his brow. "I ran the last two weeks of that river in a kind of trance. At every big rapids I thought: I am the last to see this. Then, at a portage, I hooked a lunker in the white water—a thirty-pound pike, biggest fish I've ever caught. And that was it. That was the kind of moment religious conversions are made of. I knew a fish like that could never live in the dribble Manitoba Hydro would leave behind. The dam was wrong. When I paddled into Hudson Bay, I was an environmentalist."

In the ponderosas a great horned owl calls a baritone *hoo-hooo.* Don pokes the fire with a stick until it collapses.

"Then you haven't been on the ONRC staff long," I say.

"I signed on just in time to lobby for last year's wilderness bill. I hiked into Mill Creek with Senator Mark O. Hatfield's aides. We sat on the cliffs overlooking the valley and drank a bottle of wine as the sun set. A rare woodpecker perched nearby. The day was perfect. When the bill came out of the Senate, Mill Creek was in it, with its largest boundaries ever."

Don leans back, puts his feet up beside the fire, and savors a brownie his wife has sent as dessert. "Today is the first time I've been back since the valley was saved from being logged." Then he smiles and shakes his head. "Now we've just got to save it from the cattle."

SEPTEMBER 24

9:15 P.M. Bridge Creek Wilderness. 42°F. Mileage today: 27.8. Total: 791.5.

In the morning I leave Don and hike east under the sunny skies of Indian summer. A hard day, mostly on Forest Service roads, brings me to another of the Ochoco Mountains' newly designated Wilderness Areas: Bridge Creek.

There are no trails here, so I have to bushwhack a mile through a thick fir forest up toward North Point, a tall cliff where I expect a view. The sun has set when I reach the rock-strewn barrens near the brink of the cliff. Here and there, gnarled mountain mahogany trees have struggled up from the rock, only to be sheared flat by the cold winds.

I zip my coat tight and approach the lichen-covered basalt of the rim. Far to the west, across the dark humps of the Ochocos, the silhouettes of distant Cascade volcanoes—Mount Hood, Mount Jefferson, the Three Sisters—rise from a thin, fiery river of red clouds. Luminous rays of yellow, green, and pink diffuse into the sky above the unseen sun.

After dinner I write by moonlight, wearing wool socks on my hands to keep them flexible enough to hold the pen. My tent luffs and strains in the wind.

SEPTEMBER 25

9:04 P.M. Meadow on the Ochoco crest. 42°F. Mileage today: 23.9. Total: 815.4.

At dawn the line of Cascade peaks is tipped with pink. A faint, snowy cone north of Mount Hood is 12,000-foot Mount Adams, 150 miles away. Between those mountains and my cliff lies a vast, reddish badlands of sagebrush and juniper. The forests of the Bridge Creek Wilderness begin just below me, halfway up the steep northern face of the Ochocos' range.

I pack up quickly and set out to explore. Bridge Creek itself turns out to be a narrow gully so heavily trampled by cows I dare not refill my water bottles. Instead, I strike a compass bearing through the forest for Bridge Spring. Two hours of scrambling later, I come out of the forest to a waterhole. There are nine Herefords standing in my drinking-water supply, lifting their tails. My arrival has scared the shit out of them.

In my aggravation I set a compass bearing due east, toward a forest road and a more probable spring, and march off.

Much of these Ochocos consists of grassy-floored ponderosa pine forests or open sagebrush flats. But in between are bands of fir, lodgepole pine, and larch, all mashed together in young thickets choked with limby snags and fallen trees. This is what lies due east of Bridge Spring.

Crashing through this stuff soon stripes my arms with white scratches. My backpack's pockets—even those unzipped just an inch—fill with handfuls of pine needles. Though it is a sunny day, the forest becomes so dense, my camera registers insufficient light for a picture. But at least there are no cows.

An hour's hard work brings me less than a mile forward, to the darkest, least passable part of this whole Wilderness Area. And there, hanging from a tree limb, is a long, orange plastic ribbon.

I glare at the thing. It's the kind of bright flag someone might leave to mark a route through the woods. I try to visualize the lunatic who would mark a route here. A cattleman? Impossible! A hiker? Unbelievable! At last, I conclude the flag was not left for a pathfinding function at all, although the person's hike may have begun as a path-finding mission. However, having reached this unreachable spot, I imagine the hiker tearing off an extra-long flag and hanging it promi-nently, for the same reason a mountain climber might build a cairn on a peak: simply to let those pathetic, struggling souls who come later know that—by God—he was there first.

Yet another hour eastward, I scramble out of the thickets, up a draw in the basalt cliff rock, and reach my road and spring.

After lunch, the lesser concentration required for road hiking allows me to take stock of myself, now that I've come eight hundred miles in thirty-six days. No part of my body is complaining any-more—it has conceded. My boots are freshly soled. The eastern Oregon Indian summer looks as though it could dream on forever.

Still, I notice that my only pair of jeans—new when I began—are a little worn. Every item carried in my pockets has left a whitish shadow in the denim: the circular watch, the pocket knife, the comb, the butane lighter. All are as visible as if seen by X ray.

Also, the inside cuffs of my pants legs have little ragged holes. At first this puzzles me, since the pants don't have holes elsewhere. But I observe that perhaps every tenth step my boot gives a cuff a gentle flap in passing. This happens only every tenth step, but after eight hundred miles, I've come 1.6 million steps. That's 160,000 gentle flaps. The holes are well enough explained.

The road is mesmerizing. Evening approaches. My boots rise and fall. Coyote comes.

It is the first time I have seen him on the hike. He stands before me, shaggy and gray, squarely in the middle of the road. My heart speeds up as we look at each other. Then he turns and lopes into the forest.

He leaves no tracks and no scat. But as soon as he is gone, I hear the distant croak of many frogs, though the forest here is as dry and frogless as any I've been in.

The croaking grows louder and louder. The sound comes closer and higher. I drop my pack to be ready should a herd of galloping magic frogs overrun me at the bidding of that curious prankster, Coyote.

Just when I'm sure they will reach me, the frogs turn into birds. Hundreds of them, in two long Vs. They are much too large for geese. Slowly flapping their vast rectangular wings, they repeat their litany of froggy chirps.

Sandhill cranes! Coming south over the dry Ochocos toward the great marsh-shored salt lakes of Oregon's Great Basin desert.

When they are gone I take my pack to a roadside clearing for the night's camp. I lean against the pack, watch the stars come out, and think Coyote. If I am going to believe in this "demigod of the wilderness," it will take more than burning spaceships and flocks of cranes. Perhaps he's sizing me up, testing me with simple tricks. I can wait till he's serious.

SEPTEMBER 26

3:29 P.M. Rock Creek. 70°F. Mileage today: 11.3. Total: 826.7.

This morning I pack up quickly, for I have an eleven A.M. rendezvous with a Forest Service employee seven miles away.

I sent quite a few letters before my trip, inviting Forest Service personnel to join me for a day's walk, but I only got one response. A Paulina District timber stand examiner by the name of Tyler Groo offered to show me an Ochoco roadless area not included in any of the wilderness bills.

The dirt road I follow this morning runs along the crest of the Ochocos. The summit is not a string of peaks, but rather a six-thousand-foot-tall prairie of grass, sagebrush, and pine groves. It looks like the scene of a western drama, and it once was.

Tyler Groo's district of the Ochocos is named for Chief Paulina, alias "Bulletproof" Paulina, alias the "Attila of the Sagelands." The best-known horse thief of the old Oregon frontier, this slippery Snake

Indian eluded soldiers, volunteers, and Warm Springs Indian scouts for years. Finally a rancher shot him dead in 1867 as he was breakfasting on a stolen steer near here on the Ochoco crest. The despised outlaw's bones were left to bleach in the sun. Now—such is fame— Paulina's name is bestowed on more central Oregon places than any other individual's: a lake, mountain, town, prairie, peak, and creek.

Cottonwood campground, my rendezvous point with Mr. Groo, proves to be little more than a dusty side road. There is no one in a Forest Service uniform here yet. The road is lined with beat-up old travel trailers. Old men stand in the shade talking about their rigs, about the big buck, about World War II. I recognize some of the trucks from last night, when I'd seen them driving slowly along the twilit road. Now I understand why they're here: The Ochoco deer season won't open for three days, but these die-hards are scouting the deer, watching for patterns so they can nail their buck in the opening minutes of the season Saturday morning.

One license plate reads EXPOW. A toy poodle yaps from inside an old twelve-foot Week-N-Der trailer. As I unpack my first lunch, a stubbly-bearded old man moseys up.

"Where ya headed, son?"

"Howdy." The dialect is infectious. "Thought I'd go cross-country a few miles to check out the Rock Creek Canyon." I nod toward the east.

He shakes his head. "That's mean country."

"Well, the meaner the better, maybe."

He looks at me sideways. "Back now—what the hell was it?— twenty-eight years ago I went down that way, took me half a day to get out. Heard of a guy shot an elk down there. He didn't have his meat out for a day an' a half." He strokes his wrinkled chin, watching a little Toyota drive up the road. "Some trophies still down there, though, I'll bet. If a guy—"

The deer hunter stops in mid-sentence. A man wearing long johns under a pair of white shorts has climbed out of the Toyota. Foot-long braids, tied with red rubber bands, hang down from the man's denim engineer's cap. He has a bushy beard and little wire-rimmed spectacles.

Throughout the campground, heads turn in unison, watching the stranger cross the road. A jumble of canteens, foam pads, and binoculars are lashed to his tiny rucksack. When he stops in front of me, I see a gold ring pierces his left earlobe.

"Mr. Groo?" I ask, incredulous.

"Tyler," he mumbles. "Ready for a little bushwhacking action, eh?"

"Uh, sure. Ready if you are." The question I want to ask—how a ranger looking like him ever got assigned to this conservative corner of the state—will just have to wait.

He leads off through the ponderosas, walking as slowly and cautiously as a burglar in a temple. He mutters (with a New York accent?), so that I only catch phrases over his shoulder. ". . . backpacker like you's sure easy to spot . . . union steward at the ranger station . . . no budget for primitive recreation . . ."

The gentle slope we are following begins to tilt, then nosedives over the brink of the canyon. I feel like a skier about to push off the top of an uncharted precipice. But Tyler saunters steadily on, down through a dense fir thicket that seems to part before him.

We reach twelve-foot-wide, rushing Rock Creek, and suddenly the canyon bottom is bright green with alder, false Solomon's seal, coneflower, snowberry, and wild gooseberries. "Look at this," I exclaim. "Twinflower! I thought it only grew by the ocean, or in the far north."

"*Linnaea borealis,*" Tyler says absentmindedly. "Another half mile of this bushwhacking and we'll have trail."

His muttering tone would be easy to mishear. I look at him. "Trail?" There are no trails on the map.

He takes off his little knapsack. "A good place to camp."

"But we've only come two miles! I usually hike twenty."

"You hike too much. This place feels right."

I shrug and take off my pack. I am his guest here. But I can't help asking again, "Did you really say there was a trail ahead?"

"Mmm. I've put in a few weekends fixing up an old mining ditch I found. I figured a little trail action might convince the higher-ups not to log this place for a while." As he talks, he takes a small notebook from his pack pocket and begins taking notes.

"Do you keep a journal?" I ask.

"No. Not really."

"Then what's the notebook?"

He gives a flustered shrug. "Just records of my unpaid work."

"Mind if I look at it?"

He sighs, leaves it on the ground, and turns his back to begin setting up a tiny white gas stove.

The notebook, made of waterproof paper, is filled with brief, factual entries of a hundred other trips Tyler has made into this canyon:

> *Sept. 9, 1979.* Single-bit ax. Cleared brush, recon.
>
> *Nov. 11, 1979.* Snowshoes, no tools. Found evidence of 2 hunting parties.

I flip forward:

> *June 8, 1985.* Tools: chain saw + 1 tankful gas. Worked on bridge at Rock Cr. crossing. Scared a (250-lb?) hip-high bear. Discovered fresh bones of two horses, probably the ones that strayed from the sheepherders during fall roundup. A lot of sign where they had penned themselves up in the snow near the creek. Also found a balloon with the inscription "Ken Wentworth Ford Grand Opening, Gladstone, Oregon."

I can't hold back my question any longer. "Tyler, how *did* you wind up working out here in the Ochocos?"

"Mmm," he says. "I grew up in New Jersey." He opens a pouch of backpacking food that looks like a blend of granola and spaghetti.

During dinner I learn he moved to California in the 1960s, grew long hair, and joined student protests at a remote state college. His parents responded by cutting off his funds and auctioning the contents of his room at a yard sale. He, in turn, responded with a back-to-the-earth fund-raising effort, sending summer work applications to the most remote National Forests in the country. Without even knowing quite where the Ochocos were, he accepted a job on a fire crew here.

"I liked the country, but I think the Forest Service was surprised when I asked to stay on," he muses. "There's only thirty people living at the ranger station compound, and it's over an hour's drive to the nearest town. They're a pretty tight-knit group."

"Are you saying you had trouble fitting in?"

"Well, I didn't want to cut my hair or take out my earring." He frowns. "But I did decide to chew tobacco. It was a political move."

I nod.

"Now I've been here over ten years. All the 'lifers' at the ranger station—the career guys who watch satellite TV every night and talk about the day they'll get transferred 'someplace nice'—they've all moved on." He lifts an eyebrow victoriously. "I'm only thirty-one, but when they needed someone to write a historical perspective on the district's operations, they came to me."

Dinner is done and night is falling. I ask, "Think we should have a fire?"

"Mmm," Tyler says, and looks in his homemade rucksack. He pulls out blue sweat pants and puts them on. He takes out a pair of red-and-yellow-striped hip-length leg warmers and puts them on, too. Finally he dons a lamb's-wool vest. "There."

"What about the fire?" I ask.

"I'm not a fire person."

"But I need light to write."

"Ah. To write. I'll handle this." Tyler carefully clears a six-foot circle on the forest floor down to bare dirt and builds a tiny, bright fire. "You know we require campers with fires to carry a shovel, an ax with a twenty-four-inch handle, and a water container."

I stall; he is a Forest Service employee. "Wouldn't that be pretty heavy?"

"We look the other way for backpackers. But would you know what to do with those tools if this fire torched the ponderosa over your head?"

I look up at the pine; it could happen. "I suppose if I stood in the middle of the fire I might chop down the tree with the ax. It'd take ten minutes if all went well. Even if the fire hadn't spread by then, it would when the tree fell onto these dry needles on the ground."

"No. While you were chopping it down I'd be out there with the shovel, preparing a dirt bed for it." Tyler tinkers with the miniature campfire. "You'd never save this canyon as a firefighter."

"Guess that's why I'm a writer and not a firefighter."

He sighs. "In the long run, it'll be the writers who save or lose Rock Creek."

For two hours Tyler silently constructs little tepees and log cabins of twigs over the fire's glowing center, then lets his tiny buildings burn down in a blaze of light. The single-mindedness of his purpose warms me more than his fire. He believes I must be allowed to write at all costs.

SEPTEMBER 27

6:17 P.M. Black Canyon Wilderness. 60°F. Today's mileage: 17.0. Total: 843.7.

I feel so guilty for requiring a campfire that I wake up early, spread the ashes, and cover all trace of the fire before Tyler crawls out of his bivouac sack.

We saunter on up to Tyler's mining ditch trail, which contours at the five-thousand-foot level, where the canyon's slope is dry and brown. Below, the creek bottom's bright swath of green forest looks like a biological glacier, dragging bits of red and orange fall color along on its winding path to the arid lowlands, where all will melt to brown again.

The nine-mile-long ditch itself is a monument to stubborn hand labor and lost dreams of gold. Once three feet of water flowed here, in a channel chiseled out of solid rock. Now the overgrown, dry ditch is a "cultural resource," as Tyler puts it, and an unerringly level trailbed.

When the ditch finally ends its in-gully, out-ridge windings, Rock Creek has become a lazy brook in the Ochocos' summit prairies. We reach a gravel road. Like a magician, Tyler reaches behind a tree and withdraws a bicycle with fat, knobby tires.

"My ride home," he says. "Some good action on the road back—fifteen miles downhill."

After a bite of lunch, a handshake, and a mutual thank-you, Tyler zips off down the road, his braids flying behind him. His walking stick protrudes in front of the bike like the jousting lance of a modern-day Don Quixote.

Just before leaving he told me, "The district recommendation for Rock Creek was sent to headquarters last month. It's not been made public, but we're allowed to tell people who ask." I said, "I'm asking."

He replied, "They want to keep Rock Creek roadless another ten years."

It was the treat he'd been saving for last. He rode off smiling, for he'd tilted at a windmill and won.

SEPTEMBER 28

8:26 P.M. Aldrich Mountain. 39°F. Mileage today: 20.5. Total: 864.2.

This morning I have trouble getting out of the sack to face the morning chill. One water bottle is useless—frozen shut—and the other jingles with spiny crystals.

Hiking down from the eastern end of the Ochocos through the winding, cliff-rimmed slot of Black Canyon Creek, I recall that today is the opening of the local deer season. Tyler said hikers avoid the Black Canyon Wilderness on opening day because of the hunters. But there are no hunters on these trails.

There are grasshoppers. I had never looked closely at them before. Now I see they come in three different wing colors: yellow, orange, and black with a white fringe. When they want to show off in the sun, they *ratchety-click* up in the air for a full minute. The red ones are the most frantic about this, clicking fully twenty times a second. When they're through with the aerial display, though, they're really through. Instantly all the color and motion and noise are gone. A dead brown twig falls to the ground at my feet and disappears, perfectly camouflaged. The act is not a bad solution to the age-old problem of how to show off for a mate without showing up to a predator.

After I leave the canyon, wade the South Fork John Day River, and begin climbing past sagebrush into the Aldrich Mountains, the number of grasshoppers increases. There are half a dozen in every bush. My hiking incites clusters of emergency jumps, as if my footsteps were lighting strings of miniature firecrackers. I stop to photograph a lit fuse, and discover that these emergency jumps are random, like frogs'. I zoom my camera in on a grasshopper, and bang! he takes off straight into a rock. Then he's off into a sagebrush, where he hangs awkwardly, unwilling to wriggle loose and give himself away.

Tonight, at dusk, gunshots roll across the forests from the east. Tomorrow I will be in the thick of the hunt. I may learn the emergency jump.

SEPTEMBER 29

7:01 P.M. 44°F. Near McClellan Mountain. Mileage today: 21.3. Total: 885.5.

This morning I hike four miles along the Aldrich Mountain road. Finally I find the hunt.

In the first light of dawn, four-wheel-drive rigs roll slowly past me on the dirt road, rifles out the windows. Four minutes apart, the beweaponed vehicles cruise on, always in the unsettled dust of the truck ahead.

I recall now that but for the Wilderness Areas, these eastern Oregon forests average six miles of road per square mile, with more built every year. In the 1970s it was becoming clear that wildlife had few places left to hide. Finally the Forest Service closed a third of its roads during hunting season, but it was too late. The hunters had become motorized.

Surprisingly, many of these road hunters are not old men, but rather young guys, apparently too caught up in the glory of their shiny new 4WD rigs to abandon them for mere plodding footwork. Their trucks sport fog lamps mounted on chromed roll bars. Magnesium hubcaps adorn their foolishly fat balloon tires. Their girlfriends roll down windows, bat purple-plastered eyelids, and ask, "Seen any deer?"

Young and old, the drivers all shake their heads at me and say, "No luck, huh?" I find it baffling. Here I am, thinking how very lucky I am to be in the woods on a sunny morning, headed for the yet wilder and sunnier woods beyond this road.

I am almost at the road's end, and have almost convinced myself no buck would be silly enough to wander near this noisy Maginot Line, when a tricked-out pickup lurches down the rutted track, flashing its hazard lights triumphantly. Teenage boys stand in the back, thumbs up. "All right!" they cry. "Hey, hey! Way to go!" At road's end, beside the spring, is a bushel-sized heap of viscera.

"In the act of hunting," psychoanalyst Erich Fromm wrote, "a man becomes a part of nature again; he achieves a certain, though transitory, unity with nature."

Perhaps I'll find the hunters who have achieved unity with nature after I leave the roads behind.

When 7,042-foot McClellan Mountain—my day's magnificent hurdle—looms over a pass, the road hunters are forgotten. Ahead is a hulking, treeless *mountain*—not just another blip on an Ochoco prairie. Crinkled canyons ring the mountain's broad brown shoulders. This is a bushwhacker's funhouse, waiting to be explored. I romp down a one thousand-foot canyon, up another six-hundred-foot pass, down a one thousand-foot hillside, and finally up two thousand feet to my wild summit view point amid lichen-mottled rocks. The hike is a knee and tendon tester, but things seem to be in order—not a complaint in the house.

Every tall mountain is the center of the world when you stand on top of it. But McClellan Mountain is the center of Oregon. To the west, Aldrich Mountain and the Ochocos are blue against the sun. To the north, the one-hundred-mile brown trough of the John Day River is brightened by spots of green alfalfa fields. To the south, the big dish-shaped prairie of the Silvies River stretches toward the salt lakes of the Great Basin, where rivers die. And to the east, ahead of me, Strawberry Mountain stands sudden and tall against the rough silhouette of the Blue Mountains. Hells Canyon, which I have never seen, still seems impossibly far beyond those mountains' blue silhouettes; and beyond the whisper of the coming winter.

IV.

THE BLUE
MOUNTAINS

Here is this vast, savage, howling mother of ours, Nature, lying all around, with such beauty, and such affection for her children . . ."

—HENRY DAVID THOREAU

OCTOBER 1

2:30 P.M. Trail in the Strawberry Mountain Wilderness. Cloudy,
52°F. Mileage yesterday: 14.2. Mileage so far today: 8.2. Total:
907.9.

I fretted about my food drop all yesterday morning, hiking
toward U.S. Highway 395. The precious box had been mailed to a
man I'd never met, Tim Lillebo, in Prairie City. All I had from him
was a postcard, now two months old. All I knew of him was that he
had been the lobbyist in Washington, D.C., whose Robert Redford
good looks and persuasive manner had swung many a vote on the
1984 Wilderness Bill. The man should be reliable. But I couldn't help
worrying about the irreplaceable maps, money, lightweight foods,
stove-fuel cartridges, and journal notebook in that box.

I waited at the highway's picnic area nervously. Hunters' pickups came and went. Finally a blond, tousle-haired man in jeans and a
ripped shirt stepped out of one of the pickups. He looked me over
and said, "Want a brew?"

"Tim? Boy, I'm glad to see you. Do you have my food box?"

He stopped. "Food box? Jeeesus Christ. Left it on the porch. Tell
you what, I'll haul you in, you can grab a shower and a night in a bed
before we ship you back out."

"That'd be great, but—"

"But hell." He threw my backpack into the truck bed on top a
pile of chains, oil cans, and chain saws. "Hop in."

No sooner was I in the door than he slammed the truck in gear
and started careening down the canyon road at eye-popping speed. I
ventured, "Cars sure seem fast after walking so long."

Tim grinned over the wheel. "Used to be a log truck driver.
Only turned into a goddam conservationist when I saw they were
stripping the woods to hell."

I'd always thought log truck drivers swore more than their
share. But I wondered: Did Tim clean up his language in Washington,
D.C., or was this what made him such an effective lobbyist?

We flashed past the mouth of the canyon and roared across the
broad John Day Valley to Prairie City. The town's main street had a

dozen stone buildings from the nineteenth-century, a few plank structures from the twentieth, and little else. Gaps between buildings opened onto the prairie of dead grass and rabbit brush beyond. A full-scale covered wagon perched cockily atop a saloon awning. We turned at Del's Café, tires squealing.

Tim screeched to a halt in front of an old green ranch house. Bang went the screen door. I grabbed my pack and followed. Inside, there was antique furniture everywhere, but it was all nearly buried by piles of maps, books, boxes, hunting boots, and backpacking gear. The kitchen had two stoves, one stacked with books.

He led me toward a back porch. "Here, stick your clothes in the washer. Just let me hold this hose in back while you turn it on or it'll overflow into the hall there. Right."

I stripped and tossed everything in. Tim was already ahead of me down the hall. "You want a shower, we'll have to tie up this lever with a rubber band or it'll spray everywhere."

"How about if I take a bath?"

"A bath? Hell, guess you can. You run out of hot, there's more on the living room wood stove. Need another brew? Here." He shoved an aluminum can in my hand and shut the door, leaving me naked beside the steaming tub. I had never drunk cold beer in a hot bath before, but I decided it might be a thing worth trying.

It was. When I emerged, much relaxed, I found Tim boning a chicken with the same reckless abandon that he does everything else. I looked aside, not wanting to watch him chop fingers into our enchiladas.

"You know," he said, "I've been thinking about this wilderness trail thing you're doing. It'll take more than just a trail to save the forests. I mean, even the old-growth timber sold in this area is sold at a loss. It costs more to build the roads than they get from the logs. The Forest Service admits it. That's like *paying* people to go out and rape the wilderness. But they say, 'Hey, we're keeping the local economy going, keeping the mill open, keeping up the American Way.' Dammit, it'd be better to hand out welfare checks."

"You were talking about long-distance trails?"

He glared at me, knife in hand, then went back to his work with a mischievous look in his eye. "Right. So what we need isn't just a wilderness trail, you see, it's a whole wilderness *corridor* across the state—maybe ten miles wide. No, hell, make it fifty miles wide. Just make this whole valley part of it, too. Hey, *I'd* be willing to move out, let the house go back to wilderness. And if people want to get across the corridor, let 'em walk. Or maybe ride a stage—hell, it'd get them through in eight or ten hours."

Tim's boning knife was now scalloping the air with a menacing nonchalance. "Fifty miles wide? No, a hundred! Hell, let's just make it the whole state. This country has fifty of 'em, can't we leave just *one* the way it wants to be all by itself? Everybody can move out; there's plenty of places. Then they could just let people visit, you know, but only on day hikes, so we won't get crowds. Gawd, it'd be a helluva day hike, one hundred miles from Idaho and back out that night. Maybe you'll be up to it soon, huh?"

7:05 P.M. Hotel de Bum, Strawberry Mountain Wilderness. 40°F. Mileage today: 15.0. Total: 914.7.

This morning, when Tim drops me off at my highway crossing, I calculate I've only been with him twenty hours, but his hectic pace makes it seem like a week.

I pick up the walking stick I've left to mark my place and head up a gravel road toward Strawberry Mountain. The road turns into a delightful trail beside a splashing creek in a pine forest. The autumn-red leaves spangling the forest floor are the wild strawberries that gave this mountain its name. I am puzzled by green pine-needle clusters strewn on the trail, but then look up and understand: Ponderosa pinecones grow only in the thick of needle clusters, so squirrels simply cut down cone and cluster together before absconding with the cone to eat the seeds.

While I'm pondering these natural phenomena, I suddenly spot a shape ahead by the trail that doesn't match anything in the nature books. I stop and stare with mounting fear. The thing is motionless, splotchy dark, like a bag, yet somehow I sense it's *animate*. The whole thing is halfway in the trail, where it couldn't be a stump or a bush or a—

It blinks. Two white eyes watch me.

"Hello?" I ask.

"Hi," the shape answers. Then it moves, and its parts begin to make more sense: camouflage sleeves, camouflage pants, and a black-painted face in a camouflage balaclava. When the camouflage gloves lay down a camouflage bow and pull off the balaclava, I can see the shape is a human being, resting beside the trail. In fact, I now see he's been eating granola from a green Tupperware container. Somehow this assures me he means no harm.

"You're bow hunting," I state stupidly.

"You're not?"

His remark is just as absurd as my own. Again I am reassured.

"I'm just backpacking. Mind if I rest here a bit, too?"

"Be my guest."

I break out a little granola of my own while we talk about each other and what has brought us here.

He is Del Stevens, forty-one, a captain in the Portland Fire Department, here to hunt elk in the Canyon Creek Archery Area, a corner of the wilderness he says has been off-limits to rifle hunters since the 1930s.

I ask about Del's bow, which looks nothing like the simple target-practice sticks I recall from summer camp. He shows me the fiberglass-and-graphite compound unit, mounted with pulleys and wires to make it possible to attach a eighty-pound-pull bowstring. Bolted beside the bow's contoured leather grip is a compact rack of ten camouflage-shafted arrows, their razor tips protected by a camouflage cup and their bright feather fletchings hidden by a little camouflage bag.

"You take concealment seriously."

He nods. "Every precaution helps. I won't settle for less than a standing flank shot at under forty yards, and elk are wary. I wash thoroughly before each hunt and sprinkle baking soda in my clothes to neutralize my human scent. Then see this?" He holds out a tiny can, which I quickly recognize as the source of an obnoxious odor. "It gives off the musk of urine from a cow elk in rut."

"Good lord. Elk like that?"

Del shrugs. "It takes a lot more than disguise to bow hunt. The best way to get close is to lure a bull in by bugling or barking like another elk."

"I guess I didn't know elk made noises."

From his expression I can tell my woods lore rating has just dropped. I try to recoup. "Deer aren't very noisy. What do elk sound like?"

"Well"—he crouches and rubs his hands, like a catcher waiting for a pitch—"a lonely cow sounds sort of like, *eee-yuk!*"

The sound is the broken gasp of a dying man struggling to suck in air.

I nod appreciatively. "Your elk would have to be pretty close to hear that, though. I suppose the bugle works better at a distance."

"Oh, it's not much louder, really. Most hunters bugle with a grunt tube. It's basically a radiator hose with a clarinet mouthpiece. But I just use this diaphragm."

I look at the dollar-sized disk in his hand. "You can imitate a one-thousand-pound bull elk with that little thing?"

"Here, I'll show you." Del slips the disk in his mouth, works his jaw a moment getting it in the right position, then lets loose a feeble, mournful wail. He sounds like a high school clarinetist who, attempting to play the difficult riff at the start of Gershwin's *Rhapsody in Blue*, gives up halfway through with a few dismal falling tones.

I am moved. "What does a bull elk do when he hears something like that?"

"Why, he'll bugle back. He can recognize most of the other bulls' bugles, and figures, well, here's a new rival. He'll come closer, thrashing around in the brush with his antlers to show how mean he is."

"And what do you do?"

"You grab a dead branch and thrash back to show you're a badass, too. Then you hope he throws caution to the wind and charges."

"And then?"

"And then your little bow seems like a toy. Elk are as big as horses. Bulls have been known to charge locomotives. This morning I found a three-foot-thick fir with its bark shredded and antler holes in the wood as deep as my thumb."

"How many elk have you gotten this way?"

Del sits back and sighs. "I've been bow hunting six years, sharpening my skills. Last year I shot my first."

"Oh?"

He leans over to tell the tale. "I was camouflaged at a stand while a friend spooked a cow elk my way. The elk stopped just five yards from me and stared, her nostrils flared. I didn't dare blink or even raise my bow. I counted to thirty. My eyes got dry. Then she jumped away on all four legs at once. But after thirty yards she stopped to look back toward my friend—and in that instant I let an arrow fly. It went just behind the leg, through the lungs and heart. There was no blood, no sound. I don't even think she knew what was wrong. She trotted a few yards, then walked, then coughed. I didn't try to follow, knowing adrenaline can keep a dead elk running for miles. Five minutes later I heard her legs kicking by reflex. I found the arrow, blood-covered, the razor tip bent, just four feet from where it'd hit the elk and gone right through."

Del drops his eyes a moment, reverently. Then he picks up his gear. "I'm camped three miles up the trail. Join me there tonight if you want."

"Thanks," I say. "I just might."

"I won't be back till dark," he adds, then jumps the creek and disappears into the forest.

Cold clouds roll in as I hike on alone. Near the seven-thousand-foot level there is a patter of hail. My wilderness map shows a dot where Del said he'd be camping, with the label HOTEL DE BUM. It proves to be a fire ring and five stumps beside a high mountain spring. I set up my waist-high, tepee-shaped backpacking tent across from Del's nylon dome. I refrain from dinner long after dark. It is late when I finally give up and eat alone.

Then I'm startled by a "Hello, Bill." A shadow slips out of the forest. Del hangs up his bow in the firelight.

I grin. "Welcome back. Any sign of elk?"

He digs out a pack of Oriental noodles and three tins of pudding. "I found a wallow."

"What's a wallow?" Again I expose how little I know of elk.

Del is patient. "It's sort of a private orgy spot for bulls. They each have a special bog where they urinate on themselves and on the brush. Then they toss the brush and mud over their backs with their antlers. I'll be waiting there tomorrow from dawn to dusk thirty feet up a tree."

"Up a tree?"

"Yeah. I've backpacked my platform in. It's a carpeted plywood triangle that spikes into the trunk and chains onto a branch. There's a seat belt so I don't break my neck if I fall asleep."

As soon as his dinner is ready, Del talks no more. I write, tilting my journal to catch the flickering light. Finally, when Del stretches back against a stump, I say, "Bow hunting takes a lot of dedication."

Del sighs, staring into the fire. "It's the future, though. With more people out there, we're going to need sports that consume less. We're trained to go out and win things, use things, get things—bull-shit. Look at the fishermen. They already put up with barbless hooks, or flies only, or even catch and release, to keep from wiping out the fish. Now, how many rifle hunters would agree to ban telescopic sights just to make it harder?" He shakes his head. "Someday there'll only *be* bow hunting, and then, maybe, no hunting at all."

The stars have come out, cold above the trees. Del's voice is almost a whisper. "Have you ever come to a beautiful glade in the woods and wished for a moment that you were a wild animal, so you could really understand? As human beings, our minds are full of dead books and trains and straight lines, stuff that just gets in the way. But an elk—thinking only of sex and urine and battle and lust and brush—he sees each tree as a tree. He *knows*."

Behind his black face paint, Del's eyes shine in the firelight. "If I were going to be reincarnated, I would want to come back as an elk."

OCTOBER 2

8:05 P.M. Dead Horse Basin. Windy, 47°F. Mileage today: 25.3.
Total: 940.0.

The stars are just fading with the dawn when Del's alarm clock rings. We pack up silently. He shakes my hand. "Good luck on your hike."

"Good hunting," I say, and mean it.

He smiles, his white teeth suddenly breaking his camouflage. "Yes, thank you."

The trail crests today at 8,350 feet—the highest point of my trip—beside windswept Strawberry Mountain, where last winter's snows still cling. Forested glacial valleys curve away from the peak, punctuated by little lakes and waterfalls, before fading into the desert below. I have crossed the tallest island in the archipelago of wilderness forests stretching across arid eastern Oregon.

OCTOBER 3

7:53 P.M. Reynolds Creek. 45°F. Mileage today: 24.5. Total: 964.5.

Today I cross two highways on my way into the Blue Mountains, but it is the day after hunting season and I see no one—not even a vehicle.

At a ridge, I stand on the edge of the Snake River watershed and look across mountains that filled pioneers with dread. The map shows Stinkingwater Pass, Starvation Rock, and the Malheur ("Evil") River.

This is the beginning of the 304-mile Blue Mountain Trail, a hiking route I'd heard about, in vague terms, for years. Until this year I'd always imagined it was just a smaller version of the Pacific Crest Trail. However, when I telephoned ahead to Loren Hughes, a La Grande jeweler who is the trail's chief promoter, he backpedaled furiously: "Well, the route's been in the plans since the sixties, but there are still quite a number of trailless gaps; in fact, there never has been any trail construction as such. Actually, I think it's terrific you plan to hike the route end to end—you'll be the first."

So I end my day's hike with a Blue Mountain Trail bushwhack, down a forested valley toward the much-needed water of Reynolds Creek. The forest is a maddening thicket of little lodgepole pine trunks, all spaced about twelve inches apart, except where the winter snows have bent them over like fence rails in the maze of pickets. I claw my way downhill in the gathering dusk until I reach the broad, mossy—but perfectly dry—creek channel. Where's the creek? I hike "downstream." The mystery deepens as the valley does. Miles later, in the last gleam of daylight, the creekbed erupts in gushing, moss-choked springs. The banks and hillsides are suddenly cascades of clear water and green moss cushions. I find a tiny flat spot and camp amid the welcome sound of water.

I lie on my back. The dark pines seem to point toward the middle of the sky, where blue Vega reigns, my straight-up star. Then a woman's voice sings out, making the hair on my neck stand on end like a scared cat's.

The hysterical wail rises again. I sit bolt upright and stare into the firelit columns of tree trunks. Water splashes. Wind whispers. The woman's cry slowly, mournfully dies.

I lean back against a tree, steadying my breathing. Then I smile at myself, thinking how frightened I had been by a woman's cry in the dark woods, and how relieved I am to realize instead it is that haunting prankster, Coyote.

OCTOBER 4

8:15 P.M. Dixie Butte roadless area. 47°F. Mileage today: 23.5. Total: 988:0.

I awake this morning to the whir of wingbeats and a cheery *zeet-zeet-zeet!* A robin-sized dipper, or water ouzel (*Cinclus mexicanus*), as fat and gray as any I've seen, comes zipping up Reynolds Creek like a skipping stone. He stops midstream on a mossy rock, does his mandatory little knee-bend exercises, then casually disappears into the icy water.

I climb out of my tent and look down into the rushing creek. There he is, fully two minutes later, still flapping his wings and marching around underwater, stoically deflecting the torrent overhead while he pokes about for insect larvae with his deft little bill. Then he pops back up to his rock and sings a series of jubilant trills, as though there's simply no better life for a bird than flying at the bottom of roaring mountain streams.

Ouzels have no webbed feet, and no ducklike bill, but they're better prepared for water than they look. During dives, scaly trapdoors close over the ouzel's nostrils to keep the water out, and special white membranes slide over its eyes like swimmers' goggles to provide clear underwater vision. What's more, although all birds lubricate their feathers by preening oil out of glands at the base of their tails, the ouzel is able to waterproof itself with an oil gland ten times as large as those of land birds its size.

The ouzel's odd life-style has its advantages. For one thing, hungry hawks and predatory fish do not lurk in waterfalls. For another, there is virtually no competition for insect larvae in the wild cataracts that the ouzel prefers. As a result, he lives a charmed life, perfectly guileless and constantly cheery. Even in howling winter storms I've found ouzels going about their work with the same irrepressible spirit, alternately diving through the icy sludge and doing their bobbing knee bends while pouring out songs of undimmed joy.

The ouzel in the creek this morning lets me and my telephoto lens come within twelve feet of him. The picture won't turn out—it's too dark in ouzel land, and he bobs too much—but my mental snapshot of him is clearer than Kodachrome.

The day's hike ends with a bushwhack to Jeff Davis Creek on the roadless slopes of Dixie Butte. The gold miners who overran these hills in the 1860s included a volatile mix of draft dodgers and refugees from the distant Civil War. No shots were fired in Oregon, but Blue Mountain place names record the mental struggle. Dixie Butte lies in the midst of Grant County, between McClellan Mountain and the Union County line.

Like a gold miner checking the day's pannings, I crouch beside Davis Creek, greedily counting the hard candies in my lunch bag. Fifteen a day. In cold weather I will need them all.

OCTOBER 5

7:40 P.M. Summit Camp, North Fork John Day Wilderness. 46°F. Mileage today: 22.4. Total: 1,010.4.

An elk day! At first I think all this tremendous crashing in the woods must be clumsy cattle. But then I spot fleeing orange rump patches through the trees. One three-point bull crashes ahead of me five times in a row—not because he is sharing my trail, as cattle often do, but rather because he has had the bad luck to keep choosing the direction I was walking. By our fifth meeting, he seems unnerved by the whole business and gives me a haughty glare.

Later, I come upon a friendlier cow elk in the trail. She trots ahead a few yards, then stops. I stop, too. If I had been wearing all of Del's elaborate camouflage, I couldn't have got a clearer shot at her.

As it is, however, she shoots me a dewy-eyed, wondrous look that gets me right through the heart. She even comes back a few steps and holds out her long ears like antennae, trying to pick up more data on me.

I am not a wildlife photographer. I can catch frogs, flowers, and a few other things with less mobility than I. This patient elk is about what I require in a four-legged subject. I swing off my heavy pack, unzip the camera bag, and rummage about for the telephoto lens. All this monkey business would try the patience of a mushroom. Finally my elk finds her legs, just in time to go down in history as a blurry rump.

By noon I'm wading the Middle Fork John Day River. A great blue heron gives a raucous squawk from the reeds, flaps its five-foot, pterodactyl-like wings, and circles downriver, S-necked, in search of safer frogging grounds. I wash half the "tan" from my dust-smeared arms and face, then sit to study the map. Ahead are the Greenhorns, a range of Blue Mountains in a "Scenic Area" reserve. I count the contour lines and whistle. I've four thousand feet to climb this afternoon. That'll take both lunches and all fifteen of the day's hard candies.

I trudge up a dirt road, looking forward to the "Scenic Area" and trail promised by the map. At the boundary there is a locked gate and a NO MOTORIZED VEHICLES sign, but the area ahead is anything but scenic. The "trail" is a grimy, bulldozed, ore-hauling track with bashed and splintered trees on either hand. A mile farther I find the Tempest Mine—a sulfurous junkyard of rusting dump trucks, trailers, and Quonset huts.

At first I am outraged at the failure of the weak "Scenic Area" designation, knowing full-fledged Wilderness status might have spared this high valley's beauty. Then I am incensed at the thought of a more economic tragedy here: Federal law allows miners to take over public land like this and destroy trails without paying the government back a dime.

These public lands belong to me and every other U.S. citizen. But strangers can stake free claims on our property any time they want and turn it inside out with bulldozers. Incredibly, the law says we, the owners, can't prosecute for this vandalism; on the contrary, if the miners can prove there is any remaining value to the land, we have to deed it to them free and clear.

United States mining laws were forged in the anarchy of California's gold rush. Back then, miners considered the land theirs because the nominal owners, the Indians, weren't "using" it—that is, they weren't using it up. Times have changed, but not much. Now the government is in the Indians' position.

When I finally puff to the crest of the Greenhorn Range, the cat roads are gone. I have reached the vast, newly designated North Fork John Day Wilderness.

OCTOBER 6

8:19 P.M. The Bigfoot Hilton; North Fork John Day Wilderness. Drizzling, 40°F. Mileage today: 25.2. Total: 1,035.6.

Ominous black clouds are hurrying across the sky this morning as I hike through rolling forests toward the remote canyon of the North Fork John Day River. Bit by bit I am forced to dredge up half-forgotten rain gear from the bottom of my pack.

My hand grows numb holding my blasted walking stick. I remember this same stick blistered my palm in the Cascades while I limped along on my right leg. Now that my tendons have recovered, why do I need it? I try to tell myself it's time to throw the stick away.

At least I swear I won't bring it home. In the city it would be an embarrassing trophy—or worse yet, just a stick again. I will leave it at Hells Canyon or wherever winter turns me back.

The trail dips down toward the sound of roaring water and disappears into a meadow. Ahead, at the river's edge, is a half-finished steel-and-plank bridge. Three young men are pounding up hefty timber railings and filling the bridge abutments with wheelbarrow loads of rocks.

"Good work!" I say, climbing up to the temporary plank surface. Below, the river foams waist-deep over sharp boulders the size of chairs. I had expected to wade here.

"Five dolla' to cross," a bald-headed young worker says, wrinkling and unwrinkling his brow, sending creases all across his bedrizzled scalp. "Either that or a joint."

Another worker rolls a wheelbarrow past, his muscled arms bulging illegible tattoos. "Don't mind Pinky."

"Are you guys with the Forest Service?"

The third young man grunts. "Barely."

These are the first people I've seen all day; I drop my pack on the far side of the bridge and try to drag more conversation from them. It turns out they are members of Second Growth, a reforestation cooperative in Eugene. Since trees can't be planted successfully in summer, they decided to spend the summer building bridges for the Forest Service. Three weeks ago, the Forest Service trucked them to the North Fork John Day trailhead and left them to backpack the rest of the way in. The forty-foot steel trusses and the planks were dropped at the bridge site by helicopter the same day. Since then, they've been on their own, with nothing but a blueprint and a promise they'll be paid minimum wage for their hours—if they finish before the winter snows.

I look at the bridge with new admiration. "You must have worked like beavers to do this much in three weeks."

"Hey, here's an extra shovel."

I smile. "Which way's the trail toward the Elkhorn Range?"

The man with the tattooed arms shrugs. "Don't know. All I know is where my trailhead is."

A wet dog comes over from a smoldering campfire nearby and sniffs my pants cuffs. "You mean you've been here three weeks and haven't hiked around yet?"

"That's right. Couldn't tell you where we are if you gave me a map of Oregon."

"Have you been liking it out here at all?"

For the first time the man grins. "Been loving it. There's the river. There's the canyon. There's the work. There's a little fishing. Lots of good weather, until now."

"What do you do for entertainment in the evenings?"

Pinky looks up, wrinkling his scalp. "Smoke dope and bullshit. What else is there?"

Just then, the man with the tattoos drops his shovel and stares out across the meadow. Two green-uniformed backpackers are approaching. "Holy shit," he whispers. "It's the Forest Service guys."

The Forest Service guys are a fortyish man with a handlebar

moustache and a younger woman with long blond hair. The man walks up to the half-finished bridge and surveys the progress. "Surprised you're still working."

The worker wipes the rain drizzle from his brow. "We've got to get done before winter, you know."

"That's why I'm surprised. Expected to help you break camp. Radio says we're in for the first heavy snow of the season tonight."

"Holy shit," the worker whispers again.

The woman smiles. "But don't believe it. It's way too warm."

I cling to her argument at once. A blizzard is the last thing I need in these remote mountains.

The tattooed worker grimaces upward, as if boulders had been predicted to fall from the sky. Then he looks in despair at the bridge and his co-workers. Pinky has begun to laugh, tilting his bald head back and forth. He stops only when the tattooed man threatens him with a raised shovel.

I turn to the Forest Service man. "Pardon me, which way's the trail toward the Elkhorn Range?"

The ranger looks at me more closely. "You're going to walk away from this job *that* way?"

It takes me a moment to understand. "Oh, I'm not with the bridge builders. I'm just hiking through."

"I see." He straightens his moustache. "Well, you won't need the bridge in any case. It only leads to the Silver Butte Trail. Your trail stays on this side of the river through the narrows. You'll ford three miles from here."

I groan and go across the bridge to fetch my pack.

Pinky rolls his eyes at me. "Five more dolla'. No dope, hey?"

I shake my head to him as I pass. "Sorry. Good luck."

It is mid-afternoon before I reach the correct river crossing: sixty seconds of knee-deep ice water and sharp, slippery rocks. I accomplish it barefoot only because my soles are armored with calluses from walking more than one thousand miles in fifty days.

On the far bank the sun breaks through the swift, dark clouds— such warm clouds, they really must mean rain—and the sunlight gilds a hidden tin-roofed cabin of huge unbarked pine logs.

I'd been told I might find miners' shacks along this gold-panning river. The Wilderness Act forbids new mining claims, but the old claims are "grandfathered in." Just prior to Wilderness designation, a flurry of river mining claims were filed here, mostly to claim summer steelhead-fishing sites. The claims themselves are recorded on scrawled pieces of paper visible alongside the trail inside baby-food jars, the lids of which are nailed to trees. The older claims are marked by rusting Prince Albert tobacco cans, little mailboxes in the wilderness. Since the nearest road is ten miles away, the miners have been unable to make as much of a mess as at the Tempest Mine. Every board and wood stove must be packed in on mules. Scenic little log cabins are the only practical structures.

With Wilderness designation, however, no more cabins can be built. In fact, I'm told the government is buying the old ones up as opportunity avails, to let them rot gracefully back into the wilderness duff.

I try the door and find it unlocked—in the wilderness tradition. I peer in hopefully but recoil at the stench of rat urine. Light from the gaping wall cracks reveals a nightmare room of ripped-up mattresses and debris.

I eat my final lunch of the day outside and hike on. I'd rather tent in the rain.

The river winds through a great green canyon where forested slopes drop one thousand feet into the brawling white water at every bend. At intervals, craggy spires jut out overhead. Where the trail snakes around the damp north slopes, the forest floor is cushioned with moss, prince's pine, and the shiny leaves of twinflower. Around the bend, on the dry south-facing slopes, there is only a sweet-smelling ground cover of brown pine needles; the great ponderosas stand apart, the better to bronze their trunks in the sun. On and on this goes—miles and miles of trail and canyon that make me want to stop and gape and shoot more film.

Gradually, however, it gets darker and starts to drizzle seriously. By this time I've passed five miserably rat-infested cabins with partial roofs and rotten floors. Now, in the rain and the gathering night, I am tempted to turn back to them. In most places, this canyon is too steep and it is now too dark to pitch my tent anywhere but in the trail. My legs are aching. But there is a glimmer of silver ahead through the trees.

I hurry on across a footbridge over rushing Trout Creek toward a very small log cabin. The narrow lodgepole pine logs look well chinked. Firewood is stacked under the porchlike overhanging front eave. A rail is propped up against the plank door. By matchlight I read the handwritten notice tacked there:

WeLcome To The BigFoot HiLTon

Our SeRvices include:

(1)—A LittLe Food.
    (2)—ALL The WaTer you can drink.
    (3)—UNLiMiTed BaThroom FaciLiTies.
    (4)—Broom Furnished wiTh Each SuiTe.
    (5)—Finest MaTTresses.

RuLes:

CurFew—9:00 P.M.
    MusT be vacaTed By noon each Day.
    Do NoT DisTurb oTher Guests.
    Please close CuPBoard.

signed—*BigFoot*

Cautiously I open the door. There is no smell of rats. The floor is neatly swept. True, the torn black plastic sheeting tacked underneath the old shake roof is not reassuring. But the stove is a monstrous sheet-metal box that looks as if it could consume anything and put out heat.

I build a fire in the stove's gaping mouth and let the orange light flicker across the room. Then I trace a cold draft to one of the three small windows and replace the missing pane with a big square skillet nearby. The thermometer tied to my backpack climbs to a luxurious 80°F. A potful of creek water boils quickly on the stove for my dinner. I spread my sleeping bag on a foam-rubber mat on a coil-spring cot, and finish my journal, content with the world.

OCTOBER 7

8:36 P.M. Same. 28°F.

I awake to a bright dawn from the Hilton's two glass windows—so bright I expect sunshine outside. But when I sit up on the edge of the Finest MaTTress, I see snow. Two inches of cold powder hangs on every branch and leaf.

I stare out the window quite a while. I had convinced myself the ranger's weather report would be wrong. It had been so warm, and the elevation in this canyon is not great—only 4,900 feet. But suddenly my plan to hike on into the higher, colder Elkhorn Mountains seems unwise. I have until tomorrow afternoon before I am expected at my next food drop, eighteen miles away. I check the map. The rendezvous point is Anthony Lake campground, elevation 7,200 feet. Ominously, the area is a ski resort in the winter.

I decide to wait here a day for better weather. The more I think of this, the better it sounds: snowbound in a log cabin deep in the North Fork John Day Wilderness. In fact, the prospect of a completely lazy day is sinfully delicious.

First chore is to light a crackling pine fire in the cavernous wood stove and get breakfast water boiling. That done, I inspect my suite by daylight. The arrangements are most satisfactory. I have four folding chairs, two rickety kitchen tables, a row of battered cooking pans, a corner filled with woodcutting tools, and a cupboard with a little flour and sugar. The Sasquatch management has provided everything but drinking glasses wrapped in paper.

I eat two breakfasts in a row, cozily sipping hot cocoa by the fire and watching snow drift past the windowpanes. Then I idly sort through my pack pockets. To my surprise there is a *Sunday New York Times* crossword puzzle hidden among the maps. I smile. Janell must have smuggled it in. She knows I sometimes while away a morning with these, though I always seem to give up, leaving twenty or thirty blank squares. Now I put my feet up on a chair, knit my brow, and set to work.

Half an hour's easy crosswording gives me a smattering of answers across the field. Another half hour cracks the puzzle's trick: All words with the syllable "ex-" are spelled with an "x" only (xpert, xhort). This discovery carries me along until I dead-end on all fronts. Thirty spaces left. I frown. I've dreamed away most of my wilderness morning on one of man's most abstract inventions, and done no better than usual.

I put on my coat and take a walk. The snow falls in tiny granules, almost like hail. It has melted from the central portion of the cabin roof because of the constant fire, and the runoff has formed a toothy row of three-inch icicles along the eaves. The river is unrecognizable from yesterday: white-banked, overhung with white-laced boughs, made mysterious by a snowy fog. A cold gust fills my collar with snow. I turn back.

I stamp white bootprints out of my lug soles at the door, hang my coat by the fire, and settle back down to my puzzle.

Inside a house my trail lunch looks more like what it really is: bridge-club snack food. So I sample the peanuts and candies, keeping the mental conversation as lively as possible at this party for one. And surprisingly the thirty blank spaces begin to fill.

By late afternoon the puzzle is finished: not a single square left blank. Is this a wilderness experience, too? For once in my life I've had time to finish the crossword. What's more, I learned that El Greco was born in Crete and that Ghana is a major producer of cocoa.

I look at these two perfectly irrelevant facts and laugh out loud. Yet such facts are more significant in the artificial world to which I must return than the very tangible truths I learned yesterday about twinflower and prince's pine growing only on north slopes. It is a strange system we have invented, where wilderness can be a hobby for a few, much like quilting or collecting antiques. One can "get into it" for a while, learn a bit, then give it up for lack of time.

Perhaps civilization itself is the real hobby. Surely the bottom line—the before, the after, the world itself—is wilderness.

Grainy snow rattles on the roof. When I step outside there are no stars. I should not have expected an October blizzard in the Blue Mountains to pass in a single day. Tomorrow I must push on to my checkpoint in the Elkhorns regardless of weather.

OCTOBER 10

10:12 P.M. Winter Canyon Spring. 45°F. Mileage the day before yesterday: 18.0. Mileage today: 27.7. Total: 1,081.3.

I was up before dawn in the Bigfoot Hilton, thinking of the snowy day's hike ahead. All was packed before I was really ready to go. It is hard to leave warmth and shelter for cold and wilderness. But as soon as I was crunching along the two-inch-deep powder in the beautiful white world outside I could hardly believe I had sat in a dark shack so long over a crossword puzzle.

Not a quarter mile down the river trail a great horned owl spread its enormous wings just ten feet above my head and glided silently over the icy river, a rat in its talons. A mile later I almost stumbled over eight elk in the trail before they gallumphed away through the snow.

The river gradually climbed out of its winding V-shaped canyon, taking me up with it, and meandered out onto a broad, high glacial valley. The trees were so thoroughly frosted at that altitude that even the bright orange of the larches dimmed to the sepia tint of an old photograph. At the foot of the cloud-bound Elkhorn Range I stopped for lunch.

It was perfect snowflake-watching weather. In the still, 22°F air, snowflakes landed softly on my coatsleeves. Some of the delicate, six-sided feather patterns were big as paper-punch holes, others as small as the tiniest confetti.

When I hiked on up to Crawfish Lake, the snow deepened to one and a half feet. Thick frost formations encrusted the trees, like white coral growing out from the northwest side of each trunk and branch. The slush-rimmed lake was a stark, black-white scene dissolving into gray fog.

The map showed no trail beyond Crawfish Lake over the craggy Elkhorns. I could not have found a trail even if one had been there. As I bushwhacked onward, snowy branches dumped their loads on my pack and coat. Snow-hidden logs sent me sprawling into the freezing white. I had not brought mittens, thinking to save weight, so instead I put wool socks over my numb fingers.

Finally I crawled up a steep, snow-covered rockslide to the 7,600-foot crest of the range. After a shivering second lunch, I boot-skied down through the drifts toward the black disk of Anthony Lake, with its campground and ranger station, where I was scheduled to pick up the next food package from my parents.

It was 19°F when I reached the lake, my beard a mass of white ice. With growing alarm I trudged through the deserted campground. There were no tire tracks in the deep snow covering the highway. I dropped my pack on the steps of the boarded-up ranger station and tried to order my thoughts. The road was closed. Without a food drop I would have to hike hungry. I would have to . . .

My thoughts were interrupted by the distant rattle of metal. I jumped up. The rattle grew louder. Around a corner came my parents' underpowered compact car, its little tire chains bravely clanking through the snow. I cheered, and my parents broke into excited waves and smiles. My mother ran out into the snow to hug me, plastic bags tied over her street shoes.

"We were afraid you wouldn't make it through," she said.

"I was afraid *you* wouldn't make it through. How did you?"

"We just had to," my father said. "Besides, we had to show the camera crew the way."

"Camera crew?"

He pointed down the road. A second car, emblazoned with the logo of a Portland TV station, was struggling up in their tire ruts. To my astonishment, two men jumped out, fumbled cold-fingered with a video camera, clipped a remote microphone to my coat, and interviewed me for the six o'clock news.

This was disorienting enough, considering five minutes earlier I had been planning a starvation hike in the wilderness snow. But then when I asked my parents about my food package, they insisted I drive with them to a luxury motel in Baker, where we ordered pizzas and beer while watching satellite weather photos on cable TV.

The blizzard passed that night, and though the weather remained too cold for the snow to melt, my hiking route would be downhill from Anthony Lake toward the snowless, roaded canyon of the Grande Ronde River and the town of La Grande. So this morning I set off again from Anthony Lake, this time with my parents taking my pack ahead in their car.

Now I realize how convenient it is for those well-publicized, charity-sponsored walkers (or wheelchair rollers, or pogo-stick hoppers, or bagpipers) who cross the country with support teams following in vans along the freeway, ready to whisk them away to motels or press conferences. My parents are waiting at my lunch stop with hot apple cider, bananas, and M & Ms. I warm up beside the car heater. They take my pack on to the day's campsite, where I'm served beer and pastrami sandwiches.

I've suggested they spend tonight with me under the stars, since it's one of the few camps I'll be making near a road. Enthusiastically they spend an hour rearranging stumps by the fire to get the best heat and least smoke. They've participated in the hike from a distance for so long, deciphering the tiny handwriting in the journals I mail back, puzzling over the photographs developed from my film. Now they are living the trip for a night.

My dear mother—like so many other people have done, she tries to lift my fifty-five-pound pack, groans that she cannot, and then begins to list the equipment I am not carrying but should: "What you really need is an . . ." alarm clock . . . flashlight . . . binoculars . . . fireplace grill . . . hat . . . citizens' band radio.

In the dark beyond the campfire rises the low, distant howl of Coyote. "Listen!" I whisper. "Do you hear it?"

They pause, intent, but either age has dimmed their ears to the wilderness prankster's strange call, or the call is meant only for me. When an owl close by finally raises its voice, they smile. "Oh yes. 'Who-whooo.'"

OCTOBER 11

4:19 P.M. Birnie's Jewelry Store, La Grande. Mileage today: 18.8. Total: 1,100.1.

There is a ticking of clocks. A soothing voice comes from a friendly, round-faced man behind an ancient oak-and-glass display case. "If you have any trouble with it at all, it's under warranty, so just bring it in. Thanks a million." Loren Hughes, the promoter of the Blue Mountain Trail, makes change for a customer while I wait in his La Grande jewelry store.

He straightens his bolo tie and smiles over his bifocals at me. Then he guffaws. "Bill Sullivan! Recognized you from the TV news. Have you been finding your way along the Blue Mountain Trail?"

"Pretty well so far, thanks." I shake his hand. "I'm a little worried about the route from here to Hells Canyon, though."

The soft voice is reassuring. "No problem. It's real open country.

You just pick your way through. I'll point it out on a map. I've just got some repair work to do before closing. Can you wait?"

"Sure."

He sits at a desk cluttered with miniature tools and tiny manila envelopes. As he squints through a magnifying eyepiece at a watch, he says, "So tell me about your trip."

I do, and then take the opportunity to ask, "How did you come up with the idea of a Blue Mountain Trail?"

He doesn't look up from his disassembled watch. "It wasn't my idea. That route's a century old. It was made by horse thieves who wanted a way to sneak stock from Washington to the railroad in Nevada."

I find it hard to imagine herding horses through some of the trackless forests I've hiked, but do not express my doubt. "Then you're mostly interested in the route's historical value?"

He humphs. "I'm interested in conservation. Saving that trail's like saving what little wilderness is left out here. Did you know the lumber guys call me 'Fifteen-Cent Hughes'?"

Loren can't see me shake my head, but continues. "Once I filed an appeal on seventy-eight Forest Service timber sales with a single fifteen-cent stamp. They had to throw out their whole five-year plan."

I watch him tinker with the tiny gears and wonder about this meticulous man. I risk a simile. "Sometimes I think understanding the interrelationships in a wilderness must be like trying to understand the gears of a watch. Have you felt that, too?"

His tools prod and click within the watch. "Not really, I'd say watch repair and wilderness are about as different as night and day."

I search for a more navigable conversational channel. "So, have you always lived here in the Blue Mountains?"

"Actually, I grew up in western Colorado."

"Oh?"

"My parents got 'dusted out' by the Dust Bowl. My great-uncle went out scouting new land for forty of us in the family. He came back and said, 'You've got to go to Oregon. The air's so fresh out there, when you breathe your pants flop.' So we all went. And like every other boy in eastern Oregon I figured out pretty quick the purpose of life was to hunt and fish in the wilderness and play football in town."

"But then—how'd you get into watch repair?"

"I started out in college aiming to be a football coach, until I realized football season is hunting season, too. So I switched to watch repair. After two years' study I telephoned Mr. Birnie, the old jeweler who owned this store, and asked if he had an opening. He asked, 'Do you smoke or drink?' I said no. Then he said, 'You're hired. My man quit last month.'

"I did a month's back work for the old jeweler in my first two weeks. He was so happy he decided to take a vacation he'd been putting off for eight years. And you know, it was funny. I'd just met my future wife then, and on the day old Mr. Birnie left he sold me my wife's engagement ring. Then he went to Idaho, had a heart attack, and died. I only knew him those two weeks. I've always felt like he'd given me the keys and the ring—like he was giving his blessing— before passing on."

Loren closes the watch's back and slides it into an envelope.

"Didn't you ever regret getting a job that keeps you indoors?" I ask.

"That's just it. The store keeps me in forty hours a week, but it gives me the resources to spend the other hundred and forty-eight hours out at my ranch, up in the hills, or fighting to save wilderness."

A grandfather clock beside Loren's desk bongs, and then all the clocks in the shop begin chiming five o'clock. As he goes to lock the door, he says, "Now let me show you those maps."

OCTOBER 12

7:46 P.M. North Fork Meacham Creek. 34°F. Mileage today: 25.1. Total: 1,125.2.

Today my New Oregon Trail crosses the Old Oregon Trail. Through the 1840s and 1850s, as many as three thousand people a year rode or walked with their wagons across the Grande Ronde Valley into the fearsome Blue Mountains. To the south, the craggy peaks of the Elkhorn Range were completely uncrossable for wagons. But here the Blue Mountains are a high, grassy, brown tableland, crenellated on all sides by a maze of branching, V-shaped canyons. The settlers arduously winched their wagons up to the tableland, crossed the range's flat top, and winched themselves back down.

Loren has routed me up a brushy elk path in one of the mazelike canyons. Toiling along, I begin to suspect he has overrated the quality of the last one hundred miles of his Blue Mountain Trail, perhaps to convince me this section of the larger New Oregon Trail would be easy to string together.

I struggle about the base of Mount Emily, a massive chunk of tableland named after one of two historical figures. Some local folks insist that a skinny settler near here blessed the mountain with the name of his three hundred-pound wife. Others claim that a more attractive, looser-living Emily lived alone on the mountain's slopes, and that the peak was named by the young men of La Grande because they went up so often to Mount Emily.

The evening is cold and clear. I build a hot, sparkless fire from the pitchy wood of an old snag. The light casts shadows on all sides, as if I am invisibly surrounded by the Old Oregon Trail pioneers who must have camped near here a century and a half ago. I think how much my own trip's scenery and challenges have been like theirs, yet how different are our goals. Most of those pioneers traveled in massive armadas, with perhaps one thousand people and one thousand guns—a force scaled to the vast wilderness land they had to cross. What kept them going was not a love of wilderness, but rather a vision of the island of civilization awaiting them in the green Willamette Valley.

OCTOBER 13

8:18 P.M. North Fork Umatilla Wilderness. 38°F. Mileage today: 22.2 Total: 1,147.4.

Hiking over the tablelands today, I realize why the northern half of the Blue Mountains is so very different from the craggy southern half. Up here the range has been buried and leveled by the great Columbia River basalt floods. The rimrock is part of the same lava flows I saw weeks before in the Deschutes River Canyon. Subsequent river erosion of the mile-deep flows has left this corner of Oregon jumbled with some of the deepest canyons on earth.

I end the day at the bottom of one of those canyons. My elevation is only 2,400 feet—as low as I've been since the Kalmiopsis. Gone is the sagebrush of the arid uplands. The North Fork Umatilla River is crowded on either bank by familiar, nondesert plants: alder, Oregon grape, sword fern, wild ginger, nettle, yew, and wild cherry. The leafless blue elderberry bushes sadly display sagging clusters of old berries, like street vendor's grapes unsold at day's end. The smell of decaying leaves marks the season's demise, and conjures memories of other autumn forest walks when I was merely working up an appetite for the turkey and pumpkin pie cooking at home.

Ten days from now, if the weather holds, and I hold, I'll be camped in Hells Canyon below the terminus of my hike, Hat Point. I can't help but think how I'll wave my stick and cheer at the trailhead there, or how I'll throw open the door at home and embrace Janell.

OCTOBER 14

7:18 P.M. South Fork Walla Walla River. 53°F. Mileage today: 22.0. Total: 1,169.4.

I have crossed into the ancient tribal homeland of the Nez Percé. In their language, *walla* is "running water" and any repeated word is diminutive. So tonight, camped in a mountain canyon beside the *walla walla,* I am at "Little River."

The Nez Percé were the most peaceful and powerful of all the tribes between the Rockies and the Cascades. In their winter villages they hunted, gathered camas roots, made pemmican (jerky-huckleberry cakes), fished for salmon, and selectively bred Appaloosa horses—famed even today for speed and agility. In the summers they were the only far western tribe to trek across the Rockies to the buffalo grounds of the Great Plains.

The domain of the Nez Percé, recognized by treaty in 1855, stretched from here across Hells Canyon to the Bitterroot Mountains of Idaho. In the next week I will be walking to the sacred heartland of their realm.

By legend, Coyote—creator of people—made the Nez Percé last. The trouble began long ago, when a voracious monster came down from the north sucking up all the animals. Coyote alone survived by tying himself to the tallest peak in northeast Oregon. The monster couldn't suck him up. The monster was so impressed he made friends with Coyote and let him walk safely down his huge throat. Once inside, Coyote tore out the monster's heart and freed the animals. Then he celebrated by tearing the monster into quarters and throwing the pieces to the four directions. Where each piece landed, a race of people was born.

It was then that Fox said, "Coyote, you forgot to create any people here in the middle, at Hells Canyon."

After Coyote had thought about that a moment, he replied, "All I have left of the monster is his blood. I'll wash it off and let the drops fall here. They will become the Nez Percé—few in number, but strong and pure."

OCTOBER 15

10:11 P.M. Wenaha-Tucannon Wilderness. 56°F. Mileage today: 37.5. Total: 1,206.9.

I leave the Walla Walla before sunrise, knowing I must cross the crest of the Blue Mountains again today. Dawn slices over the top of the tablelands all at once at seven A.M. The flat orange line slowly sinks down the slopes, as if someone had pulled a plug at the canyon bottom and the darkness was draining out below.

Crossing the high tableland, I endure seven miles of unmelted snow from last week's blizzard, then descend to the east into the Wenaha River Canyon, where the temperature is a balmy 70°F. Huge yellow cottonwoods and elegant snowberry bushes line the river's beautiful trail. Despite only eleven hours of sunlight, I walk twelve hours today, at a pleasant pace, and am surprised to find I've sent my pedometer needle around twice. By the campfire I inspect these legs that carry me 37.5 miles in a day: They are now so intensely packed with sinews and muscles that the veins no longer fit inside, but rather bulge out in a raised blue network.

Tonight, in the Wenaha Wilderness, I am in the ancient *ha* (domain) of Wenak, leader of a small Nez Percé band. There was no single head chief for all the Nez Percé until negotiations with the white man required one. Then the leaders chose a missionary-tutored Nez Percé named Lawyer, who negotiated away rights to 88 percent of their tribal lands in 1863, leaving only his own arid Idaho homeland as the tribe's reservation. The headmen of the Oregon bands refused to sign the new treaty. They lived on in their remote valleys and canyons for fourteen more years, until President Grant issued an ultimatum: They must cross Hells Canyon to the reservation within one more month or be moved by force. Sullenly, the Nez Percé of Oregon rounded up their Appaloosa herds and packed up to leave home. On that desperate final trek their leader would be Hinmaton-Lalaktit—Thunder Rolling in the Mountains,—known to the white man as Chief Joseph.

OCTOBER 16

10:25 A.M. Troy. 68°F. Mileage so far today: 5.9. Total: 1,212.8.

I reach the end of the Blue Mountain Trail this morning at Troy, a handful of houses and a gravel road lost at the bottom of the Grande Ronde River Canyon. It's time I checked in with a friend, who agreed months ago to drive eleven hours from western Oregon to meet me at Hells Canyon at the end of the hike.

The only public telephone is in the tavern. A waitress is stacking firewood on the porch. Inside, two cowboys look up from their pool game.

"Hello!" I holler over the crackling line. "This is Bill Sullivan! Are you still planning to meet me at Hat Point on the Hells Canyon rim next week?"

A weak voice finally breaks through the static. "Didn't I already tell you? I was out cutting firewood and felled a tree on my head . . ." Crackling interrupts the words, and then, ". . . some trouble with amnesia."

"Are you all right?"

"I'm recovering. But *who* did you say you were?"

I fight down a surge of panic. I remind my friend who I am, but he tells me his head is covered with stitches. I think: Hat Point is a very rough hour's drive from the end of paved Oregon backroads. It is no place for an injured man to be driving to—and certainly no place to end a hike without a dependable rendezvous. Nor can I ask my parents to come again; they used up their vacation on the long trip here last week.

Tonight, in the "ghost town" of Flora, I'll be at the last telephone before Hells Canyon, where civilization ends. By then I must think of someone to call for help.

6:30 P.M. Flora. Mileage today: 20.8. Total: 1,227.7.

It is drizzling as I hike up the gravel road climbing the desolate three-thousand-foot canyon rim behind Troy. My last food package is supposed to be waiting in Flora with one Carol Wulff, the mother-in-law of my mother's friend's daughter. It is a tenuous connection, but I knew no other mailing address in this remote part of the state.

Cold, dry farm fields of stubble cover the tableland beyond the canyon. The road angles toward a half dozen abandoned, weathered buildings in a field: a boarded-up schoolhouse, a steepled church surrounded by weeds.

On the edge of "town" stands a farmhouse with a tractor and several tool sheds. As I approach, a middle-aged woman throws open the door. "Come on in! Join me for elk spaghetti." She wears pink jogging shoes and a blue sweatshirt that reads: THIS IS NO ORDINARY FARM WIFE YOU'RE DEALING WITH.

"You must be Carol Wulff?"

She laughs. "Who else?"

In fact, so far she seems to be the only inhabitant of Flora. I follow her into a modern kitchen and plunge gratefully into an unexpected dinner made with flavorful elk hamburger.

"This is marvelous." I accept seconds.

"You're hungrier than a hired hand in the wheat harvest."

"You raise wheat?"

She nods. "'Course with winter coming, my husband's already on the road, driving truck again."

I think: Then she must spend the winters here alone. I try to imagine living in a snowbound "ghost town," and decide it might require more strength than any solo backpacking trip. "Just wondering—was Flora originally a mining town or something?"

"No, always just farming."

"Then what happened to the other people?"

Suddenly Carol waves out the window. "Here's Mom. She'll love to tell you about it."

A little white-haired woman opens the screen door and peers in. "Anyone home?" She has little round glasses and cherry cheeks. A hanky is stuffed in the pocket of her sensible white sweater.

"Come on in, Myrtle. He's here." Carol says.

"Oh, my," Myrtle exclaims. She shakes my hand, studying me and smiling. I begin to suspect my visit has been a source of much conversation over the past months.

I answer a number of Myrtle's questions about my hike, and then Carol says, "Bill asked about how our town got started."

"Oh, did he?" Myrtle settles down in an easy chair. "I can tell you about that 'cause my dad came here in 1888 and took up one of the first hundred-and-sixty-acre land claims. He left Illinois for his health, you see, and tramped around the country with his bedroll on his back until he heard the government had free land out here for settlers. Like most of the rest, he built a dirt-floor log cabin, planted a garden, and scythed wild hay to feed a cow and a pig in the winter."

"There were a lot of people here then?"

"My, yes." The old woman leans back with the memory. "Right after World War One, and all through the twenties, there was a second batch of free homesteading all through eastern Oregon, so we had a family on nearly every quarter section. We had three general stores, all with dry goods and men's shirts and stockings. You made your own dresses, of course. There was a Farmer's Hotel and a Baker's Hotel. We had a bank, a flour mill, a newspaper, and two churches. There was even a millinery, where a woman made frames and put hats together. And we had two blacksmith shops for shoeing all the horses and sharpening the plows. It was 1915 when they built the big two-story schoolhouse down the street—high school upstairs, grade school down."

Myrtle sighs. "Life was simpler then. It was beans and taters and bread. I was tickled to death if I got an orange on the Fourth of July."

"Did the town go bankrupt in the Depression?"

"No, no." She straightens her dress with her worn hands. "All through the Depression most the people stayed. They didn't have the money to leave. Oh, a few lost their places to taxes, but that was the only expense they had. They even grew their own tobacco. No, it was prosperity that drove them out."

"Prosperity? I don't understand."

"After World War Two the road came in to Lewiston, made it so people could get in and out in a day. The kids heard all about those high wages out in the cities, went off to jobs or college, and never came back."

Carol breaks in, "Not all the kids, Mom."

Myrtle smiles. "Someone had to stay on and buy the old farms."

As Myrtle speaks, a distant bell begins to toll. At once she is on her feet. "Oh, that's Clyde ringing the old school bell. I bet he's heading off to bed. Nice meeting you."

"The pleasure was mine." I wish her good night, but am suddenly preoccupied; the bell has reminded me of a call I must make.

10:25 P.M. Same.

Loren Hughes has come to my rescue, agreeing to meet me at the end of Hells Canyon. But he insists he can only come on a weekend. His jewelry shop ties him down during the week. Today is Wednesday. He sets our rendezvous for five P.M. Sunday.

This leaves me less than four days—less than four days to backpack 134 miles up and down, through the deepest canyon on earth!

I hang up with an unsteady hand. I have never even seen Hells Canyon before. What *is* down there anyway?

V.

HELLS CANYON

*". . . [The Snake River here is] one continued
rapid about 150 yds wide it's banks are in
most places solid and perpendicular rocks,
which rise to a great hight; it's hills are mountains high . . ."*

—Capt. Meriwether Lewis, 1806

9:24 P.M. Unnamed meadow. 38°F. Mileage today: 40.4. Total: 1,268.1.

I leave Flora by starlight at 5:55 A.M. to get a head start on the long hike ahead. The road zigzags through the frozen fields of the "ghost town's" high prairie. Then, suddenly, the prairie ends.

Gaping before me is a monstrous, jagged chasm two miles wide and half a mile deep. It is Joseph Canyon, the sacred site of Nez Percé coming-of-age vision quests. In all probability, Chief Joseph himself came here as a boy, alone, fasting day after day, awaiting the appearance of a spirit to guide him throughout his adult life.

There are no trails in Joseph Canyon. I set off, picking my way down through the broken cliffs. Rocks tumble ahead of me down the dry, barren slopes. I wade a cold creek at the bottom, in a narrow band of pines, and begin the 2,400-foot climb out. Twice I dead-end at cliffs. Over and over I must rest against my pack. Finally I reach the far rim exhausted, and look at my map. Hells Canyon is still thirty miles away. It is nearly three times as deep as Joseph Canyon.

The sun drifts across the sky as I hike eastward along a dirt road. My boots beat a mesmerizing rhythm hour after hour. The sky purples. A thumbnail moon rises, its dark side eerily lit by Earthshine. My pedometer clicks on its second trip around its twenty-five-mile dial, but the night fills me with a strange, trancelike exhilaration. I feel a heightened awareness of the forest, the road, the stars—everything except my own legs, moving distantly beneath me.

In the dark of the woods I think about being afraid. I imagine wild animals in the dark. Fear does not come. After two months outdoors, I know the forest too well.

But then for one second the road all around me is suddenly illuminated, as if by a searchlight from above. Stunned, I look up, but there is nothing but untwinkling stars. My heart speeds up. I stare into the woods. All is dark. I wait. There are no hidden trucks with flares, no UFOs. Perhaps I do not really know the forest at all.

I feel my way into a meadow beside the road and nervously build a small fire. My pedometer reads "40.4." I trace the miles on the

219

map. I have stopped just short of my goal: the mysterious edge of Hells Canyon.

But what the devil was that light on the road?

OCTOBER 18

7:04 A.M. Same. 30°F.

It was not a dream.

I was putting away my journal at ten last night when I suddenly saw another campfire across the dark meadow to the west. I recalled the map: There were no campgrounds or spur roads near me. I had passed no vehicles on my marathon hike. No campers were within miles of me. Then I noticed with a shot of fear that this sudden camp-fire looked strangely *wrong*. Instead of flickering flame by flame, the entire light brightened and dimmed uniformly, as if it were an electrically lit fake. At moments it vanished entirely without leaving so much as an ember. It looked like no campfire on earth.

Suddenly Coyote's weird laughing howl yipped from close at hand, as if behind the eerie light. Four or five impetuous, smaller yipping voices followed: Coyote's children, all on hand for this. For what?

I thought: It is a spontaneous forest fire, begun at ten P.M.; I should go put it out. But I did not. I thought: It is a reflection of my own campfire; I should ignore it. But my own campfire had burned down to coals.

I thought: It is Coyote after all. This is his call at last. He is the one who has stopped me here with his unearthly searchlight on the road. Now he has done his best imitation of a campfire—a sloppy job, but good for mere magic—and is inviting me to come to him. Perhaps he will teach me the secrets of the wilderness, of the spirit forces of creation itself. Perhaps he will hide and laugh when I fall into some preposterous joke.

I was about to get up when a wave of rationality stopped me. I thought: My legs are too tired from the forty-mile day to walk farther after will-o-the-wisps. I thought: The meadow may be too boggy to cross. I thought: The light is dimming now anyway. Coyote's fireball at Smith Rock was only a burning spaceship. His frogs in the Ochocos were only sandhill cranes. Perhaps this display, too, was something with a perfectly simple explanation.

I knew it was not. Yet I let Coyote's light die. I crawled into my tent and did not look again before being overwhelmed by sleep.

Coyote did not come in my dreams. I learned no secrets. I suffered no prank. The offer I had wanted was there, but it passed untaken.

Why couldn't I go to him? It is a question I am still asking myself.

Perhaps I am still too dulled by civilization to listen, too tired to believe. Perhaps there are things I was born too late to learn. Science, with all its reason, may succeed in picking our world apart—but, like a student dissecting an animal in a lab, it will never find the essential spirit. Some secrets are destined always to remain, not beyond us, but behind.

12:58 P.M. Eureka Bar. 72°F. Mileage so far today: 14.5. Total: 1,282.6.

There is no trace of Coyote's campfire across the meadow as I pack up this morning. Disappointed, I hoist my pack. Then I walk a few yards to the east through the forest, and stare.

I have camped on the ragged edge of a broken planet. Fourteen layers of basalt rimrock retreat downward in jagged, treeless terraces. A vertical mile below, a tiny black curve is a piece of the mighty Snake River. Beyond, crumpled badlands on the Idaho side spread into the distance, an endless pattern of sharp black shadows.

In the trance of last night's hike, I could easily have walked over this cliff, where the road peters out. A cold sweat makes me shiver. The lights of last night have kept me from hiking off the end of the world in the dark. Coyote, the spirit of the wilderness I came to find, is here.

I remember the prank message he left for me one thousand miles ago in the dust of a Siskiyou trail. I may never know him, but he knows me.

He has been with me from the first.

Then another thought catches me. I look at my watch. There are just fifty-seven hours left to reach my rendezvous on the far end of this chasm, ninety-three miles away. Could the end of my trail be just fifty-seven hours away? I set off down the trail to the Snake with sudden anticipation. It is as though Janell herself were waiting for me at the Hat Point trailhead, with love and comfort and rest.

At the same time, the beauty of the rugged wilderness before me makes me wish I could stay here, drifting, with no other goal than finally to learn Coyote's mysteries. In the past days the dilemma has been gnawing within me: Is there no way to bring the magic of the wilderness home?

Hour after hour I hike down the brown, sagebrush-dotted slopes. As the elevation plummets, the entire climate changes. I can still see the snowline high above on the rim. But I strip to a T-shirt in the summery air. Prickly-pear cactus covers the sunniest slopes. Monarch butterflies flutter past, unaware that the rest of their tribe have long since gone south to California for the winter.

Down and still down! Hells Canyon is a third of a mile deeper even than the Grand Canyon. What's more, Hells Canyon was *not* originally carved by the Snake River. Geologists insist the Snake didn't used to flow here at all—that it cut straight from southern Idaho to California. As the earth flexed, and mountains rose across eastern Oregon fifteen million years ago, a tributary of Idaho's Salmon River cut this huge, dead-end canyon, keeping pace with the rising mountains on either side. The same mountain-building process dammed the Snake's old outlet across southeast Oregon. A monumental lake formed, covering most of southern Idaho. When the rising waters of that ancient lake breached the lip at the head of Hells Canyon, the entire lake poured through, deepening the channel and overwhelming the Salmon River on its way to the Columbia.

My trail leads down a gulch and straight to an ancient, gnarled apple tree with huge fruit. Suddenly I realize how thirsty this canyon's warm climate has made me. The apples are absolutely flawless. No blight or worm could spread to this Methuselah, for there is probably no other tree of this species within fifty miles. I eat the delicious gift, marveling that civilization once reached even here.

The sound of thunder a mile down the gulch turns into the rushing, growling Snake River. I hike out onto the long gravel beach of Eureka Bar. Green water roars past in great standing waves. A rough white line thirty feet up the sheer cliffs of the Idaho side testifies to unimaginable floods.

It's hard to believe this gravel bar at the bottom of Hells Canyon could once have been the site of a city of two thousand. But behind me, rising like an Incan ruin against the hillside, are the terraced foundations of a seven-tiered gold mill.

Eureka, Oregon, was not built to mine ore, but rather to quarry the endless bonanza in the pockets of eastern stock investors. Like all the best "strikes," Eureka began with a miner's tale.

The story goes that the Nez Percé reported there were rocks glittering yellow in the sun at the bottom of Hells Canyon. Miners who had gone to hunt the rocks found only fool's gold—chalcopyrites. But in June 1899, the story was repeated at a campfire within the hearing of two miners who knew chalcopyrites are valuable as copper ore. On swift horses the two men raced each other to stake the first claims in the new Eureka.

The copper ore was never very good, but the story was. It brought in about three years of eastern investments. Just as interest was lagging, the local miners broke exciting news: There was gold in the copper ore! Stock sales soared. Fortunes were made by the locals, who built a 125-foot sternwheeler to transport the refined gold out to Lewiston. A great cable had to be anchored in the cliffs above Mountain Sheep Rapids to winch the boat through that fearsome gorge, where the entire Snake River is compressed to a sixty-foot width. After several successful test runs, the boat was loaded with the gold-mill machinery that would finally enable Eureka to begin shipping gold. Coincidentally, on that very run the boat fouled its sternwheel on the cable, turned sideways in Mountain Sheep Rapids, bridged the canyon, broke in two, and sent the mill to the bottom of the river. The eastern investors were bankrupted. And the city of Eureka vanished as swiftly as a stranger who writes bad checks.

I hike two miles to the end of the gravel bar, and am surprised to find a young man fishing where the Imnaha River joins the Snake. Mules nearby have evidently carried in his gear. He rummages about in a tackle box while a pair of lazy-looking hound dogs watch.

"Hi," I say.

"Howdy, Bill."

I study him more closely. I've never seen him before. "Do you know me?"

He straightens up and shakes my hand. "Ed Hughes. My dad said I might find you down here."

My head reels. Finding me in the vast distances of Hells Canyon must have been a monumental challenge! Loren Hughes would only have undertaken it in the direst emergency.

"What did your father need to tell me?"

"Tell you?" Ed shrugs. "He just said I might find you down here. This is my regular fishing spot."

"Oh." In a way, I'm disappointed. "I didn't know Loren had any sons."

He prepares a hook with a huge worm and a fuzzy red feather. "I reckon there's five of us."

"All conservationists too?"

"Yeah, we stand up for dad." He raises back the pole to cast the line. The hook snags the closest hound dog's lip. Yelp! Ed lays down the pole to unhook the dog. Silently, he casts again.

I watch the line stretch out in the muddy green water. "What kind of fish do you expect to catch out there?"

"Little Dolly Vardens probably. They're green with—"

Suddenly the pole bends double. Ed's eyes grow wide. *"Fish on!"* he shouts, dancing down the beach, alternately pulling the pole and reeling in. When a big silver fish leaps from the water, Ed flashes me an ecstatic V-for-victory sign.

A few minutes later, he has netted the twenty-two-inch steelhead onto the dry gravel of the beach. "Oh God, oh God, oh God," he whispers. "I'll have to break the whiskey bottle out now. She's a keeper."

"A keeper?"

"See, the fin's clipped. It's an old hatchery fish. All the native steelhead are catch-and-release." He is still whispering, on his knees.

"Is it—?"

"Shh." Ed strokes the sides of the beautiful silver fish as it flexes in the gravel. He feels its fins, shaking his head with wonder.

At the same time a roar is growing in the canyon. I look up, but there are no airplanes in sight. The sound echoes closer and closer. Then one by one, five jetboats round the bend, bouncing up the white water of the rapids like waterskiing Winnebagos. Each bears the legend: BEAMERS LANDING, EXCURSIONS AND TOURS. Each carries a dozen elderly passengers, all waving like mad. And each boat's guide is blaring loudspeaker messages to his passengers over the general roar: ". . . before your return to Lewiston . . . scenic mouth of the Imnaha . . . a treat to spot backpackers on this remote shore . . . truly a wilderness experience . . ."

9:49 P.M. Deep Creek. 54°F. Mileage today: 31.8. Total: 1,299.9.

The Snake River's inner gorge is too precipitous for any path beyond Eureka Bar, so the trail detours up the Imnaha River for five miles. Here the route is flanked by rugged, one thousand-foot cliffs. Every ledge and slope is resplendent with the fiery autumn-red leaves of nonpoisonous sumac, a profuse, palm-shaped shrub.

At the Imnaha bridge, the trail joins the route of the Nez Percé tribe's 1877 retreat under Chief Joseph. I follow the trail over the steep, barren shoulder of Cactus Mountain and stare down at the route ahead, which disappears into the chasm of the Snake River's inner gorge like a rope into a mineshaft.

Chief Joseph brought four hundred people and three thousand head of Appaloosa and cattle over this trail, hurrying to meet the army's deadline to leave Oregon. White settlers rushed in after them, claiming pastures and branding the horses the Indians left. The Snake River was in flood stage. Joseph ordered rafts built of hide bundles, heaped the rafts with baggage, and had young men on the strongest horses swim them across. Women, children, and old people followed on horseback into the raging river. Finally the remaining thousands of head of stock were driven into the water to cross on their own or drown. Miraculously, no human lives were lost.

After the tribe had regrouped and climbed the Idaho side of Hells Canyon, they stopped two miles short of the reservation for a "last council in freedom." Chief Joseph went back to check on their cattle. When he returned, he found the tribe preparing for war. Three young hotbloods, taunted by an old warrior, had murdered settlers in a nearby cabin. The U.S. Army was advancing. Joseph convinced the tribe they must first meet the troops with a white flag of surrender.

A hundred cavalrymen and a detachment of Idaho volunteers marched into the canyon where the Nez Percé were camped on June 17, 1877. Their first act was to shoot at the Indian with the white flag. At once, the well-prepared Nez Percé opened fire from all sides, killing a third of the white soldiers while suffering no losses themselves.

Thus began the Nez Percé's historic flight toward permanent sanctuary in Canada. For four months Joseph led them northeastward through Yellowstone National Park and across the plains of Montana. As they went, they paid for all the supplies they obtained, harmed no noncombatants, and moved peaceably, except in brilliant defensive battles. Their conduct won sympathy across the nation. The people of Billings, Montana, welcomed them as heroes.

The final, crushing defeat came just thirty miles short of the Canadian border. Chief Joseph said in surrender, "Our chiefs are killed. . . . The little children are freezing to death. . . . My heart is sick and sad. From where the sun now stands, I will fight no more forever."

Even the general who had pursued them urged repatriation to their tribal homeland. In vain. The Nez Percé were sent to Oklahoma, where many died of malaria. Then they were moved to Washington State, where Chief Joseph died of what the reservation doctor termed simply "a broken heart."

I reach the Snake River again as the dark blue sky is turning to purple. I drop my gear at a white-water boater camp. There is a small sandy beach, a picnic table, and an outhouse. There is no firewood; I burn dead sagebrush twigs for light.

As the hour draws nearer when I must leave this starkly beautiful canyon, I can better understand the Nez Percé's great loss. In a way, it doesn't matter that there are no army guns behind me. Tomorrow will be my last council in freedom.

OCTOBER 19

8:59 P.M. Muir Creek. 53°F. Mileage today: 33.3. Total: 1,333.2.

Today my trail traces the rushing river southeastward along sunny shores and immense brown ridges toward the easternmost point of Oregon. Eight big mule deer stand at attention when I hike into a grassy glen. There is no forest for them to hide in. They train their big jackrabbit ears at me, then spring away on all four legs across the slopes.

Later, on a ledge among cliffs, I nearly step on a snake, thinking it to be a stick. I freeze, then back up slowly. Hells Canyon is said to be full of rattlesnakes.

The snake calmly slithers into the trailside rocks. It has alternating black and brown blotches on its back like a rattler's, but its head lacks the distinctive spade shape necessary for folding back a rattler's long fangs.

A gopher snake.

Too bad. I've wanted to see a rattlesnake on this trip. Oregon's rattlers (*Crotalus viridis oreganus*) are very shy. Authorities insist they are absolutely incapable of such spuriously attributed feats of daring as crawling into a sleeping bag for warmth. Nor are they as venomous as the aggressive diamondback rattlers (*Crotalus atrox*), which live south of the Great Basin, from Texas to California.

Not seeing a rattler in over thirteen hundred miles makes me think of all the other animals I have not seen. I didn't see an eagle. I didn't see a fox. Or a beaver or a weasel or a badger. Who *has* seen a badger, really? Children grow up learning what these animals look like and how they live, but most children will grow old and die without having seen one in the wild.

Day is just starting to fade when I hike into a chasm so narrow I could throw a stone across the roaring white water of China Rapids and hit Idaho. The trail has been blasted out of the face of sheer granite cliffs like an open-sided tunnel. Far above, wild badlands and rimrock tiers stack up to the sky. At the most perilous-looking bend, my compass shows my trail—after two months of eastward progress—following the river *west*.

I've made it! I've hiked from Oregon's westernmost to its easternmost point! I let out a triumphant yell that echoes up the cliffs. Jubilantly I take my own self-timed photograph.

Then I think: The hike's not over yet! I've less than twenty-four hours to reach Hat Point, and I can't camp here—unless I sleep on the trail's ledge and fill my water bottle at the end of a rope.

Quickly I hike two more miles through the twilight. When I hear my boots splash in a creek that runs across the dark trail, I feel my way through the brush to a steep cobble beach. There I construct a rocky terrace for my tent. Beside a small driftwood fire I look at the map and groan. *Hat Point is still twenty-eight miles away and six thousand feet up!* Backpacking there in a single day will be the equivalent of carrying half a sack of cement on a marathon, and then up all the stairs in the Empire State Building five times.

I have camped beside Muir Creek. I will need every bit of inspiration that that rugged naturalist can offer.

OCTOBER 20

4:57 P.M. Hat Point. 39°F. Mileage today: 28.3. Total: 1,361.5.

I awake at 4:45 A.M. and lie in bed watching the stars through the tent flap. Betelgeuse and Aldebaran, my winter favorites, are setting. A shooting star leaves a brief glowing streak. At five, I pack my things for the last time and sit with a bowl of hot oatmeal, waiting for enough light to see the trail.

At 6:18, Coyote's howl echoes off the huge shadowy cliffs—an eerie wilderness farewell. I shiver and set off, knowing I must average nearly three miles an hour if I am to reach my five P.M. rendezvous.

For three miles the dim trail skirts riverside cliffs. Then it crosses a sandy river bar of rabbit brush and dried teasels. Finally, at a rock cairn, it ducks into a side gulch and begins to *climb.*

At two thousand feet, I startle a herd of seventy-five elk across the treeless slopes. Behind me the Snake River has shrunk to a thin curve at the bottom of Hells Canyon's immense inner gorge. But I am only a third of the way up.

At four thousand feet the snowcapped peaks of the Seven Devils rise above the distant blue of the Idaho rim, like clouds in a sky I have yet to reach. It is already two o'clock.

Step, step, breathe. My legs bulge with heated muscles. I lean on my walking stick up the endless switchbacks. Far ahead I can see my goal, a dark shoulder of tableland jutting out over the canyon. And above the snow-dusted forest at its summit I can just discern the fire lookout tower, where the trail will end.

EPILOGUE

OCTOBER 21

2:30 P.M. On a Greyhound bus; last stop before Portland.

Windshield wipers slap. Furloughed soldiers and old women jostle their baggage in the aisle. I stare out the streaked window at a restaurant parking lot. In three hours I will be in Janell's arms, hearing the welcome squeals of Karen and Ian. I will have all the food and hot baths imaginable.

Can my trip really be over? The world here seems as strange as any dream: the seas of cars, the crowds of people, the great inactivity as everyone sits.

"Excuse me, is this seat taken?"

I look up. A youngish woman is standing in the aisle.

"No, no. Please go ahead."

"Thank you." She sits primly and opens a newspaper. The title rustles at me: *Earth First! The Radical Environmental Journal.*

I recall Lou Gold, the bearded Earth First! activist in the Kalmiopsis, and think how positively opposite this tidy young woman seems. "Pardon me, are you really an Earth Firster?"

"Not really." She glances at my worn-out clothes and shaggy beard, as if for the first time, and smiles. "Are you?"

I laugh. "No, no. I've just finished a backpacking trip in the wilderness. I'm on my way home."

"How exciting. Did you go very far?"

Somehow my adventure seems suddenly absurd. "I guess I walked across Oregon."

"Why, that must have been three hundred miles!"

"Well, actually, the way I went, it was thirteen hundred."

She shakes her head—but it is not in ridicule, as I first suspect. "Oh, I'd love to do something like that someday. How long did it take?"

"Two months and three days."

"Where did you finish?"

"At the edge of Hells Canyon." I recall finally puffing up to the crest of Hat Point on a thin crust of snow—just three minutes ahead of my rendezvous hour. The parking lot was empty; the fire tower vacant. I just had time to collapse beside the trailhead signpost when a pickup truck rattled up the road. Loren Hughes leaned out and smiled. "You made it, eh?" Then he held out a beer and a hamburger, as if in apology. "Hope I didn't rush you, getting here on a Sunday." I told him, "That's all right, Loren." And I meant it, too. The challenge of Hells Canyon was a fitting end to my trail.

The young woman folds away her paper. "It must feel strange to come back after that long. What will you miss most?"

How should I answer? The slow, rosy sunrises? The thrill of discovering what lies over the next ridge? I look down. "You'll laugh. There was this walking stick I found. Just an ordinary stick, but after I carried it eight hundred miles I got to know it like a friend. It was as if it stood for all the forests I'd come to know. I left it leaning against the signpost at the end of the trail."

She nods thoughtfully. "I understand."

I look at her. "Really?"

"Oh, I'm not very much of a hiker," she adds quickly. "But I do read a lot about forests."

As soon as she pronounces the word forests "farrests," I guess she is from the East Coast. I ask her about herself.

She is Meg Larson, about thirty-five, from Baltimore. She says she never camped, or skied, or cared much at all about the outdoors until she came out west.

"I moved to California to work on Jerry Brown's campaign," Meg recalls. "One of my co-workers said, 'Hey, let's go to a Sierra Club meeting.' They had a singles night there—wouldn't you know they'd do that in California? Everyone wore Birkenstocks and went out together for beer afterwards. But they talked so much about acid rain and nuclear waste it got depressing."

"Yes, it's a hazard."

Meg straightens. "When I came to stay in Oregon I decided to think positively instead. Have you heard of Beyond War?"

"I'm not sure."

"Well, it's a group that says the threat of nuclear war really boils down to people's own attitudes. They say we should start thinking good thoughts and sending out positive energy."

I nod. "Do you think it will work?"

She frowns. "I'm a little discouraged. The history of people is so full of violence and aggression, I'm not sure everybody can change."

"Sounds like a goal, though."

"Oh, yes. And you know, the destruction of wilderness is really just a symptom of the same problem. Our tools have become so powerful we're able to destroy the environment far more effectively than ever before. It's like a sci-fi movie where harmless ants are expanded to a thousand times their size and become horrible monsters. Yet everyone says, truthfully, 'I'm not like that. I don't hurt the forests or kill the whales.'"

She looks down. "I used to go around telling my friends, 'I wish I had the opportunity to lie down in front of the bulldozers to save old-growth forests.' But then I got the opportunity. And I realized I couldn't really do it."

She sighs. "So instead I do what I *can* do. Just little things, I guess."

"Like what?"

"Oh, 'walking lightly.' I don't have a car or a television. I live downtown and ride the bus. I recycle my garbage. I don't buy Saran Wrap or paper towels. I even take my paper bags back to the grocery store and re-use them until they're all worn out."

"I suppose if enough people—"

"Even one person makes a difference," she insists, suddenly adamant. "One more beer can in the lake *does* matter. The important thing is that I can change myself. It's not the beer can in the lake; it's the fact I did not throw it."

I think: Of all the varied people I have met on my long trip, Meg may be the one who speaks to my own feelings about the wilderness best. Meg alone—who perhaps has never been in a wilderness at all!—has solved the riddle of bringing the spirit of wilderness back with me into the city.

I remember my strange encounters with the wilderness prankster. Then I smile. No wonder Coyote followed me the length of my hike. He was a part of me all along.

The bus pulls in on a rainy freeway to Portland, over the huge arch of the Fremont Bridge. The city is a child's toybox dumped across the land, full of wonder and jumble. Fifty-story chrome-and-glass space ports jostle nineteenth-century brick warehouses and cop-per-steepled churches. We drop into a gleaming new bus-transit mall as the sun breaks through, sending a misty rainbow arching over the whole sweep of city skyline.

Meg puts on her hat, cocking it briskly, and shakes my hand with a smile. "It's been pleasant talking. Good luck." And we step out into Oregon's largest city, wilderness clinging to our minds.

APPENDIX:
Gear and Food Lists

Equipment:

Backpack (5 lb)

4′ × 6′ waterproof pack cover

Two-man tent with rain fly (3½ lb)

Sleeping bag with waterproof cover (5 lb)

Hard foam sleeping pad (3 oz)

Butane backpacking stove

Large spoon

Plastic bowl

Plastic cup

2-cup whistling teapot

1-pint water bottle

2 one-quart water bottles

Stuff sack for food

Clothes:

Raincoat

Rain pants

Down jacket

Jeans with belt

Corduroy cutoffs

2 pairs underpants

2 T-shirts

Light cotton shirt, long sleeved

Heavy wool shirt, long sleeved

3 pairs light socks (85% cotton, 15% nylon)

3 pairs heavy socks (85% wool, 15% nylon)

Lug-soled hiking boots

Light jogging shoes

Small Gear:

Toothbrush

Comb

Soap in soap container

Swiss army knife

Compass

Mirror

Whistle

100 water-purification tablets

SLR camera with zoom lens

Knapsack for camera

2 rolls film

50 ft nylon cord

Pedometer

Thermometer

Digital clock

3 Band-Aids

Roll of surgical tape

Elastic bandage

Sewing kit (containing a spool of thread, pins, needles, and safety pins)

Disposable cigarette lighter

Watertight pill bottle of wooden matches

Paper matches

Wallet folder with $50 and identification

4 ballpoint pens

Notebook

Packet of maps

Stamped envelope, postcard, and manila mailer

Extra clevis pin for backpack

Additional at Each of 8 Food Drops:

Roll of film

2 butane cartridges

2 paper matchbooks

$5 bill

Unsigned blank check

Stamped envelope, postcard, and manila mailer

Maps of next trail section

Notebook of next trail section

Food (see below)

Food Totals (60 Days)*:

> 20 lb quick oats
>
> 5 lb raisins
>
> 3 lb powdered milk
>
> 5 lb cocoa mix
>
> 12½ lb granola
>
> 4 lb salted peanuts
>
> 3 lb salted sunflower seeds
>
> 4 lb pitted prunes
>
> 12 lb pilot crackers
>
> 8 lb hard candy
>
> 2½ lb jerky
>
> 60 vitamin pills
>
> 23 freeze-dried dinner entrees
>
> 21 bags herbal tea
>
> 38 three-oz packages ramen Oriental noodles
>
> 4 lb soy meat substitute (4 flavors)
>
> 6 lb instant rice
>
> 6 lb potato flakes
>
> 2 lb dried soup mix

Menus†:

BREAKFAST

> 4 oz quick oats

---

* Includes emergency rations.

† After twenty days I used surplus emergency rations to increase the quantities in all menus 50 percent, and I poured the potato flakes into gopher holes.

⅓ oz instant milk

1 oz raisins

1 oz cocoa mix

6⅓ oz

LUNCH

2½ oz granola

¾ oz salted peanuts

½ oz salted sunflower seeds

¾ oz pitted prunes (2½ pc)

1 oz pilot crackers

1 oz hard candy (6 pc)

½ oz jerky

Vitamin pill

------

7 oz

DINNER A ($\times$ 23)

3½ oz freeze-dried dinner entree

2 oz pilot crackers

⅓ oz hard candy (2 pc)

Herbal tea

------

6 oz

DINNER B ($\times$ 19)

6 oz ramen Oriental noodles (2 packs)

1 oz pilot crackers

½ oz soy meat substitute

⅓ oz hard candy (2 pc)

Herbal tea
_____
8 oz

DINNER C (× 19)

4½ oz instant rice

¾ oz dried soup mix

¾ oz soy meat substitute

1 oz pilot crackers

⅓ oz hard candy (2 pc)

Herbal tea
_____
7½ oz

DINNER D (× 19)

4 oz potato flakes

1 oz instant milk

¾ oz dried soup mix

¾ oz soy meat substitute

1 oz pilot crackers

⅓ oz hard candy (2 pc)

Herbal tea
_____
8 oz

ACKNOWLEDGMENTS

There is irony in the fact that a long solo trip requires the involvement of so many. I am indebted to the Oregon Natural Resources Council for endorsing the New Oregon Trail from the first and providing me with the staff support of Marc Prevost, Don Tryon, and Tim Lillebo. The Oregon State Parks' Recreational Trail Advisory Council likewise offered much encouragement and has since proven a tireless friend in promoting the trail concept. The Eugene *Register-Guard* paid the expenses of my expedition—$250—in return for a series of articles I wrote later; for that expression of faith, editor Dean Rea is to be commended.

Many of the individuals who held food packages for me, or hiked with me, or allowed me to interview them have been mentioned by name in the book itself. A more complete list, with my grateful thanks, must include Jim Rogers, Carrie Osborn, Bob Keefer, Lou Gold, Len Ramp, Betty McCaleb, Ron, Jack and Lucille Brownell, Chris Binns, Bob and Nancy Lee, George Murray, Elsie Butler, Ed Kaiser, Joe and Kay Softich, Debbie Demming, Bob Bagley, Mark, Irene Day, Owenuma Blue Sky, Lindsey and Brett Corklin, Tyler Groo, Deborah Ritchie, Del Stevens, Bigfoot, Ray Summers, Loren Hughes, Carol and Myrtle Wulff, Ed Hughes, and Meg Larson.

J. Wesley and Elsie Sullivan provided so much help I can't itemize it all. I still squirm to think of the unheralded trials my absence caused for my wife, Janell Sorensen, and our two children, Karen and Ian Sullivan. I also wish to thank those who read the manuscript: Janell Sorensen, Wes and Elsie Sullivan, Norman Barrett, Barbara Emashowski, and Talbot Bielefeldt.

Finally I am indebted to the works I have used for research— more excellent books and maps than I have room to list.